FRAGMENTED WORLDS, COHERENT LIVES

THE POLITICS OF DIFFERENCE IN BOTSWANA

PNINA MOTZAFI-HALLER

Foreword by John L. Comaroff

D1715493

Bergin & Garvey
Westport, Connecticut • London

Library of Congress Cataloging-in-Publication Data

Motzafi-Haller, Pnina.
  Fragmented worlds, coherent lives : the politics of difference in Botswana /
Pnina Motzafi-Haller ; foreword by John L. Comaroff.
    p. cm.
  Includes bibliographical references and index.
  ISBN 0–89789–880–X (alk. paper)—ISBN 0–89789–881–8 (pbk. : alk. paper)
  1. Tswapong (African people)—Social conditions. 2. Tswapong (African
people)—Ethnic identity. 3. Tswapong (African people)—Politics and
government. 4. Migration, Internal—Botswana. 5. Social change—Botswana.
6. Botswana—Social conditions. 7. Botswana—Politics and government.
I. Title.
DT2458.T93 M67   2002
305.896'306883—dc21   2001058321

British Library Cataloguing in Publication Data is available.

Library of Congress Catalog Card Number: 2001058321
ISBN: 0–89789–880–X
      0–89789–881–8 (pbk.)

First published in 2002

Bergin & Garvey, 88 Post Road West, Westport, CT 06881
An imprint of Greenwood Publishing Group, Inc.
www.greenwood.com

Printed in the United States of America

The paper used in this book complies with the
Permanent Paper Standard issued by the National
Information Standards Organization (Z39.48-1984).

10 9 8 7 6 5 4 3 2 1

In memory of Moses Basebi
And of my parents—Farha and George Motzafi

Contents

Foreword

From beyond its borders, Botswana appears unrelievedly dull. Its animal population aside, it is, by African standards, decidedly unexotic. A place of large plains and largely plainspoken people, a place not known for extravagant *couture,* for elaborate, tourist-magnetic rituals, or for hip cultural products, Botswana does not draw much attention to itself. True, its August windstorms have a tearing, red-sand-in-your-face magnificence. True, its booming summer rains and deadly, fork-tongued lightning leave an imprint on the senses. True, its workaday repose is occasionally broken by a national scandal, by an outburst of populist antigovernment pique, by a sudden jolt of occult violence. True, there is more youthful anger in evidence in its towns and cities than ever before. But, such things apart, life here has long evinced a remarkable serenity, an evenness of mood underscored by the subdued pathos of the hunger that pervades so much of the countryside. Although Botswana has managed to sustain one of the more durable democracies on the continent, it has always lived in the shadows of its more newsworthy, noisy neighbors. Happily so.

And yet, beneath its surfaces, hiding in the light of everyday life, lies a world of enduring fascination, a world of quiet cultural depth, a world troubled—indeed, fragmented—by unruly and world historical forces, a world, nonetheless, in which indomitable people fashion coherent, meaningful lives, shoring up their meager material resources by seeking to create social wealth. It is on a journey into that infinitely complex, labile world that Pnina Motzafi-Haller takes us in this, her memorable first book.

Or, at least, into part of it. It is the part inhabited by people known as
Batswapong, a population of agro-pastoralists and perennial migrants who
live in the east-central region of the country. The choice is not arbitrary.
And it does not hark back to an anthropology, now irremediably anachro-
nistic, of "little societies" living in isolated, discrete places. Quite the opposite: Motzafi-Haller takes pains to show that Batswapong—who have long
occupied the middle ground in a hierarchy of relations of domination, sus-
pended between Sarwa, the so-called "Bushmen," and their Tswana
rulers—have had constantly to construct, negotiate, and accomplish an
identity; the term itself, "identity" that is, referring less to a thing *an sich*
than to an order of relations. In dissecting this process of fabrication, which
she shows to be profoundly gendered, Motzafi-Haller takes care *not* to take
"traditional" African identities for granted. To the contrary, she demonstrates, in exquisitely fine-grained detail, how the phenomenological condi-
tion-of-being-Tswapong is actually conjured into everyday life; into everyday lives constrained by a politics of scarcity and political domination, lives
fashioned by people whose creativity at the game of survival is honed at
once by necessity, desire, and a genius for culturally inspired improvisation.
Note, here, the shift from singular to plural, from everyday life to everyday
lives; it is intentional, marking the fact that the population which has come
to know itself a Tswapong is continually parsed by the exigencies of social
distinction.

This, in short, is an ethnography of production. Located in a deeply
reflexive, reflective sensibility about the nature of ethnographic accounting,
and in an acute reading of the various theoretical flows that currently swirl
around the anthropological mainstream, it is about the production of material existence, about the production of family, home, and habitation, about
the production of persons, people, and populations, about the production
of collective consciousness, about the production of sites, spaces, and
places. In this respect, it is Janus-faced, being grounded simultaneously in
the classic concerns of the great tradition of social theory, the concerns of
Marx, Weber, and Durkheim, and in an anthropological postmodernity that
has shifted its analytic object from nouns to verbs; from culture, society,
community, selfhood, caste, class and the like to the processes by which
social and discursive objects are objectified, realities realized, persons per-
sonified, concepts conceptualized, regimes regimented. This is especially
appropriate in describing the world inhabited by Tswapong—note the
absence of a definite article, of *the* Tswapong—for whom movement and
uncertainty are less an aberration than a state of being, less the exception
than the rule. Indeed, their predicament makes, in existential terms, a point
that Akhil Gupta and James Ferguson's *Anthropological Locations* makes
in a methodological key: that the spatial order of any life-world is never
given, never to be presumed. Like social context, it is something to be ana-
lytically determined.

In interrogating the fragmentary, labile, uncertain world inhabited by Tswapong, Pnina Motzafi-Haller achieves two things of great note; these in addition to the distinctly non-trivial accomplishment of laying bare the architecture of the processes of social production to which I alluded a moment ago. One is substantive, the other, if I may be forgiven the obviously awkward formulation, theoretical-methodological.

The substantive achievement is to provide an answer—a context-specific answer to be sure, but an answer nonetheless—to the Problem of African Impossibility. The problem, baldly stated, is this. How, given their almost non-existent financial resources, their dire ecological straits, their meager opportunities to produce or to earn, and their fragile social wealth, do millions of Africans, those at the nether end of the economic spectrum, actually survive their material conditions? After all, according to the "rational" canons of Western social science—and to normative models of income, expenditure, exchanges, and consumption—sustaining life under such conditions would seem flatly impossible. And yet it is not. Africans everywhere, even in highly adverse circumstances, make lives, produce value, fashion identities, husband social wealth, construct habitable worlds, create cultural products. The ethnographic challenge is to ascertain how, precisely, they do so, how the Problem of African Impossibility is resolved in the practice of everyday life, in the aspirations that drive it, in the improvisations that are demanded by it, in the face of hazards that threaten constantly to disrupt it. Motzafi-Haller does more than just address the Problem. She shows how, sometimes wittingly sometimes autonomically. Tswapong make coherent, sustainable lives out of almost nothing at all. How, in other words, they transform the impossible into the possible.

The theoretical-methodological achievement of *Fragmented Worlds, Coherent Lives* lies in Motzafi-Haller's deployment of the life-history as an ethnographic technique, a narrative genre of report whose intention is to offer up accounts of a social world that, by a process of simultaneous aggregation and objectification, reveal more than the subject of its telling. For my own part, I have been very critical of life history in the past. Biography, after all, is a bourgeois, Judeo-Christian mode of reckoning, of textualizing and decontextualizing, of rendering serial and consistent human lives that are typically inchoate, contradictory messes of minutiae; it is, recall, one of those "synoptic illusions" against which Bourdieu warns us, the illusion not merely of false coherence, but also of the construction of the radically individualized subject *both* as the author of her or his own life and as the atom of the lived world. In this neoliberal age, in which history is rapidly being reduced to memory, in which identity is understood increasingly in a therapeutic, Lacanian key, in which the social is dissolved by the ideological force of the market, the dangers of reducing ethnography to personal stories is painfully obvious. Motzafi-Haller succeeds in avoiding this trap. More positively, the manner in which she elicits and deploys those stories fuses the methodological with the theoretical; hence my awkward hyphen-ation. The claim of this book, and it is a compelling one, is that, in narrat-ing their biographies as they do, and in giving them palpable shape, Tswapong women instantiate the process by which a fragmentary world is itself conjured into social existence, shaped, made habitale. Produced. The production of individual lives, in other words, and the production of social life are shown—dialectically, dialogically, experientially, ironically—to be the conditions of each other's possibility.

Note, one last time, *possibility*. This, as I have already intimated, is a book about the impossibly poignant lives of people trying to make a life possible for themselves. But it is also more than that. It is an essay that makes a strong case for the continuing possibility—against increasingly strident claims made about the political, moral, narrative impossibility—of "thick" ethnographic description in the Time of the Postcolony, the Time of Reflexive Anthropology, the Time of the Other. As such, it is no less than an argument for an ethical, ethnographically grounded anthropology, an anthropology for the African present and future. For this, and for all its other virtues, it demands to be read.

John L. Comaroff

Acknowledgments

My research in Botswana began when I met Moses Basebi in 1981, a year before I came to live in his village Mokokwana. I was exploring a place to locate my intensive ethnographic research, and I had not known at that point if I had the funds to support my research plans. Moses said something that I recalled two decades later because it sums up the deepest gratitude that stands at the core of my work in Botswana. He said: "We can offer you all we have, but we cannot give you more than what we have." I lived in the home of Serefete Batlang, Moses's sister, for more than a year between 1982 and 1984, and the story of the Basebi family stands at the center of this book. I have not changed the names of these people who offered me "all they had" because they were real people and I felt they should be able to read what I wrote about them individually, and not in the abstract. I owe Moses, to whom this book is dedicated, and his family the deepest gratitude. They fed me, supported me during hard times, and welcomed me into their lives.

The people of Mokokwana village and Leoketsa L. Selaledi, the village headman, accepted me into their homes and welcomed me when I returned to visit them over the years. Leoketsa's father, old *kgosi* Lekutile Selaledi, was a dear friend until he passed away in 1984. A special mention must go to the members of the Maunatlala Land Board who allowed me to join them on their trips around the region, offered me direct access to all their official files, and invited me into their meetings. Many people across the Tswapong region hosted Moses and me during our travels in the region and shared with us their stories, past and present. I thank all of them, those whose names appear in this book and many others whose names do not but whose hospitality and friendship enabled my work in their villages.

Funding for the initial phase of field research was provided by the National Science Foundation, the American Philosophical Society, and a special grant from Brandeis University. My return to Botswana in 1993 was partly financed by the organizers of a conference that convened in Grahamstown, South Africa. I would like to thank Ed Wilmsen for inviting me to that conference and for reading and commenting on many early drafts of this book. I returned to Botswana and to the Tswapong in May 2000. I would like to thank Richard Werbner for inviting me to a conference he organized in Botswana where I presented some of the materials contained in Chapter 7 of this book.

Most of the writing of this book was done while I was a research fellow and a lecturer on anthropology at Ben Gurion University, at the Blaustein Institute for Desert Research in Sde Boker. I would like to thank Niza Yanai, my colleague at the Department of Behavioral Studies who read and commented insightfully on the introductory chapter, and John L. Comaroff, who read several drafts of this book and wrote its Foreword.

Finally, I would like to thank Wolfgang Motzafi-Haller who drew the maps, all the figures, and tables for the book.

Abbreviations

BNA	Botswana National Archive
CSO	Central Statistics Office
GOB	Government of Botswana
NDP	National Development Plan
NMS	National Migration Study
PDL	Poverty Datum Line
TGLP	Tribal Grazing Land Policy

Introduction

Migration and displacement have been the most profound and agonizing experiences in the lives of people in southern Africa for more than a century. Throughout the twentieth century, blacks in South Africa and millions of migrant workers from its periphery in independent countries like neighboring Botswana left their impoverished rural homes and families in search of employment in white-owned farms, urban homes, and mines. How do these people create and re-create the fragile tissue of their communities, families, and identities in the context of such ceaseless personal and communal upheavals and dislocations? What does community mean in such contexts? What happens when the relationships between communities and places are redefined in the postcolony? This book explores the ways in which people in one rural periphery in Botswana have forged a sense of place and collective identity over the past two decades. It aims to shed light on the experience of displacement and impermanency in the lives of these people and to analyze the production of identity, difference, and place in a world of shifting hierarchies of power and domination.

Movement between villages and outlying agricultural zones, to and from cities, and across international boundaries has been a major part of life in Botswana for generations. Since the early 1940s, anthropologist Isaac Schapera and others have documented patterns of migrant labor to South Africa and its effects on family life and local power relations. Strongly influenced by "world systems" and "underdevelopment" theories, political scientists and historians like Jack Parson (1981) and David Massey (1980) have examined the deleterious effects of labor migration on economy and society in Botswana. More recent research, including the ambitious National Migration Study of 1981–1982 (GOB 1981, 1983), has been useful in documenting the complex pattern of internal and international movement in the postindependence era. Yet what has not been recognized, partly because of prevailing theoretical paradigms, is that mobility here is not an aberration in what are otherwise stable, unchanging communities. The incessant movement of people has always shaped the way in which they have interacted and developed their sense of distinctive identities, both personal and collective. This calls for an ethnographic method that deals directly with mobility and the experiences of dislocation as an intrinsic feature of everyday life. Fragmentation in time and space, as the ethnographic record will show, does not mean the lack of coherent lives but a different way of constructing personhood and of acting in the world. This ethnography offers an analysis of how residents in the Tswapong Hills region in Central Botswana made sense of their deeply fragmented world in a particular moment in their postindependent history.

The Batswapong are agro-pastoralists and migrant workers who, like other Tswana-speaking groups, live in clustered village settlements surrounded by agricultural and grazing areas in the east central hilly region of Central Botswana. While their social and political organization shows similarities with that of other Tswana communities, the residents of these peripheral hills had been, in precolonial times, tribute-paying subjects; they occupied a position only a step above that of the ethnographically better known Basarwa ("Bushmen") within the hierarchical Tswana sociopolitical order. While many studies have focused on the centralized Tswana polities and on the plight of their "Bushmen" serfs, little has been published on minority subject groups such as the Batswapong, on their local world, their relationships with their former overlords, and their engagement with colonial and postcolonial forces.

ETHNOGRAPHIC AND HISTORICAL OVERVIEW

This study explores the interplay of space, memory, and identities within the Tswapong region. This region is a relatively well-watered hilly region, one of five administrative units within the large Central District of Botswana (see Map I.1). The total population of the region, including residents in land areas, cattle posts, and clustered village settlements, was about 20,000 in 1981. A decade later, the regional population grew to almost 25,000. Settlements in the Tswapong region tend to be small, located at the base of the hills and near water sources. Arable lands, cultivated by the residents of the village communities, are close by, at a distance of one to several hours walk from the village residence. The average size of the resident population in a Tswapong village settlement in the early 1980s was about

MAP I.1   The Tswapong Hills in Botswana

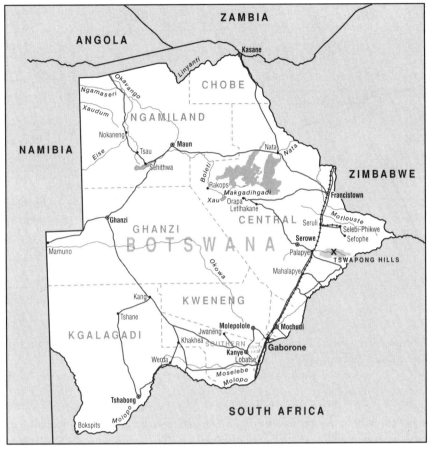

Source: Adapted from newafrica.com/maps.

700 people. The arable land cultivated by residents of one village community tends to fall within one or more named land area blocks, which "belong to" that village community. The movements in and out of villages and into a second dwelling constructed in the arable zone in this region are quite different from those occurring in the large agro-towns elsewhere in Botswana with populations of up to 30,000 people. The close tapestry of village-plus-agricultural-land units in this densely populated region also means that grazing areas consist of a few narrow strips of pasture on top of the hills and outside the residential and arable zones to the northwestern regions along the Lotsane River and next to the Elibi and Seoka streams. A

MAP I.2   Villages in the Tswapong Hills Region

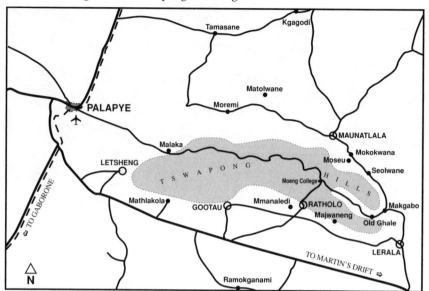

few pasture areas are also located to the northeast, around the village of Tamasane. (See Map I.2.)

The region reflects many of the economic patterns that characterize rural Botswana as a whole. It offers no employment opportunities in the form of locally based industry or other nonagricultural production. While the most economically active population in the region is still engaged in agriculture, agricultural production does not provide a sufficient basis for the economic survival of the regional population. Cash employment is extremely limited in the region and is mainly available in the larger villages. A large proportion of the potential workforce in the region is inactive; a larger number still must seek employment outside the region, in South African mines and in urban centers within Botswana. Since the mid-1980s, the growing mining sector Botswana, particularly the town of Selebi Pikwe, has become an attractive workplace for Tswapong residents.

A further characteristic of the contemporary regional socioeconomic structure concerns inter-village variability. On the whole, the larger the village, the higher the average income of its dwellers. Rooted in preindependence times, such inter-village differentiation has multiple implications for struggles over territorial and tenural arrangements unfolding in the region since the late 1970s.

In terms of ethnic classification, the population of the region is diverse. In 1952, Schapera (1952:185) commented: "The tribe called Tswapong is really a collection of several groups named generally after the hills in which they live." Indeed, despite the label "Batswapong" (used more often as a self-referent since the late 1980s), the residents of the hills define themselves as members of more specific ethnic and totemic collective entities. Some, like the original groups who established the village of Maunatlala, refer to themselves as Babirwa; others in the village of Seolwane are known as Batalaote. Other small groups that constitute a ward, or part of a ward, within established village communities trace their origin to, and are thus known by the collective name of, other Tswana groups settled outside the region, such as Bakhurutshe and Bakaa. Those who are considered to be the original inhabitants of the hills are often known as Bapedi, and their histories of migration into the region and of splitting once they settled continue to be a subject of intense public debate. The internal hierarchy of coresidential groups and the constant attempts to redefine it are central to the understanding of the emerging pattern of tenural and sociopolitical relations in the Tswapong region. A key to contemporary struggles over space and place in the region is found in historical accounts of residents who argue for their respective, legitimate, collective rights over particular spaces.

Taken together, the history of these diverse regional groups was significantly transformed at the point of their incorporation, after the 1860s, into the larger, more powerful political center of the precolonial Ngwato polity. Tswapong agriculturists paid tribute to the remote Ngwato center, and although they were allowed to maintain a large measure of control over their internal affairs, control over the region was ceded to Ngwato rule. The Ngwato ruler could, and often did, move dissenting groups from one locality to another within the region and, toward the turn of the twentieth century, had increasingly introduced new groups of settlers into the region. The cumulative outcome of these processes has been an increasing pressure over land and an emerging instability of relationships that once linked groups to particular tracts of land in the region. The establishment of the British Protectorate in 1895 over the whole area of present-day Botswana and the transformation of Tswana polities into "tribal reserves" with fixed geographical boundaries and limited jurisdiction over their subject population had further contributed to this sociopolitical and tenural process of transformation.

The two-decades-long postindependence history that stands at the center of the analysis offered in this study must be evaluated in the context of this longer regional history. By the late 1970s, almost a decade after independence, the impact of a major land reform and several legislative reforms was beginning to be felt in the Tswapong region. Increasing commodification of space and increasing capital investment in arable production resulted in a dramatic shift in the relationships between people and spaces. The most powerful result of this process of shifting definition of rights to residential and agricultural land has been the emergence of several new village communities in formerly open agricultural and grazing zones. Three new village settlements were added to the existing fourteen villages by the early 1990s. The process of emergence of these village communities in formerly open agricultural zones, the struggles—both material and cultural—articulated in the course of this process of tenural transformation, and the shifts in conception of locality, identity, and memory that this process signaled, are closely documented and analyzed in this study.

In analyzing the construction of space and identity and in situating cultural difference within shifting hierarchies of power and domination, I seek to understand how ideas of gender, personhood, and collective memory have been defined and reformulated during this period in the Tswapong region.

THEORETICAL REFRAMING

I first came to know the people whose lives I attempt to understand in this book in the early 1980s (between September 1982 and January 1984, following an exploratory research period in November 1981) when I began full-time participant observation research in the Tswapong hills region. In the summer of 1993 I went back to the same sites and followed the developments in the lives of the people I knew and in the structures of power and meaning that shape their lives. The decade that had elapsed between these two direct fieldwork experiences had produced not only two sets of data that bring to this study a critical time depth, it also marks a dramatic shift in the theoretical and analytical frameworks brought to bear in my effort to understand my empirical data. The result of this theoretical shift has been not only a novel interpretation, a fresh look at the empirical data I had recorded at two points in time, but also the reintroduction of bodies of ethnographic knowledge I had deemed irrelevant for earlier analysis I produced before my second visit (Motzafi-Haller 1988, 1993a, 1993b). Critical in this respect has been my use of life histories, analyzed in the first chapter of this book, and my analysis of the oral history narratives produced during interviews collected by Tswana history students from the University of Botswana. The analysis that closes the book, which explores the construction of ethnicized gendered identities, also draws on novel data and interpretive frames.

Since the early 1980s when I began working in Botswana until the moment of writing these words, social theory and practice have undergone a critical revolution in the way knowledge is produced and presented. This study is set, as it must be, against the profound questions and epistemological challenges posed by postmodernist ideas and by feminist responses to these ideas. Over the past two decades or more, postmodernism in its various guises has posited critical challenges to mainstream social theory. Above all, it rejected the search for broad generalizations and the tendency of modernist thinkers to develop "master-narratives" to explain social phenomena and called instead for the acceptance of the partial nature of all knowledge claims. The contingent and constructed nature of knowledge production has drawn attention to the manner in which individuals interpret their experience and create meanings in specific contexts of power. This shift in focus leads to a greater interest in processes of construction of partial identities and the notion of difference. These insights, although not easily encapsulated into a coherent abstract general theory, have yielded exciting new theoretical and analytical tools that have altered the way we think about societies and social realities, about cultures and how to represent them.

This book contextualizes some of the theoretical debates emerging in the aftermath of this "post" era—postmodernism, postcolonialism, poststructuralism—through closely detailed ethnographic research. Yet, it reflects only those epistemic and theoretical elements in contemporary critical theory that I found relevant for my work and that I have actively internalized as a writer and researcher. The process of selection, of making use of some aspects of postmodernist ideas while rejecting others, of internalizing feminist perspectives and marrying these to my anthropological work has taken many long years. During these years I have worked not only on my Botswana ethnography, but on two additional research projects in which my positioning as a researcher and author were quite different from that in which I have found myself in Botswana. In the first research setting I have been working as a "native anthropologist" exploring issues linking gender, ethnicity, and class analysis in my native Israel (see Motzafi-Haller 1997, 2001). In the second research setting I returned to Africa, to Burkina Faso (formerly known as Upper Volta) and to issues of rural social change. This time I am part of a collaborative research endeavor that engages three young Burkinabe researchers who are actively conducting field research on topics of their choice within several regions of the country. My ongoing work in these two research projects has been shaped by, and has directly shaped, the kind of epistemological and conceptual questions I place at the center of this book: How do we understand the social reality of marginalized people? How and who can represent their fragmented, indeterminate, continuously emerging reality? How can we make the life worlds of people remote from power palpable to readers without losing sight of the political and material conditions that shape their environment?

The following section presents four key analytical questions I seek to explore in my work. The discussion is not intended to explicate these theoretical and analytical principles in the abstract but to show how I have used them in constructing the narrative of this study.

GENERAL ANALYTICAL ISSUES

Contingent Realities and the Question of Representation

The lives of the people among whom I lived have been, as the ethnographic record I shall present shows, deeply fragmented, and their worlds, which necessitated movements between impoverished rural areas and industrialized centers that claimed their labor, have been deeply alienating. In attempting to understand their experiences of impermanence and displacement, I could not assume an ordered, coherent world. In depicting their lives and worlds I opted to enter the narrative at a range of "entry points," of places from which to provide a partial view of these lives. Thus I enter the narrative in each chapter from a different perspective. Before presenting a detailed exploration of life stories of members of a single family, I analyze the context within which these and all other biographical narratives were recorded. I point out the ruptures, gaps, and silences inherent in these narratives. I then move to a political-economy view that attempts to examine from outside the conditions that shape these lives. Then I reenter the story by examining historical narration articulated by local elders and offer a look at a selection of "local moments" that depict tensions within several focal sites in the region.

One central feature of the analysis offered here is that it questions the very notion of community and communal identities and focuses on the multiple struggles to impose meanings by positioned individuals. Throughout this analysis I select for closer examination the way gender is interwoven, defined, and resisted in a range of moments during the two decades in which I followed events in the region. The pieces—the partial analyses that explore the construction of space, memory, and individual and collective identities—are not intended to provide a complete narrative, a coherent story about "The Batswapong" or about historical transformations occurring in the region over two decades or more. They are, by definition, fragments, glimpses into a world lacking clarity, a world characterized by alienation.

Throughout this study I problematize the manner in which I came to know what I argue that I know. I stay away from the established anthropological practice of citing unnamed informants or stating general cultural realities in phrases such as "The Batswapong do X" or "Among the Batswapong it is common that." Instead, I begin all my analyses with particular, specific events and anecdotes—with experiences and moments of incomprehension I shared with people. I then proceed to examine the complex negotiations and twists of meaning in each particular situation. I seek to analyze these local events as part of a historical process of contradictions unfolding in larger contexts of power.

Writing Life-Worlds within Political Economy

At its most general level, this ethnography attempts to bridge the gap between studies that have attempted to depict, in Marcus and Fischer's words (1986), "other cultural experience" through an examination of narrativity, personal histories, and the way the world is experienced by social actors on the one hand and studies that have analyzed the hybrid world of these marginalized people in southern Africa in terms of world historical, political economy models on the other.

When I began working in the region, the focus of my research was to identify transformation in the relationships of people to land in the aftermath of a major land reform. I was working within a theoretical framework that focused on historical processes and the political economy of such processes. Within this analytical and theoretical framework there was little place for the personal stories I documented. But these accounts, as we shall see in the opening chapter, contain a powerful insight into the way life was experienced in the Tswapong. Once I set out to explore the meaning of these accounts and to theorize their links to the wider processes I had documented, it became amply clear that I needed to account for their complexity and to problematize the process of genesis behind these narratives. The recent debates within feminist and cultural theory about the ways personal narratives of subaltern populations are to be comprehended became central to this book.

Over the past two decades, this interest in the silenced, marginalized voices of the oppressed has led a growing number of researchers to make increasing use of narratives, life stories, and records of personal experience. Feminist critics, for example, noted that women often experience the world in particular ways that are not reported and that are often silenced by mainstream writing. But this growing body of work on narrativity faces, in its turn, several important criticisms. Within anthropology, a burgeoning literature has developed an important critique that calls into question the simplified, conventional views about individual experience and the concepts of selfhood and identity as bounded, fixed essences. This literature drew attention to the social and cultural specificity of subjectivity. Eloquent in this regard is Catherine Lutz's work (1988). Lutz develops a theoretical argument about the socially constructed nature of identities and emotions, as does Dorinne Kondo's more recent ethnography about the way selves and identities are "crafted" in contemporary Japan (1990). Other feminist theorists (particularly DeLauretis 1986; Scott 1988; Spivak 1988) have taken this critique a step further by showing not only that identities and narratives produced about personal experience are historically and culturally specific, but that "the construction of identities cannot be discussed in the abstract, separately from power relations" (Kondo 1990:43).

The book opens with personal narratives that depict the fragmented nature of lives of men, women, and children not because these narratives tell us about the "true feelings" of the people with whom I spoke, but because they are particular discursive nodes that articulate through their specific narrative conventions and forms the various ways in which gender, displacement, and life are experienced. I thus begin the book by asking what these stories say about the construction of gender and ethnicity, about space, and about collective identities in a shifting world of power. Only then do I move on to examine these concepts and processes from other data sources (local moments, oral interviews, events). I seek to understand the construction of collective identities in Chapters 3 and 4; the issue of space is examined in the following two chapters, and an exploration of the making of gender and ethnic identities is offered in Chapter 7.

Writing in the late 1990s, I struggle to understand how this fragmented world was experienced and acted upon by the men and women who inhabited this impoverished margin of the global economy. I attempt to do this without losing sight of the political and material conditions that shape these life-worlds.

Social Space and Memory

The evidence of transformation in spatial relations was the focus of my initial investigations in the region. I began by exploring how people have dealt with state reforms that redefined patterns of local leadership and altered access to land, both arable and residential, following a major land reform. My analysis of the unfolding process of territorial and tenural changes shows that subjectivities have been constructed across a range of different sites, across time, and through a complex process that has invoked historical legacies in the service of contemporary struggles. State impingement into the Tswapong region has taken the form of provision of social and physical infrastructures and the constitution of a system of registration that imposed novel fixity on an inherently fluid spatial organization. Foucault's insight (1984) that links spatial relationship with concerns of control and social power has been central to the analysis I develop of such historical empirical data.

In a series of critical works published between 1970 and the mid-1980s, Foucault (1970, 1975, 1984) focused his attention on the relationship between power and space. In theorizing about the links between space, power, and knowledge, Foucault explored not only the evolution and "production" of social spaces (such as military hospitals, factories, and planned towns) but also examined the impact of such spaces both on individual behavior and on the mechanisms of political and social control.

Drawing on Foucault and the work of social geographers Harvey (1992), Soja (1988), and Gottdiener (1985, 1987), I explore the ways in which space was produced and transformed in rural Botswana. For if space, as Foucault has argued, is always a container of social power, then the reorganization of space, which I document in this book (specifically in Chapters 5 and 6), must indicate a transformation in social relationships and in the distribution of social power. I examine how the apparent change in spacial relationships has been structured and how it affected the redistribution of wealth and power in this region.

Feminism and Postmodernist Sensibility: Linking Gender to Other Lines of Social Differentiation

The infusion of race and class into feminist analyses has been one of the most heated and prolific debates in contemporary feminist writings. However, few studies examine the way gender is constituted as a category of social difference within specific historical and political settings and as one axis within several other, mutually defining axes of social difference. This study attempts to do just that. My treatment of gender in this study begins with an exploration of the way it is experienced and articulated by both men and women. The analysis proceeds to examine the working of other lines of social difference along ethnicity, class, and clientship in their historical specificity. I return to a focused interrogation of the construction of gender and its embeddedness in spatial and institutional contexts of power in Chapter 7 where I explore the way Basarwa femininity is constituted and resisted in a marginalized community. Basarwa, as the analysis developed in this book shows, is a category created in particular contexts of power relations in Botswana and not a given, essentialized ethnic category.

The analysis of the manner in which some women were constructed as "Basarwa" by hegemonic Tswana discourse and the particular implications of such classification in their lives, I argue, cannot be performed before one grasps the historically specific contexts that shape other axes of social difference in Botswana, namely clientship, ethnic hierarchies, and class. In developing this argument I draw on more recent feminist theorizing that has called into question the liberal feminist orthodoxy that has ignored difference among women (Spelman 1990). This brand of feminism, most often advocated by minority feminists, argues that race, culture, and class must be incorporated into feminist analysis (Anthias and Yuval-Davis 1990; Collins 1990; Emberley 1993; Fox-Genovese 1994; hooks 1990).

The feminist analysis I seek to enact in this book is an analysis that recognizes the importance of multiple lines of social difference and the local complexities of such divisions without neglecting larger political and economic structures. It explores the making and unmaking of social difference as an interplay of multiple, mutually constitutive identities, individual and collective.

THE PLAN OF THE BOOK

I begin with a detailed exploration of the setting that yielded eighty-seven narrated biographies of adult residents in one small Tswapong village. This context is necessary for framing the detailed stories of lives of members of one family—the Basebis—presented in Chapter 1. Through these strikingly varied life stories we grasp the experience of dislocation and movement of men, women, and children and their resources across space and through time. These detailed life stories are contextualized in Chapter 2, where an outline of the three-pronged production economy in Botswana that includes cattle, cultivation, and labor migration is presented. Then, using detailed village census data, I proceed to locate the position of the Basebis and their neighbors on that national socioeconomic grid. Chapter 3 presents detailed data on the movement of people and resources in and out of some eighty homestead compounds in a single Tswapong village over a decade. This profile is traced at two moments of time, 1983 and 1993, to make possible an examination of the political and economic conditions under which distinctive identities, both personal and collective, are constructed. It also examines the third domain of identity formation, the village-centered household, and explores its links to the notions of family and conjugality. The exposition of the malleability and fluidity of the notions of family, household, and conjugal relations provides the underpinning for the following chapters that examine other sites of identity formation—the village community and its association with larger constructed social units and relations.

Using my own and other unpublished oral data, I document in Chapter 4 the shifting definitions of group identities with reference to the changing political economy in and beyond the region. Based on a critical reading of transcripts of oral interviews carried out in the Tswapong region by University of Botswana history students in 1980, this chapter examines the way contemporary struggles to define communities and the control over segments within these communities is articulated in historical narratives. It also explores the power of indigenous narratives to express resistance to dominant ideologies and to give voice to subjective formulations of space, memory, and collective identities.

Building on the analysis presented in Chapter 4, Chapters 5 and 6 examine the ways in which people struggle to establish spatial and temporal meanings—and how they enter into the politics by which culturally distinct places are produced. In Chapter 5, I document the manner in which unfolding changes in spatial relations over the last two decades have become the focus of intense social struggles in Botswana. Based on ethnographic and historical research spanning more than a decade, I describe how the organization of space and place in the Tswapong region gave. way to an ever more shifting, uncertain definition of rights to residential and agricultural land brought about, in part, by state policies promulgated in the late 1970s. In the aftermath of national land reform, with an increasing commodification of space, a radical change in relations among people and places has occurred. Several new village communities have emerged in formerly open agricultural zones, and capital investment in real estate has imposed fixidity on previously fluid, shifting arrangements. My analysis seeks to demonstrate that these processes challenge existing frameworks of power and differentiation, reconfiguring conceptions of locality, place, identity, and collective memory.

Chapter 6 takes a closer look at a doubly marginal community emerging at the edge of the Tswapong region on the South African border. This case examines two moments in a decades-long struggle of impoverished herders and former serfs to assert their claims to a settled life and the engagement of such local struggles with national and transnational forces. The analysis offers an exploration of the way collective identities, social space, and social relations have shifted in the course of the past decade or more in rural Botswana. It also probes the cultural dimension of reproducing and challenging patterns of rural differentiation. When situated in larger frames in time and space, the local story of this one rural struggle for land, leadership, and social recognition is seen as structured by and indicative of a rapid social transformation in the region. In the emerging reality, new identities are drawn, land becomes scarcer, and economic gaps sharper.

Gender, like class and ethnic divisions, is institutionalized in the fabric of Tswana society and shapes patterns of inequality. Tracing the life stories of three generations of Basarwa women, residents of a Tswapong village, and placing these stories in the larger political economy that has structured social distinction in Botswana, Chapter 7 offers an analysis of the interlocking dynamics of gender, class, and ethnic categories. It depicts the way gender intersects with ethnic definitions in a historical process that has reproduced poverty and social marginality, social identity, and group boundaries.

In Chapter 8, I draw together the ethnographic insights that link the range of entry points I have developed in this study into the lives of the people I knew. I also make explicit the paradoxes and epistemic tensions that have emerged in the process of writing an ethnography in this critical post "post" moment.

1

Fragmented Lives

Jeremea Mabati was born in 1923 in the village of Mokokwana, in his father's homestead (*lolwapa*). Jeremea was the fifth child. He spent his childhood herding his father's cattle in a remote grazing area known locally as Mokgacha-wa-dinama. He attended one year of school, so he can identify letters but cannot really read. When he was fourteen or fifteen years old, he hired himself as a "kitchen boy" in Mafeking, the colonial administrative center of the Bechuanaland Protectorate in the southern region of Botswana. After a few years in Mafeking, the white people he worked for "transferred" him (he used this term in English) to another family in the Tuli Block farms, a region of freehold farms at the eastern border of Botswana with South Africa. As a kitchen boy he was paid little, so when he had a chance, in 1952, he took a mine job in South Africa. His work in the mines meant that he was absent from home for long periods of time, but part of his wages was sent back to his family, who bought him cattle with these remittances.

Jeremea worked seven years in the mines before he accumulated enough cattle necessary to begin the process of "talking about marriage" (*nyalo*). His father provided him with three head of cattle, and his mother's brother (his *malome*) contributed an additional beast toward his marriage payment (*bogadi*). When his wife had their first child, she continued to live with her parents while Jeremea went back to another yearlong work contract in the mines. Between 1961 (when his father died) and 1964, Jeremea was in South Africa without a break. His family heard nothing from him. When he returned to Mokokwana in 1964, after several uninterrupted years of absence, he took the time to split the family herd, tended all these years by his older brother.

During the years of his absence his wife and children lived in the arable zone and shared their home with Jeremea's younger sister. Three out of the seven children born to Jeremea and his wife survived. In 1972, Jeremea ended his last contract of migrant labor and returned to Mokokwana to tend his cattle. He built a makeshift hut in the grazing areas and remained with his cattle in the remote cattle post. A year later, in 1973, his wife joined him in their cattle post, but the children remained with Jeremea's sister because her house was closer to the school they attended in the neighboring village of Maunatlala (there was no school in Mokokwana at the time). In 1975, Jeremea's wife built their first mud and thatch home in the clustered village settlement in Mokokwana. Their older son, Mpo, was sending some money from his mine work in South Africa.

Jeremea's story, recorded in Mokokwana on August 12, 1983, speaks of a life that is broken by repeated migration and dislocation, of shifting residence in several sites, and of prolonged separation between spouses and among parents and their children. Jeremea's story raises questions of enduring and general significance, given that so many people in Botswana's rural peripheries are leading similarly fragmented lives under the impact of rural impoverishment and labor migration.

Why are lives in this place so broken up, so mobile, so labile? And how do the people who lead these lives make sense of their existence and construct coherent experiences—and, inasmuch as they do, narratives—about it? This chapter sets out to explore these two questions.

TELLING LIVES

On a cool, gray August afternoon in 1983, sixty-year-old Nkalolang dressed in his best clothes—a worn, gray suit jacket and a Panama hat—walked slowly into the open, large yard of MaTuma. His wife, Matsatsi, with a dignified looking knitted shawl on her shoulders was a few steps behind him. They approached the chairs placed in the shade of my hut, in MaTuma's yard, and after exchanging greetings with MaTuma, with her brother, Moses Basebi, who acted as my research assistant, and with me, they sat upright waiting for the expected "interview" to begin. By that afternoon, I had been in Mokokwana, living in MaTuma's yard, for almost a year. Everyone in the small 400-strong resident Tswapong village was familiar with my research at that point. Since my arrival in Mokokwana in September 1982, Moses Basebi and I had completed a detailed village census, visited people in their second dwellings next to their arable fields, participated in every social public event in the village and its surroundings, and convened several sessions in which we asked about the local history of the village. In late August 1983, the word was out that now Pnina (or as they called me, "Penni") and "Mosis" (Moses Basebi's nickname) were inviting each adult resident of Mokokwana for a formal interview.

It was Moses's idea that we carry out such interviews in the large yard of his sister Serefete (known as MaTuma—mother of Tuma, the name of her firstborn son), where I resided, and not in people's yards. "It will lend more dignity to the interviews," he argued. And dignified they were. In fact, the setting of an "interview" imposed rigidity we could not overcome, nor, as it turned out, could we change the format or the idea of interviewing *all* Mokokwana adults. Once begun, these interviews had a life of their own. People were not merely being cooperative by showing up in my yard during the afternoon scheduled for them. They were eager to take their turn in such sessions. The interviews became a village event, formal, orderly, and bestowing respect and dignity on all who participated.

Between August and early November 1983, I interviewed eighty-seven adult residents in the village of Mokokwana (fifty-three males and thirty-four females), asking them to tell me about their lives. The decision to begin what I called in my notes "a systematic record of all 'personal histories' of adults living in the village" was conceived as another "database" designed to complement other systematic bodies of data I was driven to amass as a "good fieldworker." A central feature of life in the Tswapong region in east-central Botswana was the incessant movement of people out of their impoverished rural homes in search of employment in urban centers within Botswana and in white-owned farms and mines in neighboring South Africa. My systematic efforts to map out the socioeconomic patterns and the politics of space that defined this reality of ceaseless mobility and dislocation had yielded, at that point in my work, several bodies of empirical evidence, including a complete village census and a record of the varied links among members of all village-based residential units (*malwapa*)—those resident in the village and in the agricultural zones surrounding it and those absent from their rural homes. I was also working on compiling a detailed oral history of group settlement in this and other villages in the region. By turning to the records of individual histories, I was hoping to complement this objectivist database with a subjective record that might shed light on how these general social processes of movement and fragmentation were experienced by the people I knew in the region. I wanted to grasp how they made sense of their truncated world, of the long separation between spouses and between parents and their children. I wanted to grasp how they experienced life in what they called *makgoeng,* the country of the *makgoa* (whites), and how they constructed the links between their rural homes and their lives in towns, farms, mines, and factories within and outside Botswana.

My notebooks are scattered with vibrant vignettes describing a woman's reflection about her life, shared with me during a walk in the woods collecting firewood, or a man's emotional recollection of his experiences as a youth herding cattle in the open grazing areas, told in a conversation during a family meal I was invited to partake around the evening fire. But it was obvious, early on, that I could not reach such moments, such quality of reflection and personal narrative, during the scheduled interviews. I was painfully aware of my inability to draw out more detailed, personal stories and reflections.

Here is what I put down for Nkalolang Motsabi on August 21, 1983.

Born in 1921 in Motsabi's (his father's) yard. The third born in the Mogomelo agnatic descent group. Pitoro was the headman then. When he was 12 or 13 he was sent to his father's cattle post. In 1940, he went to Maunatlala elementary school and attended school for three years. In 1943, he walked to his first mine job in South Africa. He counts ten such mine work contracts in the following years. He had bought many cattle with his mine earnings, but they all died.

In 1951, when his first daughter, Kebone, was born, he worked in Kimberly. He was paid 12 South African rands per month.[1] Kebone was born in the *masimong* (the residence next to the arable field) of Matsatsi, his future wife's parents. Matsatsi stayed five years in her parents' yard and Nkalolang gave her money to feed the children. In 1956, Matsatsi and the children moved to his parents' yard. It was then that they performed what is known as a *setapa* ceremony. He provided four goats to be slaughtered in that ceremony. He gave her father two cows: one is *lerumo* (a bullet—for entering the yard [and impregnating the girl] without agreement of the parents), the second was called *sebeko* (to ask the wife with). He also gave blankets. When Matsatsi moved to Nkalolang's parents' yard, she built her own two huts in their yard and began to cultivate a part of a field given to Nkalolang. It was, in fact, his father's father's plot reserved for him. Nkalolang helped Matsatsi plough their land during the short periods that separated his consecutive labor contracts. He also came back when Matsatsi built their huts—he constructed the roofs.

In 1965, Nkalolang stopped going to South Africa. For almost a year he stayed around in the village. That year (1965), he recalls, was the year of the "big drought" when his cattle all died. A couple of years later, Nkalolang moved to Gaborone where he secured a job in the town council. His job in Gaborone enabled him to buy a single-room house. He paid a small deposit and every month five pula were taken out of his salary. Throughout his years of work in Gaborone, his family visited him and stayed in that house. When his daughter wanted to attend secondary school, she lived with him for five years until she completed her education. In 1982, Nkalolang left Gaborone "because he was too old." He was given a sum of money which he used to buy two cows.

The telegraphic account of the life story of Kebone, Nkalolang's firstborn daughter, provides another illustration for the kind of record I produced about this young woman's life.

Kebone was born in 1951. She completed her first years of elementary education in Maunatlala. She walked to school every day from her parents' residence next to their fields. In 1966, Kebone left school and went to work as a housemaid for a white person (a *lekgoa*) in Selebi Phikwe, the mining town constructed in those years. In Phikwe, she met a man from Serowe and became pregnant by him in 1971.

She came back to Mokokwana and stayed in her parents' yard because she was *motsetse* (a woman after giving birth, a nursing mother). The man sent money to support her and her child. In 1977, after having three more children they got married at the District Council offices in Serowe. That marriage is called *chatile*. His *bogadi* (marriage payment) was 120 pula paid to her father. He also promised to give a cow but, at the time of the interview, had not fulfilled his promise. In 1983, Kebone lived with her man and their six children in Phikwe.

Clearly, what I have here is far from my expected vivid narrative of how this man and his daughter "experienced" their lives. When I reviewed these notes (that made up a separate hard-covered notebook) during the years of reflection and analysis that followed my first fieldwork, I found them useless. I had not used these records in my earlier analytical work.

Years later, when I first read Renato Rosaldo's (1976) strikingly similar feeling of disappointment due to his own inability to elicit "a revelation of the dark and hidden depths" in the life of an Ilongot man, I came to realize that I needed to question my original expectations of what these interviews meant and that I must reassess my original ideas about how these individual accounts could be used to shed light on social processes I was describing. There was also the burgeoning literature in anthropology and feminist scholarship that have refocused attention on such personal narratives. This recent interest in "native voices" and "narratives of the self" has yielded an increasing desire among many contemporary anthropologists to produce an unedited record of such narratives in order to hear the "real truth" about the narrator's life. Rosaldo (1976:145) parodies this methodological naiveté, noting that placing a tape recorder "in front of Mr. Non-literate Everyman" does not necessarily mean that "he will tell the 'real truth' about his life."

Like Rosaldo, a new, more sophisticated body of work had began to ask: What happens when narratives articulated in other cultural settings do not take the form of the expected, western idea of self-reflection, or when such "voices" appear in ways that often do not articulate a coherent, flowing narrative? What constitutes a "real truth" in such personal narratives? And how do we account for the misreading and shifts of meaning that always occur when an unedited, unanalyzed "native life story" is brought, as Ruth Behar's (1993) superb study of a Mexican market woman's life story has shown, "across the border"?[2]

This chapter offers a reformulated evaluation of the individual biographical accounts I recorded in Mokokwana in 1983 and in 1993. In the interpretive framework I develop, the focus on individual lives is necessary—not merely complementary—to an understanding of larger social phenomena. Social phenomena is understood through its embodiment in actual, lived experience. An understanding of the culturally constituted nature of narratives of self stands at the center of this theoretical reformulation.

THEORETICAL REFRAMINGS: CULTURALLY
CONSTRUCTED NARRATIVES OF THE SELF

Since the late 1960s, the anthropological tendency to generalize from decontextualized statements made by undifferentiated "informants" has been challenged by scholars working in a range of theoretical positions—in post-structuralism, feminist theory, and practice theory. From their varied theoretical and analytical positions, these critics have called for recentering attention on the "subject" as an acting agent within specific cultural and historical settings. The burgeoning literature that has placed biographies and narratives of the self at the center of social analysis had, in its turn, to face mounting criticism for its tendency to treat biographies as neutral, transparent windows into history and society (Bourdieu 1987). "One problem with the genre [of life stories]," writes Ruth Behar (1993:272), "has always been its use of the Western form of the autobiography to encase the self-narrative of a person marginalized by the west." If we are to go beyond such ethnocentric and ahistorical understanding of individuals and subjectivities, Comaroff (1992:26) has argued, we must problematize the very notions of individuals and events. The question thus becomes: How are subjects constituted in varied social and historical settings?

Over the last decade or more, feminist theorists articulated a further challenge to the assumption about the unity of the "Self," the "speaking subject" who is expected to produce reflexive, coherent self-knowledge (Butler 1989; Harding 1991, 1992; Hekman 1990, 1992). Feminist ethnography has called for a consideration of the multiple, contradictory, and partial nature of identities and has argued for a theorized interpretation of experience (Weed 1989). The category "experience" in this theoretical reformulation does not necessarily reflect the "truth" about any one individual life. It is used, instead, as an avenue for reading the way individuals deal with conflicting social, political, and ideological forces.

Making use of these theoretical and analytical insights I wish to reexamine these life histories—the fragmented, hybrid accounts I have recorded—not as complete, authentic texts (which they are not), but as partial, ambivalent constructions of selfhoods crafted at the particular setting of the interviews held in the early 1980s. I shall analyze these fragmented, disrupted narratives in three ways:

1. They can be viewed as both a product and an expression of the disruptions and displacement experienced by people living within and crossing the boundaries of "two worlds"—rural and urban, country and industrial centers, here and there.

2. I shall ask what these stories tell us about varied strategies used by these people for dealing with impermanence and disruptions.

3. I will explore how people crafted their notions of gender, identity, and space within their shifting, complex worlds during the act of constructing these stories.

This approach has critical methodological implications. First, it means that these stories are to be analyzed as "speech events" and not as closed, complete textual products. In this sense, the setting of interaction between teller (who is actively constructing his or her life story and, by that very act, articulating his or her own subjectivity) and the listener/recorder of the story cannot be transparent and must be included in such an analytical frame. I will thus begin with an exposition of the setting of the interview sessions.

The second methodological implication concerns a renewed interest in the form and the style of the story told. Literature on the topic often draws a distinction between what it terms "life story" and "life history." Life stories, it is argued, connote creativity, invention, and construction, while life history assumes matter-of-fact telling of given facts, recounting a sequence of events (cf. Polanyi 1985; Jesselson and Lieblich 1995). I find such a distinction artificial and of little use for the case in point. It is embedded in western notions of individuals who are introspective, creative, and detached from the reports they produce of their lives. The setting I wish to analyze here must be understood in different terms. Creativity here is not articulated in embellished, flowing narratives, but via the very form of telling these stories. Here I find feminist epistemology more useful due to its emphasis on "silences, gaps, disruptions, or contradictions" (Chase 1995:14) that are symptomatic of situations of inequality and power.

In reading these biographical accounts I wish to examine not only what was said but also what was missing from these accounts. The form of these individual stories, when properly analyzed, might lead to insights about larger processes of domination and empowerment in this and other local sites.

AUTOBIOGRAPHY, ETHNOGRAPHY, AND THE CONSTRUCTION OF NARRATIVES

Telling one's "life story" is not a familiar cultural form in the Tswapong region. It was enacted in the particular setting of the ethnographic research project I began in September 1982.[3] The interviews were carried out almost a year after my arrival in the village and were, more than any other aspect of my research in that village, a shared product. Although I raised the idea and introduced the notion of writing down individual biographies, people in the village had, to a large extent, defined the shape and scope of the sessions within which these biographies were created. It was, in fact, a classic case of what Donna Haraway (1988) has called "situational knowledges"—knowledges produced in and for specific contexts. Viewed in this manner, the biographical accounts I present here must be seen as a particular product of the research "situation." My discussion of the research setting and the place of the biographical accounts as one kind of knowledge produced within this setting will address two specific issues. The first depicts my ambivalent position in the binary racially divided world of rural Botswana. It will also discuss the place of my research assistant in the research process.

The second part of the analysis will describe in greater detail the interview settings and the dynamic interaction among Moses, myself, and the tellers, an interaction that has actively produced the biographical accounts.

In speaking about the particular role I took in producing these accounts, I do not wish to engage in what Geertz in *Works and Lives* (1988:89) dismisses as "diary disease" or to follow the increasingly more sterile reflexive accounts about "my experience" in the field. Rather, and in accordance with the analytical framework that sees these accounts as products of speech events, as knowledge produced within and for the research, it is an attempt to map my and my assistant's respective roles as full partners in the production of these biographical accounts. Consideration of our respective positions within this focused process of knowledge production raises critical issues of epistemic and political significance.

A *Lekgoa* After All: *Lekgoa* as a Mirror

In the last day of my first extended stay in Mokokwana, in January 1984, when I made my rounds of good-byes, Mazambia, one of my best women friends, reflected about my presence in her village by saying that years from now, when she will tell the children that a *legkoa* who spoke Setswana lived in Mokokwana for more than a year, they will not believe her. A *lekgoa* is a person of non-Tswana origin, most often white. My being a *lekgoa* was, for her, the most critical defining element of who I was. The other parts of my identity—the fact that I was Israeli, Jewish, a student, a woman researcher, single, young, a friend with whom she shared many secrets—all faded away. I was a *lekgoa,* and *makgoa* (plural of *lekgoa*) have never stayed in her village or other rural sites she was familiar with, the way I did. For Mazambia and others in this rural periphery at the edge of apartheid South Africa, the color line that distinguishes between *makgoa* and Batswana was a defining fact of life. Their lives were spent working for whites in apartheid South Africa, in mines, urban homes, and farms. In all their encounters *makgoa* were powerful, privileged, wealthy people whose only dealings with Batswana (people of Botswana) were as employers, supervisors, and instructors. Batswana left home to work for the *makgoa,* but very few *makgoa* ever entered small villages like Mokokwana. When they had, their stay was brief and for a specific goal such as the recruitment of workers or sales.

Significantly, encounters with *makgoa* often required the possession of papers and official documents. Writing or providing information that was written down was associated with such inherently unequal situations that required the production and frequent presentation of papers needed as work permits. Biographical facts, such as place of birth and a range of dates indicating the beginning and end of work contracts, were critical for these written papers that secured employment or denied it.

I was, of course, deeply aware of these powerful circumstances of inequality from the outset. Toddlers cried and clung to their mothers in fear when I entered their yards, and it took months before the local children stopped running after me in the village paths screaming with joy: "*Lekgoa. Lekgoa. . . .*" People were amused by the fact that I insisted I was a *Moisraela,* a woman from Israel. They have heard about Israel as the land of Jesus via their Christian education but knew little about its contemporary existence. My own ambivalent position within this binary racial division (as a woman of Middle-Eastern ancestry, a *Mizrahi,* with a somewhat darker skin color that got me barred from entry into a public facility open for "whites only" in Johannesburg—see Motzafi-Haller 1997) was not relevant to my hosts in Mokokwana. I came from the undistinguished land of plenty, land of the whites—*makgoeng*—and I must, therefore, possess the goods, the knowledge, and the power of whites.

My struggles for acceptance in this small community centered on undermining as much as I could the extreme power imbalance embedded in this racially divided world. From the very opening public meeting held in the central village *kgotla* (the gathering central space) where my request to live in the village was discussed, I made it clear that I have no power or material resources with which to help the community. I insisted that I was there to learn, to write about what I learned, and that the only contribution my work might yield was that "those with power" might read what I have written.

Throughout my stay in the village and during my visits and interviews in other sites in the region, I explained that I was a novice, not a professional researcher, that I was a student who had to write a thesis that must be approved by my professors. I said I would need to understand things properly if I wished to "pass" (get my degree). The idea of students who work on their education and the fear of not "passing" was familiar in Mokokwana. Several sons and daughters of Mokokwana families were students in high schools, one completed teachers' training college and one was applying for the Botswana University in Gaborone. In fact, the word *pass* has become a Setswana word that is conjugated in the vernacular form.

To fit my "student" status, I displayed the tools of my craft—my hardcovered notebooks, camera, and tape recorder (that never seemed to function)—on all occasions. In one instance, a few months after I began my work in Mokokwana, an old woman stopped her conversation with me and urged her little son to run to my hut and bring "Penni's book" because she was going to explain something I should "write well." This growing sense of sharing, of taking an active role in the process of producing what I was to write about their lives deepened and took the form it had due to the particular nature of Moses Basebi's place in this project. Moses's personality and his position in the community were critical in this regard.

Moses was a thirty-two-year-old resident of Mokokwana and the only English-speaking person in the village when I began working there in 1982. I hired Moses as a translator and teacher of Setswana during the first months of research. (I had studied Setswana—the language spoken by most Batswana—for almost a year with a Tswana graduate student in Boston prior to arriving in the village.) But Moses emerged very rapidly into a partner and a most able assistant for the research. An intelligent man with a great curiosity about the world around him, Moses grasped rapidly the main idea of what I wanted to accomplish in my research. During the first months of our work together, when we recorded the domestic composition and histories of each residential unit in Mokokwana, Moses's role was never limited to simple translation of questions and answers. He was able to alert my attention to what was meant by these answers. For example, when a woman answered my opening question, "Whose yard is this?" with a name of a man and then proceeded to answer the next question by listing the names of all the children born to this man, Moses translated her words directly and then added what he understood I might have missed: the man mentioned died a few years ago, and the last three children born in this yard were in fact the biological offspring of another man. In oral history sessions we carried out in Mokokwana and later in other villages in the region, Moses took an increasingly active role in asking questions himself. We spent many evenings discussing not only the logistics of the research—what I wanted to learn next and why, where we should go, and who we should interview—but also how I thought this body of data could be used in my attempts to understand life in Tswapong. I showed Moses my notes, explained how I recorded domestic and dynastic histories in kinship charts, and shared with him my partial insights about the processes we were documenting. When we began recording oral histories in other villages within the region (and as my facility with Setswana improved), Moses became an interviewer who posited his own, independent questions. I will analyze these sessions and Moses's role in them in the upcoming chapters.

When I proposed the idea of recording personal histories of adult residents of Mokokwana, Moses was a full partner in planning and eventually in shaping the interviews. This was his village and he knew every person in it. They all knew him and his active role in the project. Moses, whose biography opens the next chapter, was one of the guys. He was not richer, nor more educated than most people in the village. His intelligence and energy won him much respect in the village, but his unsettled status as an unmarried man balanced this respect. People often had an active joking relationship with Moses. They admired his ability to speak English, a language he picked up during his fragmented work experience and not through formal training that might have set him apart as "too educated." And they clearly wanted to be part of the "being written up" idea Moses supported.

Let us draw together these lines that depicted the contexts within which the sessions took place and suggest a few ideas about the meaning of the narratives produced in such settings. Writing, and being written up, as I noted earlier, was associated with the world of power and with their oppressed place in such a world. Familiar contexts where biographical facts were reported and recorded have been at the center of the oppressive encounter between Batswana and *makgoa*, hired laborer and employer, the powerful official or representative of the law and a migrant whose presence had to be justified with documents. Here was a different kind of a writing setting, in which they had actual control over their own representation. It was a session with no imposed form, nor a limited time frame. The sessions were an inversion of the familiar hierarchical order in several ways. The sessions were held within their rural, social universe and not in alienated settings of the *makgoa* world (the employment office, for example). A *lekgoa* who penetrated this space was recording their words, but her presence was mediated by the evident interest and active role played by a local man. The *lekgoa* had no direct, supervisory power over the narrators. And the speakers were surrounded by family and friends who played an active part in constructing these biographical narratives.

Yet, despite the license to say whatever they wanted to tell about their lives, the sessions, as we shall see, evolved into a ceremony, an invented ritual of sorts that followed a few, repeated characteristics. I will first outline the more specific dynamics of these sessions and then proceed to make several observations about the emerging form and content of these narratives.

NARRATION AND SUBALTERN DIGNITY

When they walked into MaTuma's yard, they were all dressed up; some of the women had put on their colorful church clothing. The greetings were detailed and formal. Both men and women were offered chairs to face those on which Moses and I sat. Women giggled in embarrassment but never refused the chair offered them. (In public meetings and in their domestic spaces women often sit on the ground, on a mat, with their legs stretched in front of them.) Children and young adults who came to listen sat around the small circle of chairs and were often told by Moses and other adults to stay back and keep quiet. MaTuma, my "adopting mother," acted as a host, offering sugared tea and slices of white bread to my guests.

After several failed attempts to get these sessions recorded (my recorder was full of dust, the batteries usually went dead in the middle of the session, etc.), we proceeded mainly by relying on my writing. I pulled out *the* hard-covered blue notebook (that became a known object in these settings and the butt of repeated teasing comments) and declared that I was ready for their words. During the initial sessions when I began writing rapid notes for myself to describe the event and the people, I was scolded. People insisted that I must begin writing only after they had sorted out the "correct" facts about their lives. I use the verb "sort out" intentionally, for this is what people were actually and actively doing in these sessions. They took their time and involved those present in the process of constructing what they deemed an ordered sequence of events and facts about their lives.

It was an explicit "workshop," a setting where they converted their inarticulate experiences into an ordered, externalized "story." Bourdieu speaks about this process of objectification when he notes that "private experiences undergo nothing less than a change of state when they recognize themselves in the public objectivity of an already constituted discourse, the objective sign of recognition of their right to be spoken and spoken publicly" (1977: 170). The process of objectifying their life experience and molding it into a pattern, a reified story, however, occurred in the setting I describe here without what Bourdieu calls "an already constituted discourse." In this rural setting in Botswana, as in many parts of the non-western world, biographical narration and recording is not a familiar discursive practice. More suggestive, in this context, is Bhabha's notion of mimicry as an act of "double articulation." The insistence on dictating only "facts" that were collectively approved, the laconic style of these narrated facts, and the respected, dignified nature developed in the course of these sessions all attest to the ambivalent adoption of the language of power. It is an act, in Bhabha's words, "which 'appropriates' the Other as it visualizes power" (1993:86). Before developing this interpretive argument further, it is necessary to turn to the narratives and analyze them for their emerging form.

EVENTS NARRATED, GAPS, AND SILENCES

There was a significant difference between the kind of narration offered by men and women about their lives. Men's narratives always proceeded in a strict chronological order that opened with the date and place of one's birth. Women tended to begin with the present: where they resided, how many children they presently have, etc.

Men structured their life stories around a sequence of several distinct life events. The place and date of birth often contained details about one's family affiliation, and in several cases the date of birth was marked by citing who was the village headman that year. Few words were offered to describe childhood experiences. Most men reported spending their early childhood and young adolescent years herding cattle at grazing areas outside their village homes. Men often made a point in noting whose cattle they herded during those years (father's, mother's brother's, etc.) and the location of the cattle post in which they spent several years of their lives. Before reporting about their first year of migrant work, most men duly mentioned the number of years they spent in school. Most men over age forty reported staying only one to three years necessary for attainment of literacy. Younger men, born since the early 1960s (and thus school age in the post-independence years) tended to stay longer in school—up to seven years.

The most critical event reported in all biographical accounts of Mokokwana males is the first departure for migratory work. Men insisted on recording the precise dates of each contract in a long sequence of migratory work experiences. If a man had not returned at the end of several consecutive periods of labor migration, and could not therefore cite the precise dates of departure and return to his rural home, he was jeered by those present as a *lekgolwa*. No man offered such a definition of himself. Being a *lekgolwa* meant that you severed your social links and your obligation toward people left behind in the rural home. It was thus with great pride and precision that men recounted the many cycles of departure from and return to the village.

However, although the dates of labor migration were recorded in great detail, little was said about the experiences of life spent abroad. One fact mentioned by several men was the pitiful amount of money they were paid for their labor. Little else was volunteered. Even when asked directly to indicate the name of places where they worked, people evaded the question. One exceptional example will illustrate this collective silence about life in *makgoeng*. One man had spent most of his adult working life as a cook and house servant for a Jewish family in Johannesburg. Relating to my Jewish background, this man spoke often about his life with the Jewish family. He told me the names of his employers, described what he cooked for them, and spoke about how they treated him. During his scheduled interview, when he continued to speak about his life in South Africa, those present (including Moses Basebi) were ill at ease. At one point, they proposed that he was getting into unnecessary detail and effectively silenced the man. The man, I must add, was the only one who insisted on referring to me as "missus Penina" months after all in the village were calling me by my local nickname.

In contrast to this general silence about life in *makgoeng*, many details were offered about the use of money and remittances sent back home during these migrating years. Men noted how many head of cattle they had purchased, who had cared for the cattle, and how the cattle were used and by whom. Marriage payments and the exchange of cattle during various stages leading into the establishment of a marriage featured greatly in such accounts. Men detailed the precise dates in which they made various marriage payments; they noted the nature of these transactions (blankets, cattle, money) and indicated their specific amounts.

Engagement in agricultural production was also depicted in many of these biographical accounts. Men recalled what field they cultivated in what year and whether that year was a good or bad year for agricultural production. Details, like the amount of bags of grain produced in a particular year and who shared that produce, were also noted with alacrity.

Women, especially older women and those who headed their own expanding households, developed narrative accounts of their lives that did not follow the chronological sequencing so prevalent in the men's stories. Women often opened their narratives by indicating their present situation: they noted where they lived and with whom. As they laid out the social network that linked them to the father or, often, various fathers of their children, they made detailed references to the extent and kind of help each man offered in raising their children. Women, in other words, spoke through connections, and these connections were not linked to inter-family or descent lines of relationships but were directly focused on their children and on the people who helped them in raising these children (biological fathers, brothers, and adult sons).

Women, many of them illiterate, were clear about the chronology of their life story. They cited dates (reported in English numbers) without hesitation or prolonged efforts to calculate those dates. I found it extremely surprising that most of the women who reported the year of birth of their children had some difficulty reporting the age of that child.

Women traced the chronology of their lives through the dates of births of their various children and through the sequence of their movement in space. Their movement between the village home and the one next to arable fields was not seasonal but extended into several years. Often women stayed in their arable land home when their men were away from the village or when their children were too young to attend school. Single, unmarried, or widowed women tended to stay away from their village homes for longer periods of time. Their return to their village home was related to a shift in their relationship to other adults and children. These movements, between residential loci in the rural areas and between rural and urban homes (where they helped their daughters raise young children) structured the chronology of life for most adult women interviewed.

The cycle of movement in space was closely linked to their reproductive cycle. Women often tried to give birth and spend the first months after birth-giving in their natal homes. Women were more explicit than men when they spoke about children born in *bonyatsi* (lovers) relationships. Women were much less detailed in describing the various economic and social transactions that led to their own proper marriages. They seldom mentioned the amount of cattle paid for their *bogadi* or the various services and other material goods paid by their husbands to their families of origin.

CONCLUSIONS: "TWO WORLDS" AND "FRACTURED SELVES"

The laconic, fragmented, and telegraphic style of these accounts is not a failed, unsuccessful, limited narration of complex lives but the very expression of the fragmented world of which these lives were made. The act of crafting a personal narrative was an effort to convert an inarticulate experience of dislocations, of work in oppressive circumstances, of disrupted efforts to build a home and a family into a meaningful story.[4]

In the process of trying to transform their inarticulate experiences of dislocation and fragmented existence into coherent narratives, the narrators appropriated the language and discursive style of the dominant. They insisted on having these stories written down in English and sought to mimic the dry, chronological style of official record taking by providing precise dates for their migrating life cycle. But while documenting the precise dates of their periods of labor migration, they offered little information about the way they experienced life in *makgoeng*. In fact, they imposed silence on anyone who attempted to describe his life in *makgoeng*.

In contrast to the general silence about life in *makgoeng*, the narratives offer a wealth of detailed recollections about aspects of life linked to their rural existence. Men offered many details about their agricultural production, carried out before, after, and during the brief time away from their life in *makgoeng*. They relished in tracing the many transactions that led to their marriage contracts, and they recounted the amounts of beasts they bought, herded, and lost in the course of their lives. Life lived outside this rural social arena, even if it lasts for long years, is not discussed. Meaningful lives unfold in the rural home. Women who migrated to join their menfolk in *makgoeng* deal with impermanence by focusing on their children and construct their social identities within the spatial boundaries of home. The narratives are suggestive about the varied strategies adopted by men and women to make sense of their lives. These narratives speak about the way people who live such fragmented lives cope with their worlds and about the kind of identities constructed in these historical and political contexts. These narratives provide vivid evidence (fragmented and in need of interpretive frames as it is) for the manner in which subaltern people construct their hybrid identities.

The rest of this book attempts to explore how such hybrid identities articulate within larger frames and relationships. In the next chapter we begin with the examination of the meaning of family and conjugality. The chapters that follow expand these circles to include community, leadership, and larger collective identities.

NOTES

1. At the time of the interview a rand was worth about one U.S. dollar.

2. Jane Fajans's book *They Make Themselves: Work and Play Among the Baining of Papua* (University of Chicago Press, 1997) deals with similar questions and explores in greater depth the same methodological and theoretical implications.

3. I completed some of the biographies in 1993, especially those of the Basebi family that form the core of the next chapter.

4. In their most recent book (1997) Jean and John Comaroff respond to John Peel who told them to pay attention to "the most universal and primary forms of narrative" and base their analysis not only on missionary texts, but also on stories told

by people "from personal memory and experience" (1995:586). The Comaroffs claimed to have "pursued such stories in every shape and form" (1997:426), but insist that these stories "often did not yield historical narratives, *senu stricto,* other than those told in the modernist genre or in response to our prompting." I am not clear what is suggested in this last phrase. Does it mean that the people among whom the Comaroffs worked produced only "modernist narratives" and that these were not good material for historical analysis? Given the sophisticated, by now classical, analysis offered by the Comaroffs (1987) of what a "madman" conveys via his gestures and dress, I doubt that this is the case. Personal narratives can be elicited in the research process, as I did in my work, and the analysis of what they mean and how they represent the world of the narrators is extremely useful and revealing. I thus agree with Peel and those who insist that paying attention to "native voices" is important. Such narratives should be contextualized as I have done here.

2

Gender, Conjugality, and Family

The presentation in this chapter consists of two main parts. The first provides an exemplary family history, a detailed account of the shifting interconnections among the lives of members of a single family (the Basebi family) over three generations and more. The second part of the presentation moves to explore several individual life histories of members of this family, each in its turn. This organization is designed to articulate both the theoretical and ethnographic themes I wish to employ in this chapter. By examining the shifting frame of relationships within the context of a family, I seek to demonstrate that the definition of personhood among the people I knew is multiple and intersubjective. The "family," as we shall see, is itself a node of shifting relationships rather than a stable, corporate, and exclusive social unit. The second objective of the chapter is to trace a few individual histories in greater depth, beyond what was offered in Chapter 1, in order to illuminate the different strategies used by men and women, older people and the young generation to cope with poverty and fragmentation in their lives.

THE BASEBI FAMILY

Basebi was born in Mokokwana in the first decade of this century (sometime between 1905 and 1910) to a family of Pedi migrants who came from the South. He was the most senior, living member of a village ward (*kgotlana*) known as Modimoeng, one of the four major wards of Mokokwana.[1]

FIGURE 2.1   The Basebi Family

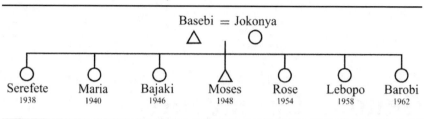

The original lineage at the core of the Modimoeng ward had shrunk to only two existing households in the village: Basebi's and that of his younger brother Sebopelo. Sebopelo died in the early 1970s, leaving behind a widow who resided with her grandchildren in the village yard (*lolwapa*) #28.[2] At the time of the first village census in November-December 1982, Basebi resided in a small, unkempt *lolwapa* (#13), together with his wife Jokonya, his unmarried son Moses (my research assistant), and the two young children of his daughter Lebopo, who was working in Francistown. Only two of Basebi's daughters—Serefete (*lolwapa* #1) and Maria (*lolwapa* #45)—resided with their children in the village. (See Figure 2.1.)

As a descendent of migrants (*bafaladi*) who had joined the dominant *kgosing* ward,[3] Basebi was mainly an observer and not a key player in internal power struggles in the village arena. In 1982, Basebi's lack of social standing in the community was further hampered by his rapidly deteriorating eyesight and his severe walking difficulties, due to a grossly swollen foot. Basebi had been absent from the village and his family was fragmented and dispersed for many years. Basebi was a young man working in a South African mine in the mid-1930s when he impregnated Jokonya, daughter of Tsiamo, on one of his visits to Mokokwana. Jokonya gave birth to her first daughter, Serefete, in 1938, and to a second daughter, Maria, in 1940. During most of this time, Basebi was away working in the mines, and Jokonya and her children remained in her parents' yard. In 1943, Jokonya left her two young daughters behind in her mother's yard and joined Basebi in South Africa. While in South Africa, the couple had two more children: Bajaki was born in 1946 and Moses in 1948.

Basebi, according to his son Moses, was a *lekgolwa* for many years. Whenever he left to go to work in South Africa, he had to be called back; otherwise he stayed on "forever." In 1950, Sebopelo, Basebi's younger brother, traveled to South Africa to bring his brother back home. Basebi, Jokonya, and their two younger children came back to Mokokwana and the conjugal bond was firmly established with a transfer of a bride price (*bogadi*) of eight head of cattle. Upon his return to Mokokwana, Basebi built a yard next to his brother's, cultivated arable fields together with his brother, and extended his family with two more children. Rose was born in 1954 and Lebopo in 1958. But in 1961, while Jokonya was pregnant with yet another child, Basebi acted out his "*lekgolwa*" reputation and "disappeared" again. Jokonya took her newborn child (named Barobi) and went south to look for her husband. Jokonya never found Basebi. She ended up working on a white person's farm in the Tuli Block.

During the early years of their mother's absence from the village, the three middle Basebi children left behind in Mokokwana—Bajaki, Moses, and Rose—were taken care of by Maria, the second-born daughter. Serefete, the eldest, had already begun her own reproductive cycle: her first child, Tuma, was born in Mokokwana in 1958. In 1960, Serefete left Mokokwana. She, like her mother, had taken her firstborn child and joined his father, Batlang, in South Africa.

When their mother left the village, the three younger Basebi children had been attending primary school. In 1963, Bajaki, who was seventeen at the time, was the first to leave the village for Francistown. After she secured a place to live and a job, she took seven-year-old Rose to live with her.

Meanwhile, Jokonya remained in the Tuli Block farms with her two younger children, Lebopo and Barobi. She supported herself and her children through her work as a hired farmhand. No one knew of Basebi's whereabouts. When asked directly during the interview session to recall the names of the places he had worked in South Africa during his many years of absence, Basebi chuckled and said plainly he did not remember the name of the places. He was, he said: "*mo nageng*"—in the bush.

In 1966, Moses and Maria decided to join their mother in her Tuli Block farm residence. Their residence in the Tuli Block farms, Maria recalls, was not a "village" (*motse*), but a group of huts where people of various origins worked—Batswana, as well as non-Setswana-speaking South Africans. "There was no chief (*kgosi*) only a 'foraman,'" she explains (the word *foraman* is the Setswana derivative of the word "foreman"). In 1967, about a year after they joined their mother at the white-owned farm, Moses, now nineteen, returned to Mokokwana alone, but there was no home to which he could return. All that was left of the family's village *lolwapa*, following long years of absence, were a few ruined mud huts. The family's *lolwapa*, had turned into a *matota*, a ruined yard. In fact, Moses recalls, there were very few *malwapa* (plural form of *lolwapa*, yards) in the village arena when he returned. These were the years immediately following the *boipuso* (national independence), and most Mokokwana villagers stayed year-round in their second homes in the arable zones. Moses thus joined his father's brother, Sebopelo (*lolwapa* #28), and his family in their residence in the agricultural zone.

Meanwhile, Rose, who was living in Francistown with her sister Bajaki, had found a job in a shop in Serowe. A few years later, she moved back to Francistown to work as a salesperson in a small canteen. In 1973, she married a local policeman, a man of Kalanga origin.

In 1972, after almost a decade of migrant work in South Africa, during which he had not maintained any contacts with his wife and children, Basebi, old and almost blind, returned to Botswana. For the subsequent seven years (between 1972 and 1979) Basebi lived with his sister in her dwelling near her fields, while Jokonya continued to live and work at the Tuli Block farms. In 1979, Moses, after more than a decade of migrant work contracts and incessant movement between jobs in Botswana, took it upon himself to bring his mother back from the Tuli Block farms. The return of the Basebis to the clustered village settlement, and the rebuilding of their village home in the early 1980s, was part of a larger process of collective resurgence in Mokokwana.

In 1981, Basebi joined his wife Jokonya, his son Moses, and his daughter Maria and her children in their newly erected village home. Soon after, the two children of Lebopo (at the time an unwed mother, living in Francistown) were sent to Mokokwana to join the Basebi homestead. Maria, the second-born daughter, noted that the arrival of her younger sister's two children strengthened her decision to move out of her parents' overcrowded yard. An unwed mother of seven children, Maria took advantage of the new land allocation law that enabled women to apply for their own residential and arable land. In 1981, she was allocated a plot within the village settlement where she constructed her own *lolwapa*.

Basebi's return to his village home after long years of absence in the South African "wilderness" (*mo nageng*), was, however, short-lived. In February 1983, Basebi left the village to seek medical help for his increasing blindness. He resided in Francistown with his daughter Rose, who supported him.

In December 1983, in the course of my second village census in Mokokwana, I recorded the following composition of the Basebi *lolwapa* (#13): old Jokonya, her unmarried son Moses, and Lebopo's two children, Margaret (born 1977) and Bonolo (born 1980). Basebi died in a hospital in Francistown in 1987. In 1993, the Basebis' *lolwapa* (#13) was deserted once more. Moses, hospitalized in Francistown, had left his wife and two children in the *lolwapa* of his wife's parents. Jokonya, his mother, had been living with Rose in Francistown ever since her husband died. Aside from Serefete and Maria, the two eldest Basebi daughters who still remained in Mokokwana, all the other Basebi offsprings (four daughters, a son, and their respective children) resided permanently in Francistown.

THE EXPERIENCE OF DISLOCATION AND THE FAMILY

These interlinked life stories speak about lives of acute poverty in what has come to be known as the "labor reserve" region at the periphery of the South African industrial center. The experience of dislocation, of movement and fragmentation, is central to the lives of members of this single, four-generation family. We have learned about incessant movement across international borders and between several temporary homes. We have heard about the varied strategies used by men and women to survive within a hostile and exploitative political economy that claimed their labor and devastated their ability to make a living in their rural homes. We have also heard about their struggles to make homes, to create meaningful lives in the midst of such fragmentation and mobility. To understand the disruptions in the lives of these people and the deep contradictions inherent in their fragile worlds, we need to understand the ways in which they constituted their worlds, lives, families, and communities.

The detailed account of the lives of members of the Basebi family shows that individuals moved in and out of relationships and situated social categories. In the process of such ceaseless movement and displacement, the family unit fragmented and again coalesced. During this process of fragmentation and coalescing, clusters of localized family units of shifting composition were constituted. In the case in point, such localized clusters have existed at different points in time: a mother and a few of her children, several siblings of various ages, a man and the family of his father's brother, or a man and his sister's family.

The Basebis had created several temporary homes at various locations. In South Africa, a fragment was created when Jokonya crossed the border to join her husband and remained with him long enough to enlarge the family by two more children. Yet, even then, a small fragment of the young family had been left behind. Children who were left by their parents were cared for by other members of the extended family. Connections with the natal home also secured a place to which family members could return when labor contracts were terminated. Resources were pulled together to enable the transition back to the rural home. Upon their return to Mokokwana, the Basebi couple and their young children moved to reside next to Basebi's brother and began to cultivate arable land that was jointly held by the two brothers.

Fragmentation often put women in a position of having to fend for themselves and take care of their children for many long years. The second phase of migration across international borders in the Basebi family history resulted in such fragmentation. While Basebi worked in a South African mine, Jokonya supported her two youngest children through her work as a farm laborer at a white-owned farm in the Tuli Block. Here again, parts of the nuclear family were left in the rural home. The rural home acted as a center from which fragments dispersed and coalesced. When the mother, Jokonya, left to work as a hired laborer on the farms, her school-age children were cared for by an older daughter. The three made ends meet via irregular small sums of money sent back by their mother and help from relatives and neighbors in the village arena.

The strategies adopted by the women left behind have varied over time. The option a woman and, perhaps, a few of her children had to join the migrant man in his workplace in South Africa became more limited when international borders were established after the political independence of Botswana in 1966. Serefete was able to join her husband, Batlang, at his workplace in South Africa during the early years after independence, but not later. Migrant labor by women as an option of survival was dramatically curtailed by the late 1960s. Since the early 1970s, young women, like the two Basebi daughters, began to leave their rural home in search of employment in the growing urban centers within Botswana. Conjugality in these urban settings, as the life stories of Rose and Bajaki detailed later in this chapter will show, produced a new set of practices and meanings.

The story of the Basebi family also illustrates the ways in which children and resources circulate among the various, shifting family fragments. Fragments of a family centered in urban areas relied on rural fragments to care for their young and provide sustenance to those left in rural homes. In their turn, wage-earning daughters in town supported their children and other members of their family residing in the village. This situation is particularly critical when the mother is unmarried, as is the case of Lebopo who resided in Francistown. Lebopo sent her children to her rural home when this was constituted in the late 1970s. In some cases, a child would be sent out of the rural areas to town. Thus, when a young woman (like Bajaki) found an employment in town, she called for her younger sister to live with her, thus relieving some of the pressure on the impoverished family fragment clustered in the rural home.

Networks of support link fragments in the rural home with their urban, wage-earning members and connect several family fragments struggling to survive in the large town. As we have seen, the two unmarried daughters (one of them the mother of the children sent to the rural home) created a shared household in town. Or in another situation, a married daughter who settled in town might offer accommodation to her younger sister until the latter finds employment in town. We have also seen in this family how Rose, once established in town, supported her father when he was in need of medical attention available in Francistown.

Families, we learn from this extended single history, are not corporate units with clear boundaries that prescribe rights and obligations of their members. The boundaries of the family ebb and flow, and family fragments cluster at shifting sites. While related people (both agnates and matrilateral kin) may cooperate in productive work and share resources such as land or labor, these associations are often short-lived and shifting. The detailed chronicles of movements in space and time of members of the Basebi family show that the family is itself a moving node of social and economic relations. The impermanence in the Basebis' lives, true for most rural families in Botswana, had dramatically shaped the way in which people interacted with one another and constructed their sense of distinctive identities, both individual and collective. The critical question thus becomes not how has impermanence disrupted families and stable communities, but rather what is the shape and meaning of individual and collective identities in these fluid contexts?

In the next section we look at the experience of fragmentation and movement across space and time articulated by individual members of the Basebi family. In presenting the individual life stories of members of the family, I wish to explore the distinctions between male and female life trajectories and those that prevailed among three generations of males and females within this family. The Basebi life stories begin with the account provided by Moses Basebi, the only son of Basebi and Jokonya.

Moses Basebi

Moses was born in South Africa in 1948. He was two years old when he was brought to Botswana by his father and mother. He did not know the name of the place in South Africa where he was born; it was next to one of the mines where his father worked. When they returned to Botswana, Moses lived with his parents and his three older sisters next to their arable field. The field was jointly cultivated by his father and his father's younger brother. Moses and his father's brother's son tended the small common herd belonging to their two families. Moses remembered walking about seven kilometers from his parents' home in the agricultural zone to the elementary school in the neighboring Maunatlala village. He completed seven years of elementary education. Moses loved school and was the best in his class. In 1962, when his mother left to search for his father in South Africa, he continued to attend school. During the years of his mother's absence, he recalled that they (the three younger children) often cooked for themselves. His mother sent small amounts of money, enough "to buy corn-meal." When he was almost eighteen, Moses searched for his mother and younger sister in the Tuli Block farm where she worked. He found his mother after a few months and stayed to work at the same farm. However, the pay for farm labor was lower than what he could earn as a miner in South Africa.

Moses signed his first mine contract job in 1968, which was for nine months and paid 29 tebe per day. (In 1982, when Moses was recalling these facts, the Botswana currency of one pula [100 tebe] was equal to about one U.S. dollar.) Moses spoke openly about his deep fear of the mine. He was terrified of the depth of the places where he had to spend a whole day digging. It was like death, he related, with no light, and he could not breathe. The Afrikaner supervisor made fun of him and called him a coward. Moses vowed never to return to the mines again.

When his contract was over, Moses returned to Mokokwana, but he did not find anything to do. He hung around the village for a few weeks and then secured better-paying mine work—for 51 tebe a day. This time, Moses managed to get himself a clerical position in the mine's office. His good command of the Afrikaner language and his clear handwriting helped convince his supervisors that he could do the job. But toward the end of the third year, Moses decided to look for a job within Botswana. In 1970, he began to work in a shop in Palapye. A few months later, he started working as a clerk in a post office at Sherwood Ranch (on the Botswana–South African border), a job he kept until 1975. The pay was low, but he was away from the mines.

While in Palapye, Moses impregnated a local woman. Moses made no bones about his evasion of responsibility. He indicated that he moved out of Palapye and took a job at Sherwood because he wished to escape paying money to support the woman and "her" child; constant demands on his salary had been made by the woman and her siblings. He had not intended to marry her and was afraid that she would take him to court and make him pay "damages," a lump sum paid to the mother toward the cost of raising a child. Moses admitted he had made several other women pregnant. In some cases he paid; in others, he "escaped."

In 1975, Moses decided to move to Francistown, where he lived with his sister Rose. In Francistown, he could only manage to get low-paying, part-time jobs (he called these "piss jobs"). In 1977, he returned to the village. Knowing that no family homestead existed in the central village arena, he headed for the lands area, where he joined his father's brother's son and began to cultivate a field with him (his uncle was deceased by then).

Two years later, in 1979, Moses departed for the Tuli Block in order to bring his mother and sisters back home. His sister Maria was a mother of several children, whom she supported alone. His mother came back first and then Maria followed with her children. They immediately began to build a new *lolwapa* in Mokokwana. Moses cleared and then ploughed the field belonging to his father. The field had been deserted for many years. The few cattle that belonged to his father from a herd jointly owned with his father's brother were not sufficient for the needed draft power. His mother's sister lent them her draft team. They ploughed together, sharing labor and draft power. Yet, despite all their work, nothing grew in the newly cleared family plot. Their mother's sister gave them half a bag of corn from her meager yield, and they made ends meet by selling two head of cattle. Their few head of cattle had been held by relatives during the many years of their absence.

I first met Moses in October 1981, when he was "hanging around the village." Moses worked as my research assistant between October 1982 and January 1984. For a few weeks in February 1983, Moses worked as a supervisor for a drought relief project.

For almost a year after I left Botswana Moses did "nothing," as he put it. He spent a few months in Francistown, living at his sister Rose's house; he returned to Mokokwana and just "hung around." In early 1985, Moses returned to work in South Africa. He continued to work in South Africa, with just a few weeks "rest time" at home for almost five years. During these years, Moses had yielded to his mother's pressure and made legitimate his relationship with a Mokokwana woman with whom he had already fathered two children. He did not provide any *bogadi* (bride wealth) cattle to the woman's parents, but bought her dresses and pots and some other property for her kin. Moses laughed when I asked him in 1993 if these were *mokwele* (formal gifts) presented by the man's kin group to the woman's family, items that signify the commitment of both sides to the union. "It was not serious," he explained. "I just gave them some presents."

In 1990, Moses took his wife and children to Francistown, where he found a job as a guard in a local firm. "I was getting fat," he says, alluding to his good luck. "It was a good job and I earned money every month." Moses wrote me several letters after 1990. He was happy and was beginning to build a stable home for his family in Franscistown. But when I arrived in Mokokwana in the summer of 1993, I was told that Moses has been hospitalized. Moses had lost feeling in his feet and could not walk. Weeks of conventional medical checkups found no obvious reason for his malady. Moses was convinced he was bewitched by his coworkers, who were jealous of his nice position. With no pay and growing debts, Moses moved out of the single room he rented in the poor part of town, and his wife and their four children were sent back to the village to live with her parents because Moses's parents' yard was deserted at the time.

Moses's life story is particularly interesting because it diverges in two critical points from the more common male life cycle I had recorded in the Tswapong region and from stories other scholars have documented in other parts of Botswana (cf. Comaroff and Roberts 1977, Cooper 1979, Schapera 1947). First, Moses had avoided migrant work as much as he could and second, he was able to openly describe his feelings about his life as a migrant, in contrast to the life stories of all the other migrant interviewees who seldom talked about that experience. An analysis of the particular circumstances that have shaped this man's life trajectory provides a good entry point to an understanding of the economic significance and the sociocultural meaning of migrant work in the lives of young males in rural Botswana. Because of the candid and detailed nature of his life story, it also sheds light on the experience of conjugality and parenthood—from the male perspective. Ultimately, this life story raises important questions about the contradictory processes of construction of individual identity and selfhood in the context of life that spans two worlds—rural periphery and labor migrancy.

Several critical themes emerge from the way Moses constructs his life story. The most central is the manner in which Moses weaves together the fragments of his life, the sequence of disruptions and dislocations, into a single tale of his life career. Moses emerges from the story he constructed as a man who struggled to control an inherently unstable, confused, and fragmented world. His story speaks of the need, shared by most males in Botswana, to migrate to South Africa to secure employment. Labor migration is a critical phase in the lives of most young men because it is often the only avenue they have to accumulate enough to begin the cycle of their own independent household unit.

Moses had obviously failed to create his own autonomous economic and social base until quite late in life (his late thirties). He had made repeated efforts to create a life without labor migrancy. In the process, he relied on his own abilities and on family support—material and social. In South Africa, soon after his first contract, Moses had crafted a privileged space for himself in the hated universe of mine work. In Botswana, he had moved between clerical jobs and sporadic efforts to make a living through agriculture. Moses had cultivated land and shared labor with some of his matrilateral kin *(ba ga etsho mogolo)* and with his agnatic kin *(ba ga etsho)*. When he was in the hospital, he relied on his new affines to care for his wife and children. Yet despite his skills and his creativity, his limited success in building a life without migrancy (success measured in terms of his ability to build an independent social and economic base) attests to the irreducible, unavoidable place of labor migrancy and the almost complete reliance on wage economy in the lives of men in this study.

A second critical element that is unique to Moses's life story and thus illuminates, by contrast, other stories I have recorded, is his ability to speak about his work experience as a migrant. As I noted in Chapter 1, one of the things that impressed me about the life stories told by Mokokwana men was their ability to report the precise dates in the sequence of their movements to and from work sites in South Africa, without a moment's hesitation or a fragment of a thought one might need to calculate, to reconstruct the date of an event. Yet, these men volunteered little information about their lives in South Africa, and little was ever said about their personal feelings of living and working in South African mines, farms, and urban centers. The most powerful illustration for this collective silence, this tendency of glossing over such life experience abroad was Basebi's (Moses's father) claim that he could "not remember" any of the names of the places where he had worked in South Africa. Like him, most of the men interviewed spoke about their migrant lives as an existence in *sekgweng* (in the bush), and they spoke about South Africa as *"makgoeng,"* the country of the *makgoa,* the white people.

Moses's vivid account about his deep fear and profound hate of the mines and his repeated attempts to escape migrant labor contrasts with the silence accorded such experiences by the others. The gaps in their stories are made more evident when we consider Moses's reflexive account.

Moses constructed his life story with its repeated movements across space and time not as a truncated, disrupted account, but as a prolonged process of crafting a social self. The movements between rural and urban settings, migrant work, and reintegration into village social life was the texture from which his goal of creating meaningful life in Botswana was made. Through-out his movements, Moses maintained his social obligations as a son and a brother—but clearly not as a lover and father. His sustained commitment to his natal family contrasted with, and maybe was borne out of, his irre-sponsible conduct as a father and partner. His father had been a *lekgolwa*—a person who had cut his social links with his dependents in the rural areas. Migration and long separations, in other words, do not *necessarily* tear the fragile tissue of social relationships in this setting. Adult male lives are frag-mented when they leave their families and search for employment many miles away from rural homes and families, but separation in space and time does not necessarily lead to social and individual isolation. The concept of *lekgolwa* seems to encapsulate the ever present fear of disconnections and social isolation. A *lekgolwa* is a man who has failed to create coherent life. Unlike the *lekgolwa,* most men struggle all their lives to *maintain* social interdependence and keep their responsibility towards kinfolk despite pro-longed separation. Basebi, during his *lekgolwa* years, defaulted on his responsibilities and created a space, a vacuum which Moses, the only son, had to fill.

Moses had not been a *lekgolwa*—he had maintained and built up his links with close kin and others in his rural home. Yet Moses had not been as successful in maintaining his social responsibilities toward women and the children he had fathered. It is important to emphasize that Moses was not proud of moving on, or in his words "escaping" the demands these women placed on his limited resources. In other words, he perceived his conduct as socially improper. The problem lay not in some cultural disap-proval of having children with a woman without legitimizing the bond in marriage. The improper conduct of people like Moses rested on their repeated pattern of avoiding a socially prescribed responsibility toward these women and their offspring.

Moses seemed to draw a distinction between the fleeting relationships with the women he met during his brief stays in their villages and the for-mal marriage *(nyalo)* he had eventually entered into with a Mokokwana woman in the late 1980s. In order to grasp the meaning of his relationships with these various women, one must understand indigenous notions of con-jugality. Anthropologists have often described the processual nature of Tswana marriages (J. L. Comaroff 1980, Kuper 1975, Roberts 1977, Schapera 1940, 1950, 1963). One cannot comprehend Moses's and many other Tswana males' conduct in terms of western bourgeois ideas of a pre-marital frivolous life in contrast to an eventual, if delayed, proper marriage. Instead, his many liaisons with women run a continuum that characterizes the nature of Tswana heterosexual relationships (cf. J. L. Comaroff 1980, Roberts 1977). On one end of this continuum stand the casual unions Moses created with a series of women, having no intention of sustaining such bonds.

Moses was a *legodu*, a thief who metaphorically sneaks into the yard of the girl at night, unseen, without social recognition. Moses's conduct (at one point he estimated having fathered nine children prior to his marriage), however, had gone beyond such ambivalent cultural approval in two respects. First, he repeated the pattern too many times and thus gained a reputation as an unreliable man. Second, Moses had too often breached a basic norm that requires a man to compensate the women's pregnancies and provide limited child support. While women could and often had sued men for such compensation, Moses took advantage of his transient position to escape his responsibility. Moses's narrative speaks about the tensions of conjugality and the meaning of parenthood from the male perspective. The stories of his sisters, diverse and varied as they are, give the female-centered perspective.

The life stories of Moses's six sisters fall into two contrasting pairs: those known as married versus those known as unmarried and those who created their homes in their natal village to those whose main residence became the urban center. We begin with the two women who constructed their homes in the village arena. The first, Serefete, is a "properly married" woman; the second, Maria, is an unmarried, single head of her own large rural-based household.

Serefete

Serefete was a slightly built, severe-looking woman when she accepted me into her home and eventually became my "adoptive mother." I lived in Serefete's homestead from the first day of my arrival in the village and returned to it almost a decade later. Serefete's yard was one of the more impressive homes in the village. Serefete spent days decorating the walls of the huts with designs she made of colorful sand and mud and built small arches to enclose sitting spaces in front of these huts. In 1983, Serefete's yard included a well-constructed hut that stood empty. I was invited to reside in that hut and became part of the family.

Serefete was born in 1938, the first child of Jokonya and Basebi. She grew up in her mother's mother's yard. Her father, Basebi, spent years in the South African mines. When Serefete was five, she was left behind when her mother joined Basebi in South Africa. When her parents returned to the village, Serefete was almost twelve years old. Serefete had completed two years of elementary school. In 1958, Serefete gave birth to her first child. The father, Batlang, was a young villager who had already begun his migrant life cycle. Batlang never paid *bogadi*. In 1960, taking her firstborn son with her, Serefete went to South Africa where she joined Batlang for three years. In 1963, Serefete came back to her natal village with her firstborn son, in order to give birth to her second child while Batlang remained in South Africa. Serefete made a point in explaining that she was a *motsetse*, a woman convalescing in Batlang's parents' yard after giving birth. The

implication was that their relationship was in the process of being legitimated as marriage.

Batlang, however, like Serefete's father, Basebi, tended to be a *lekgolwa*,
a man who stayed for years in South Africa unless made to come back.
Indeed, after her return home to give birth in 1963, Serefete saw Batlang for
only one month in 1966. Then Batlang remained in South Africa for almost
four years without visiting his family. In 1970, Serefete decided to travel to
South Africa again and join Batlang. They lived together in South Africa for
another two years until 1972, when pregnant with her third child, she
returned to Botswana to give birth. Batlang followed her to the village only
a year later, this time to remain in Botswana.

From 1973 and until the end of 1976, Batlang and Serefete lived with their
children at Batlang's sister's, in her lands area home. In 1977, soon after they
built their village home (*lolwapa* #1), Batlang left to work in Gaborone, the
capital. Serefete gave birth to two more children in 1975 and in 1978. In 1981,
Serefete's oldest daughter, Kay (born in 1963), interrupted her second year in
a Gaborone high school and came back to the village to give birth to her first
child. Serefete convinced Kay to go back to school after a year of nursing the
child (the father was a "kid from school" and no effort was made to contact
his family). The child was "given" to Serefete, and Kay returned to school.

In 1983, Serefete was among the more fortunate women in the village.
Her husband sent money from his town employment, and her son was gainfully employed in South Africa. Her three younger children were attending
the local school. When she needed to plough her field, Serefete used some
of the remittance money sent by her husband and son to arrange work sharing with a neighbor.

In 1986, Serefete accepted Gakelebitse, mother of her son's (Tuma) new
baby, into her yard. Young Gakelebitse lived with Serefete until 1990, when
Tuma secured a job as a guard in Palapye. He took his growing family with
him and they lived in the company's housing.

Serefete was told about her husband's death by a neighbor who had traveled all the way to Mokokwana to bring her the bad news: Batlang was hit
by a car as he crossed a road in Gaborone. In 1993, Serefete was alone in
her village *lolwapa*. Her sons were all in town. Tuma was married with
three children, and younger Zoo and Ishe were living and working in
Palapye and Gaborone, respectively. Kay, now an unmarried mother of
three, worked as a cleaner in an office building, and the youngest, Kebato,
attended school in Palapye and lived with her sister Kay.

Serefete's life was relatively privileged in the small rural community.
Serefete managed a small household with remittances sent from both a
gainfully employed son and a husband. Batlang was publicly known as her
husband, a!though no transfer of *bogadi* (marriage payment) had ever
occurred. As a "wife" and not a *nyatsi* (lover), Serefete could and often had

made demands on Batlang's income. Despite this obvious economic and social advantage, marriage did not dramatically distinguish Serefete's and other "married" women's daily lives from the daily lives of "unmarried" women. When we look at Serefete's life story, it becomes clear that she saw little of her husband. Aside from short periods of transient residence in the village, Batlang lived elsewhere and Serefete's daily routine centered on her children, kin, and neighbors. Serefete was clearly the manager of the household. She used cash income generated by her husband and son who worked elsewhere to enter into labor arrangements that enabled her to cultivate the family's field and maintain the family's herd. She made the key decisions about whether and when to begin ploughing. She disciplined her children and paid their school fees. She built mud huts and walls in her *lolwapa*. When she was short on cash, she brewed beer (*bojalwa*) to sell. She even implied that "there is no person who does not have a lover."

We also see how Serefete's own reproductive cycle touches and almost overlaps that of her daughter's. Serefete, like two other women her age I knew in Mokokwana, nursed her own grandchild. In both cases, the daughters/mothers of "children-left-behind" were unmarried women in their teens. Serefete's efforts to help her daughter achieve a high school certificate so that she might enter the workforce in a relatively advantageous position failed. The important point is, however, that despite her displeasure with her daughter's second pregnancy, Serefete offered an unconditional home to her daughter. The role of women of Serefete's generation as anchors for the dispersed family fragments and the shifts in such role in recent years will be discussed in the next chapter.

Maria

Although Serefete was poor and her life complex, she seemed privileged when compared to her sister. Maria, a cheerful and strong woman, tells a story different in many ways. Maria's *lolwapa* was a few steps away from her older sister's yard. The new yard was not enclosed by any fence, and Maria and her large household slept in a single plain mud hut. For months in early 1983, I observed Maria shape mud bricks into a wooden frame and allow them to dry in the open air. Maria planned to use the bricks for building a second hut. An image is embedded in my memory. It is a photograph I took of Maria smiling feebly in the midst of half melted mud bricks strewn around her. Maria could not afford to buy a plastic sheet necessary to protect her bricks from the sporadic rains.

In 1982, Maria Basebi was the head of a large household (# 45). She lived in her newly erected homestead with her seven children and two of her grandchildren, born to her eldest daughter in 1979 and 1980. Maria's life story illustrates many issues raised in the expanding literature regarding female-headed households in Botswana. Maria, like Serefete, had built her life centered in Mokokwana and its rural surroundings. Maria was born in 1940 in the cattle post of her mother's father. In 1943, she was taken with her mother, Jokonya, to South Africa. In 1950, when she was about ten years old, she came back with her parents to Botswana. They resided next to their field; they did not have a village home at the time. In 1954, Maria began attending school in the village of Maunatlala, walking from her parents' homestead in the Maipafela fields area to school. She completed five years of elementary school education. Maria was living in her parents' fields homestead when she gave birth to her first child in 1960. A year later, her mother, pregnant with her last child, left home to join her husband, Maria's father. Maria, a young mother herself, was left to care for her younger siblings.

When asked who was the father of her first child, Maria shrugged shoulders and said the man lived in the cattle post.

> Q: Was he the father of your second child born in 1962?
> A: No!
> Q: Were damages paid (in support of the child)?
> A: Not really. I don't know. (laughter)

Her answers were frozen and short. I knew I was embarrassing Maria by posing these questions. Maria managed to say that the father of the second child "helped a little," but only for a while. Maria gave birth to a third child before she decided to look for work herself.

In 1966, Maria began looking for work in the neighboring white-owned farms and soon after locating her mother, she joined her at the farm where her mother was employed. Her subsequent children were all born in the farms. The fourth child was born in 1968, another girl in 1970, and two more boys in 1973 and 1979. In 1979, her firstborn daughter, Modiro, became pregnant. Jokonya, Maria's mother, returned with pregnant Modiro to their natal home. Maria stayed on the farms until 1981.

Initially, after her return to Mokokwana, Maria settled with her children in her mother's homestead in the village. She was able to raise some corn and sorghum in a field plot known as the plot of Jokonya's mother. Moses, her brother, helped Maria in cultivating this field.

In September 1982, when she felt it was becoming too crowded in her mother's yard (her own daughter had two children and her younger sister was also bearing children in the yard), Maria moved away to establish her own yard. That same year she also applied for her own field from the newly elected subregional land board.

In the fall of 1983, Maria took one of her daughters and stayed in the cattle post area, where she managed the herds of—in her words—"a man from Maunatlala." The man, others in the village insisted, was her lover (*nyatsi*) and the father of her last-born son. The Maunatlala man was married and his family resided in the large village of his origin. In the yard in

Mokokwana, Maria's younger children were looked after by Modiro, her older daughter and mother of two children of her own. This village-based unit was partly supported by occasional money sent by the father of Modiro's two children, a man from Majwaneng (a Tswapong village about an hour's walk away from Mokokwana). The man expressed his intentions to marry Maria's daughter. A few of his relatives initiated marriage negotiations in November 1982. A decade later, when I visited Maria in 1993, her daughter, now mother of three children, was still living in her mother's yard. The marriage negotiations were stalled. Modiro supported her children by working as a maid for a teacher in Moeng, a high school located about a forty-minute walk from the village.

In 1993, Maria headed a household composed largely of the children of her unmarried daughters. In addition to the three children of her eldest daughter, Maria's third daughter, a mother of two, left one of her children with her mother. She took her second child with her to Gaborone where she was "looking for work." Another granddaughter, born to Maria's fifth daughter, was also living in Maria's yard, while her mother sought work in Gaborone. Among Maria's four sons (second, fourth, sixth, and seventh), only the youngest (born in 1979) was still living with her. The other three all worked and lived in Francistown.

The biographies of the younger four Basebi sisters differ from the two life stories of Serefete and Maria. These four younger women centered their adult lives in urban settings. The life of Maria contrasts sharply with the lives of her two "properly married" younger sisters, Bajaki and Rose, but has interesting parallels with the urban unmarried youngest two sisters.

Bajaki

I met Bajaki only once, when she came on a rare visit to Mokokwana in 1983. Bajaki was a woman of few words. She could not understand what I, a *lekgoa*, was doing in her sister's *lolwapa*, and she acted reserved and at times hostile when I asked questions. Her biographical account is therefore short, and the story I recorded for her is extremely thin.

Bajaki was born in South Africa in 1946. She does not recall this fact and was "reminded" it by other family members present during the interview. Bajaki had seen little of her father, Basebi. She stayed in school long enough to learn to read and write (she dropped out of school in her second year, but claimed to never have attended class regularly). Unlike her two older sisters Maria and Serefete who stayed in the rural areas most of their lives, Bajaki left for town when she was seventeen years old. She joined a young woman she knew from Mokokwana who was caring for the children of a school teacher in Francistown. Two years after she arrived in town, Bajaki became pregnant. The father was a man of Kalanga origin. They were married six months after she gave birth to her first son. It was a marriage registered at the local council, and she was given a golden wedding ring. The man was gainfully employed and when he was transferred by his employers to Serowe, the regional capital of Central District, they built their home there.

In Serowe, the couple lived among Kalanga-speaking people, and Bajaki was quick to learn their language, called Sekalanga. Her children all attended school; the oldest, who was seventeen at the time of the interview, was completing Form II, the second year of high school education.

Bajaki maintained little contact with her family of origin and with people in Mokokwana. Her husband, she insisted, had not paid bride-price because they were married "with a ring." The gainfully employed Mokalanga man did maintain his links with his in-laws. Still, I learned from Moses that Bajaki's husband sent Moses several small sums of money "to help him live."

Rose

Rose, like Bajaki, was married "with a ring" to a Mokalanga man. She was a large, energetic, and assertive woman. I interviewed Rose in her spacious home in Francistown in 1993. During my first fifteen-month long stay in Mokokwana in 1983–1984, Rose never came to visit. The interview was conducted in English. Rose and her son wrote me several letters after I left Botswana in 1993.

Rose, the fifth child of Basebi and Jokonya, was born in 1954 in the village of Mokokwana. She was eight years old when her mother Jokonya left the village and settled in the Tuli Block farms with the two younger children. Rose was taken by her older sister Bajaki to live with her in town. She attended school in Francistown while Bajaki worked. Bajaki, however, had little money and many times Rose was sent home from school because she could not pay school fees. Despite these difficulties, Rose completed six years of elementary education, more than any of her sisters and just one year less than her brother Moses. Her relatively high level of formal education opened for her the opportunity to work for a family business owned by Batswana of Indian origin. While working for this family, Rose learned some English, which she uses today in her job.

When she was twenty, Rose was married "with a ring" (registered at the district council and not via marriage payment) to a local policeman, a man of Kalanga origin. In 1993, Rose lived in a large, five-bedroom house in Francistown. She had permanent employment at a local factory, and she augmented her income by renting two residential units she constructed at the back of her house. In 1993, all of Rose's children completed high school, a level of education that, at the time, secured a decent-paying clerical position. The family also owned a house in Gaborone, the capital, where her husband was working at the time.

Lebopo

I met Lebopo several times in 1983, when she came to visit her family and bring her children clothing and food. Lebopo was taller than her sisters and very shy. She spoke nothing but Setswana. During my 1993 stay in Francistown, Lepobo spent many hours with me and with Moses in the hospital and in her younger sister Barobi's home.

In 1993, Lebopo explained the difference between her life and that of her married sisters in the following way:

Now I have five children. Each child stays with me for two or three years and then I send him back to live with my mother [in the village]. When I am *motsetse* [a woman who just gave birth], my mother comes to be with me in town. If a woman is married, the children will be sent to her *bomatsalagwe*, the family of her in-laws.

Lebopo joined Barobi in 1989 in Francistown because Barobi was sick at the time and Lebopo was *motsetse*. In 1993, Lebopo found employment in a blanket factory and lived with Barobi. Their mother, Jokonya, came to live with them in Francistown. In 1984, Lebopo gave one of her children, third-born Bonolo, to her childless sister Barobi. Lebopo's two first children had been living in Mokokwana with their mother's mother Jokonya since 1979, where they attended school.

Lebopo decided to keep her fourth-born daughter Tsetse with her in Francistown. When Serefete, Lebopo's eldest sister, had to live alone in her Mokokwana yard, Lebopo sent Tsetse to help the aging Serefete. She insisted, however, that Tsetse was not a "given child" (*ngwana o ke mofil-weng*), that Tsetse was only temporarily living with her older sister to help her with errands and that when Serefete would not need Tsetse's services any longer, the child would go back to her mother.

Ruth Barobi Basebi

Ruth Barobi Basebi was the last child born to Jokonya and Basebi. She was born in 1962 in Mokokwana. When I interviewed Barobi for the first time in 1993 (she never came to Mokokwana during my first research in the village), Barobi was a portly woman who suffered from advanced stages of diabetes and was almost blind. Despite her relatively young age (she was thirty-one at the time) Barobi was a known *maprofiti*, a healer, whose services were sought after in the shantytown of Francistown where she resided. Her curing powers were linked to her association with the New Apostle church.

"I 'enter' the church a lot," Barobi told me as we walked the muddy streets of what Moses called (borrowing a term from apartheid realities of South Africa) "the location," a shantytown at the edge of Francistown. Barobi had discovered her curing (*go alafa*) powers in 1983, when she was living in Mahalape, a large village in the southeastern region of Botswana.

"What brought you to Mahalape?" I asked. She was a *nwetsi*, a "bride" of a man from Mahalape. She was to marry the man and thus lived with his parents. She met the man in Francistown in 1980, and when their relationship deepened, she followed him to his natal village. For two years, between 1980 and 1982, Barobi stayed there (she says *"ke ntse hela"*—I simply stayed there). She was expected to build a family with the man, but she bore no children. By 1983, she began to become seriously disabled as her eyesight and her health rapidly deteriorated. At the same time, her involvement in New Apostle church activities were intensified. Her "teacher" was a woman *maprofiti* (from the word "prophet") of Ndbele origin, known as MaHunt. The full name of her teacher was Elizabeth Tsosani. Barobi learned to use her curing powers from MaHunt. In 1986, the man she lived with left her "because I was blind," she reported in a matter-of-fact way. She returned to Francistown and for a short while lived at her sister Rose's house. In 1987, she was able to build her own *mukhukhu*, a house made of mud walls with a zinc roof. By 1991 as her reputation as a sought-after healer increased, she could afford building a five-room home with large glass windows inserted in the cement brick walls. At the back of her yard she built two separate units, one with two rooms, the other a single room unit, which she rented out.

Barobi never bore any children, yet her yard was always bustling with people and children. In addition to neighbors, the two tenant families, and the many visitors who came to seek her curing services, Barobi lived with her 12-year-old son "given" to her by a church-going friend and another son given to her by her sister Lebopo. Unlike her sisters, Barobi was barely literate and had never held a paid position in town.

CONCLUSIONS: GENDER, CONJUGALITY, AND IDENTITY

The gender imbalance in the Basebi family—one son and six daughters in the middle generation—allows us to explore in greater detail not only the variability between male and female strategies of survival, but also the variation among the women's lives. It is clear from these stories that strategies for making a living and creating homes vary within this small family group. On the whole, strategies used by men are different from those of women, and earlier generations had a different set of options to choose from in comparison to men and women coming of age in Botswana in the 1980s and 1990s.

When read in light of the analysis of biographical narratives presented in Chapter 1, it is evident that Moses's story is more textured and detailed than most of the life stories of males I recorded in the village. It was also not typical. Moses, as we have seen, constructed his life story as the narrative of an outsider, of a man who was drawn into social patterns of migrant work and marriage despite his inner resistance and innovative strategies of escaping such patterns. The eccentricity of Moses's life brings to light the inherent tensions built into male lives in this rural periphery. Without any possibility of making a living based on agricultural production, these men are forced out of their rural homes to employment that is often hundreds of miles away from home. Employment within Botswana was extremely limited and required skills most rural men did not have. The long period of separation between migrating men and their families gave rise to a range of coping strategies. In the preindependence era women have joined their men next to their worksites, returning each time to give birth and care for the young children in their rural homes. Men constructed their lives around social relations centered in the village. They invested in cattle, ploughed their fields whenever they could, and supported those left behind with their wages.

Basebi's life story shows how difficult it is to maintain such a balancing act, to keep links with the rural home while working and living in the mines and urban world hundreds of miles away. Basebi and many other men opted to give up one end of this truncated existence—they became *lekgolwa,* for they cut their ties with their rural home. This balancing act also meant that there is an inherent tension between the demands on a young miner's wages by his family of origin and his need to establish his own future family. Moses's complex life presents a particularly apt example for such contradictions.

Taken together, the individual stories of Basebi and Jokonya and their seven children raise the question of the meaning of marriage and other forms of conjugality as they are experienced in the lives of rural men and women in Botswana. A large anthropological and policy-oriented literature deals with the issues of marriage and extramarital sexuality (Comaroff and Roberts 1977; Schapera 1933, 1938), the impact of labor migration on women (Brown 1983, Gulbrandsen 1994, Massey 1980, Schapera 1947;), changes in the practice of bride-wealth payment (Comaroff 1980; Kuper 1982; Schapera 1957), and the current predicaments of what policy makers call "female-headed households" (Kerven 1979, 1984; Peters 1984). The force of these interlinked life stories of members of this one family over three generations is in enabling us to grasp the significance and complexity of these processes in specific lives. Reading these biographical accounts, we learn that marriage in these regions is indeed a long process and that the paying of *bogadi* (bride-price) is not the only way of establishing the legitimacy of such a bond. We also learn that unmarried mothers are supported by some of the men who father their children but that such support is sporadic and unreliable. We see a significant difference between life of urban and rural women but also recognize multiple links—material and social—that bridge the urban/rural divide.

These stories enrich our understanding of what it means to be an "unmarried head of household" in Botswana in both urban and rural settings. Thus Maria's story gives voice to a woman's lifelong experience of building a home in the rural areas. Lebopo's story provides a nice contrast to Maria's. Lebopo, like Maria, was never married. Her meager and irregular earnings meant, however, that she could not keep her children with her in town. Barobi's unique tale of blindness, childlessness, and curing powers opens for discussion less common strategies of survival and construction of selfhood. Finally, the two sisters married "with a ring" in town—Rose and Bajaki—mark an emerging trend. Marriage is with an outsider, in both cases with a man from a non-Setswana speaking ethnic group. There are no negotiations or any transaction of bride-price between the families in such marriages. Yet members of the family continue to rely on these daughters when they venture into town.

The next chapter turns to the village, regional, and national socioeconomic and political contexts in order to place the stories of the members of this single family in larger frames.

NOTES

1. The history of the village and its composition is described in greater detail in my Ph.D. thesis. For the history of each village ward, consult in particular Appendix 2-a in Motzafi-Haller 1988.

2. My records contained detailed information about all village yards. All village yards (*malwapa*, plural of *lolwapa*) were numbered. I had kept the reference numbers in order to enable cross-referencing of the units discussed.

3. *Kgosi* is king or leader. The name *kgosing* is common to all village wards that are the wards of the village headman (the *kgosi*) and his family.

3

Making a Living, Making a Home

Tuma was twenty-five and had been working in South Africa for almost seven years. During these years Tuma had saved some money in cash and invested it in six head of cattle, managed at the time by his mother, Serefete. In Christmas 1982, Tuma came home for a few months, before he could begin his next work contract.[1] He brought many presents for his younger brothers and sisters and several clothing items for Moses, his maternal uncle (*malome*). One evening, a few days after his arrival, Tuma came to speak to me in my hut, which he built for himself and which I rented from his mother. In embarrassed, truncated sentences while repeatedly checking if I understood what he said in Setswana, he talked about his school years, the exact dates of each of his migrant work contracts, and the money he had brought back from South Africa. Based on my other interviews in the village, I was beginning to grasp the nature of the multiple links tying young migrants like Tuma to their natal homes. But there was a particular urgency in Tuma's voice. He kept on saying that he wanted to marry Gakelebitse, a neighbor's girl (from household #7) and that he must make her pregnant during this short Christmas vacation. He *must* do this, he said. Otherwise he would not succeed in his plans. Did I understand?

It was clear to me that Tuma did not speak about romantic love but about a more precise and urgent idea that had to do with publicly affirming his rights over Gakelebitse and his need to begin an independent home in the village. I also sensed that, in his eyes, making Gakelebitse pregnant was the best way to establish such claims. But I could not, at that long evening conversation, figure out what was the cultural logic that informed the strong emotions Tuma was trying so hard to articulate. Tuma, I know today, was talking about his need to create a home, about his urge to put an end to his migrating phase of life, about establishing a new identity of a mature man that went beyond and redefined his social position as a youth with no roots. But I could only grasp these processes and Tuma's particular position in these processes in hindsight.

I had the same feeling of inadequate understanding a few days earlier that same Christmas of 1982 when I talked to Tuma's younger sister, Kay. Kay was twenty. She was living with her father in Gaborone when she came on a rare short visit to her natal home. Kay had already had one child "from a boy in class." At seventeen, Kay gave her son to her mother and went back to school. Her first son, Dromio, was almost two years old in 1982 and very attached to his grandmother. The favorite way of teasing little Dromio was to point to visiting Kay, who he rarely recognized, and say: "Look now, *this* is your mother." Dromio would hang on to Serefete, his mother's mother, ever more desperately as his not much older uncles and aunts (who were four, seven, and nine years old at the time) burst into loud laughter.

Kay was pregnant again. And again, the biological father was not discussed; he was another "boy from class." This time, however, Kay told me, she was going to keep the child herself. "My soul wants him," she told me, looking deep into my eyes and inquiring if I grasped her point.

To understand Tuma's urgent need to impregnate Gakelebitse before he returned for what he decided was his last migrant work year and to grasp Kay's decision to drop out of school and raise her second child in her natal home, it is necessary to appreciate the cultural meaning of conjugal relationships and of parenting at that particular historical moment in Botswana. To comprehend their views of their life paths and the cultural logic that structured their decisions, it requires, above all, an understanding of the processes through which both males and females craft a sense of home and social identity in a shifting world of social relations. To do this, we must begin with an account of the larger socioeconomic and political factors that impose long separation between spouses and structure such endemic fluidity.

This chapter intends to lay out the shape of these socioeconomic and political frameworks. It begins with a detailed outline of the three-pronged production economy in Botswana that includes cattle, cultivation, and labor migration. Then, using detailed village census data, it proceeds to locate the position of the Basebis and their village neighbors on that national socioeconomic grid. It closes with a closer look at two village-centered households. These narrowing three circles of socioeconomic analysis—the national, village-based, and household—contextualize the individual stories of Tuma and Kay. It also provide the larger setting for the life stories presented in the former two chapters.

SOCIOECONOMIC PROFILES: A NATIONAL OVERVIEW

Eighty years of colonial rule marked by "extreme neglect" resulted in independence in 1966, in a situation "worse off in terms of both social and directly productive infrastructure than any other ex-British territory in Africa" (Colclough and MacCarthy 1980:28). With per capita income of about $80 at independence, Botswana was one of the poorest countries in the world. At independence, almost 90 percent of the population was resident in rural areas engaged in agricultural production (both arable and animal husbandry). Despite an increasing rate of out-migration from rural areas to the growing urban centers of Botswana over the past three decades, most Batswana continue to live in the rural areas. Table 3.1 records the changing rate of urban and rural residence in Botswana for the 1970s, 1980s, and 1990s.

The main productive assets in the rural areas are land and livestock. Arable production is carried out by the majority of the population of Botswana. Yet, aside from a small number of commercial farmers, who are most often found in several specific ecological zones in the country, arable farming in Botswana is largely limited to the cultivation of subsistence crops, mainly maize, sorghum, and beans. Agriculture provides a livelihood for more than 80 percent of the population but supplies only about 50 percent of food needs and accounts, in 1996 estimates, for only 4 percent of the GDP. Low and erratic rainfall, poor soils, and high evaporation rates set severe limits on productivity of arable agriculture in even the more favorable eastern regions of the country (Sims 1981:132–135). In 1975, a Food and Agriculture Organization (FAO) study recorded that 91 percent of households in eastern Botswana, where agricultural production predominates, said they infrequently or never produced enough to feed themselves. The general failure of rural households to meet their subsistence needs based on arable production has been documented by several studies carried out in subsequent years. In the early 1980s, the National Migration Study (1982) found that only 10 percent of all rural households in the country were able to subsist on crop production alone (see also Cooper 1980:29–34). More recent data (Molutsi 1986) suggest that rural households produce only 23 percent of their own food needs and that, on the whole, more than 60 percent of all rural households fall below the poverty line.

TABLE 3.1   Population in Urban and Rural Areas, 1971–1991

	1971	%	1981	%	1991	%
Total population	574,094	100.0	941,027	100.0	1,326,796	100.0
Urban population	63,540	11.1	166,268	17.6	316,642	23.7
Rural population	510,554	88.9	774,759	82.4	1,010,154	76.3

The second major economic sector in contemporary Botswana is the cattle industry. Botswana is known as one of the largest meat processing and marketing countries in Africa (Colclough and McCarthy 1980:120–124). In 1990, the cattle population in Botswana numbered some 2,700,000 head, increasing within one year to 2,844,000 head in 1991. By 1993, the revenues from the cattle industry were third in size in the total export revenue of the country, after diamonds and copper-nickel exports (GOB 1993). However, cattle rearing, like crop production, is rarely a sufficient source of livelihood. According to one calculation, only a "mere nine percent of all cattle owners [in Botswana] would be able to live off their income from cattle alone" (GOB 1982:38). Cattle ownership is vastly skewed in Botswana. In the mid-1970s one estimate recorded that 5 percent of the rural households in the country owned 50 percent of the national herd, while 45 percent owned no cattle at all. Almost a decade later, another nationwide survey indicated that "between 44–54 percent of the rural units claimed not to own cattle," while 12 percent of rural cattle owners "own fifty percent of the cattle, by value" (GOB 1982:38).

In sum, the vast majority of rural households cannot rely on agricultural production (both arable and animal husbandry) for their survival. As a result, the dependence of the rural population on wage income is acute. In August 1997, the most recent National Development Plan, for the years 1997/8 to 2002/3, concluded (GOB 1997:24) that "Cash earning still remain the main source of income for most households in Botswana." On the whole, an estimated 80 percent of all rural households in Botswana have at least one member who has earned cash on the job for at least part of the year. Yet given the extremely limited number of regular wage-earning opportunities in the rural areas, most wage earners need to migrate out of their rural homes to find jobs within Botswana and abroad, in urban centers, farms, and mines in neighboring South Africa.

The dependence on employment in South Africa as a source of cash has been part of Tswana life since the late nineteenth century (Schapera 1947; Massey 1978, 1980; Parson 1981, 1984). Labor migration to South Africa had gradually increased from relatively modest levels in the 1930s (about 10,000 workers) to about 70,000 workers in 1970. By the late 1970s, a third of the country's male labor force was employed in South African mines (Colclough and McCarthy 1980:171). The rate of out-migration to South Africa had reached its peak in the early 1980s only to drop sharply by the early 1990s. In 1982, the total recruits for South African mine employment numbered 21,456. A decade later, in 1991, there were only 14,263 recruits (GOB 1991).[2] Political changes in South Africa and the growth in employment opportunities within Botswana in the expanding local mining sector and in the government sector resulted in this sharp drop in the rate of out-migration to South African mines.

TABLE 3.2   Estimated Monthly Cash Earnings in Three Economic Sectors
            (in Pula)[3]

	1983	1988	1991
Agriculture	75	99	197
Mining	308	525	857
Construction	168	270	396
Average cash income	N/A	369	549

Employment in the mines, within Botswana or abroad, provides an important inflow of cash to rural households. As Table 3.2 shows, mine employment is three to five times more lucrative than cash income earned in agricultural production. A miner earns about twice as much as a worker in construction, the second most lucrative employment in Botswana.

Earlier studies estimate that cash earnings by migrant mine workers contributed about one-fifth of the median rural household income (GOB 1976, Colclough and McCarthy 1980:173). More recent evidence shows that mining constitutes about 42.3 percent of the 1991 GDP per capita income.[4] Unemployment rates remain a problem, despite the rapid growth in GDP.[5] Unemployment rates for 1996 were estimated at 21 percent.

When viewed from the perspective of the single rural-based household unit, the three economic sectors in Botswana—wage employment, arable production, and cattle raising—are closely integrated. Most rural households in the country must combine access to all these three sources of income to survive. There are, however, important variations among households in the relative share of each income source in their livelihood. As shown on the next page, Table 3.3 provides data relevant for the mid-1980s.[6]

Table 3.3 presents income distribution data among Botswana households clustered into four major income profiles and distinguishes between rural and urban households. The distinction between rural and urban households presented in this aggregate statistical data is problematic, however. A more complete discussion that outlines the complex relations between the village residential units known as *malwapa* (singular, *lolwapa*) with the larger unit of consumption and production, the household, is offered in the next section. At this point it is important to keep in mind that rural and urban people are often members of the same multifocal household units. The income profile of urban households is seldom isolated from that recorded for rural-based households. Members in these two sectors are often part of a larger unit of production and consumption.

Keeping this in mind we can examine the data presented in Table 3.3 and add that the monthly income of less than 100 pula per household, which defines the lowest income category, falls far below the poverty datum line

TABLE 3.3   Income Distribution of Households in Urban and Rural Areas[7]

Households	Urban	Rural	Total
Less than 100	14.3%	37.0%	31.0%
100–600	63.3	56.1	58.1
600–2,000	17.8	6.7	9.5
2,000 and over	4.6	0.2	1.4
Median income	546 pula/month	219 pula/month	306 pula/month

(PDL). More than 30 percent of households in the country fall within this category. The poorest households are more often found in rural areas. Moreover, within the second category of income, with monthly income ranging from 100 to 600 pula per month, two-thirds of all households in this income category stand at or below the PDL. The third income profile category, which includes the households with income ranging from 600 to 2,000 pula monthly—termed "upper middle income"—consist of less than 10 percent of Botswana households. The richest households, with more than P2,000, constitute the upper 99th percentile category.

Another important observation, critical to our subsequent discussion, concerns the patterns of income generation characteristic of each of these four income categories. The poorest households rely heavily on income in kind: gathering and hunting, in particular, constitute about 70 percent of their total income. Remittances from miners take the second place, and the third most important source of income for these poorest households is farming (considering crops and livestock together). The "lower middle income" households tend to rely largely on gifts and remittances from employed members, while crop production and cattle rearing constitute their second most important income source. Gathering, beer brewing, and hunting are third. In the third income profile group (only 10 percent of the population), cattle rearing and cash employment seem to hold almost equal positions. Crop production is also an important income source in this income category. Finally, the richest households seem to rely most heavily on cattle rearing. In this category, trading is second in importance, while employment and arable production come last.

This brief summary of the varied income profiles of Botswana households raises three points. First, there is a strong interdependence among the three major sources of income for most households in Botswana. Few households can subsist on one income source alone. Second, to survive, members of a village-centered household *must* migrate out of the village settlement to other sites within the agricultural zone outside the village, into towns and large villages within Botswana, and often to mines and farms in neighboring South Africa. The ongoing flow of people, labor, and resources between the village *lolwapa* and the second and, at times, third residential units located in the agricultural zone or in urban centers occurs and must be understood as part of a larger political economy that links rural and urban sites within and beyond regional and national boundaries.

The third observation concerns the centrality of crop production and thus the lasting links to rural homes for the majority of people in Botswana, especially for the lower middle income and upper middle income categories. This last observation is central to the questions of collective identity construction and struggles over communal rights to land that I raise in subsequent chapters. It suggests that despite the rapid rate of urbanization, struggles over land in the rural areas have not lost their importance or centrality in people's lives. Rather, such struggles, at once material and symbolic, are carried out and must be understood not only in the context of shifting relationships among groups and identities within the region, but also as processes articulating larger ethnic and class divisions in the country. The purpose of the next section is to place the position of Mokokwana villagers within this national economic profile and to analyze the meaning of the rural-urban link from the perspective of residents of one rural community.

SHIFTING WORLDS AND COUNTING UNITS

In the following pages I will present detailed data documenting the movement of people and resources in and out of some eighty homestead compounds in a single Tswapong village over a decade. Such a systematic, complete village-based census sheds light on larger patterns and processes documented in the national profile sketched earlier in this chapter. It provides more precise illustration of the dynamics that link residents in a village-centered homestead, or *lolwapa*, with other members of the wider unit of production and consumption, the household. This villagewide profile is also designed to provide a systematic database and a necessary context for the individual life stories described in Chapter 1. How unique are the life stories of the members of the Basebi family? Were Tuma's career decisions shared by other young migrants? What was the reality of life for unmarried mothers like Kay? More generally, this detailed socioeconomic profile, based on data recorded in the early 1980s and early 1990s, enables an examination of movement and instability of social units and relationships in real historical time.

However, the use of census data raises analytical questions and narrative tensions that stand at the core of the theoretical theme developed in this book. Indeed, the use of census data, which by its nature must rely on counting units—residential units, households, family units of varied complexity—assumes unproblematic, pre-given social units and identities. Yet as anyone who worked in Southern Africa (Ferguson 1992, Murray 1981, Peters 1983a) and elsewhere (Baerends 1994, Peters and Guyer 1984) knows, rural households are fluid, interacting social entities with unclear boundaries. In their comprehensive review of the theoretical and method-ological implications of the household concept, Peters and Guyer (1984:xiv) caution against the practice of assuming that "there is a domes-tic unit or household which is simultaneously a production unit, consump-tion unit, and investment unit." Following their lead, and the more recent insightful analysis offered by James Ferguson (1992) of the cultural nature of inter-household material and social flows, the following exposition pro-ceeds at two levels. First, an exploration of the relations between domestic units, dwelling units, and the larger consumption and production units of which they are part is offered. Based on this detailed data a complete empir-ical record of socioeconomic patterns pertaining to the whole village is laid out. The final segment of the chapter will return to a few of the individuals whose life stories were explored in Chapter 1 and explore their movement within the frames linking domestic units, consumption, and production arrangements. This time, individual lives are seen as they are interwoven within family and household units.

UNITS OF ANALYSIS: LOLWAPA, FAMILY, AND THE HOUSEHOLD

To present a socioeconomic profile of Mokokwana, or any other local rural setting in Botswana, it is necessary to start with the key social and eco-nomic unit, the household. A working definition of a Tswana household must be discussed in relation to two other closely interconnected primary units, the family and the residential unit, or *lolwapa*. There is an important difference between the *lolwapa*, the coresidential unit observed in the vil-lage settlement, and the larger income generating and property holding unit that makes up the household unit. In essence, the household is the primary unit of production and consumption. Many members of the household, but not all of them, are connected through ties of kinship and/or marriage. Research in Botswana has firmly established that "while many dwelling units are at one and the same time households, not all households are con-tained within a single dwelling unit" (GOB 1983:554). To comprehend the complex relations that tie together the dispersed members of the household, it is useful to start with the observable physical dwelling unit and examine its composition as a core from which family and economic ties are extended.

The 1981 national census recorded 221 people who occupied, at the time of enumeration, only forty-four of the existing seventy-two *malwapa* in the village of Mokokwana. In an obvious omission these census records do not mention any land areas associated with the Mokokwana village settlement. The village of Mokokwana, like other small and large villages in the Tswapong region, is made up of a clustered residential settlement and sev-eral named expanses of arable land known to belong to the village. The clustered residential settlement of Mokokwana, the *motse* (in this context the word means a village, but it also means a "home") is situated about seven kilometers from the larger administrative center of Maunatlala and very close to the hills. The arable cultivated fields area, known as *masimong*, consists of four named zones stretching to the north and northeast of the clustered village settlement. Most of the residents of Mokokwana hold a second dwelling unit they have erected on or next to their cultivated field in this arable zone.[8] This second "land dwelling" is often made of less durable materials and constructed with less care. A few Mokokwana residents have a third dwelling unit in the grazing areas that stretch to the northwest and directly north of the arable zone.

My first house-to-house census carried out about a year after that national census, in December 1982, recorded 345 people who belonged to seventy-six *malwapa* in the village settlement of Mokokwana. A decade later, in the summer of 1993, I recorded twelve new *malwapa* in the village arena. I also noted that four *malwapa* that had existed in 1983 were dismantled by 1993.[9] All but one of the twelve new *malwapa* were constructed by young couples who moved out of an existing *lolwapa* of their parents. Six of the women in these young couples were themselves Mokokwana residents, and the other five originated from neighboring villages.[10]

A *lolwapa*, often translated as "compound" or more accurately a dwelling unit, is a well-defined physical space in Tswana villages. Its boundaries are often marked with a fence (made of wooden poles or the more expensive wire fence) that encloses a large, open yard. A *lolwapa* contains one or more single-room, square or round sleeping huts. All but two *malwapa* in 1982 in Mokokwana contained huts made of mud with thatched roofs. The use of cement bricks and zinc roof was more common in large Tswapong villages until the early 1990s. Aside from several sleeping huts, each *lolwapa* also includes a roofless enclosure made of bulky wooden poles that serves as a cooking space *(setlhagana)*.

The number of residents in Mokokwana *malwapa* in 1982 ranged from one to twelve people who belonged to one or more fragments of nuclear families. Most Mokokwana *malwapa* were composed of individuals belonging to two or three generations. Complete nuclear families resided in less than a quarter of all village *malwapa*. About 10 percent were occupied by members belonging to one generation; among these, five *malwapa* were occupied by single elderly people, and four housed childless couples. The largest number of the village *malwapa* contained three generational composites consisting of several fragments of nuclear families plus dependents.

The movement of people in and out of the village-centered *lolwapa* results in great variations of Mokokwana *malwapa* over time. In comparing the results of two complete population censuses conducted in the village in a one-year interval, I found that only 36 percent of the village *malwapa* maintained the same number of residents throughout that year. Most *malwapa* (64 percent) experienced some turnover in their internal composition in the course of that year. There were five births and one death, and in three other cases a coresidential unit recorded in my first census divided into two dwelling units prior to the second census. Taking these demographic changes into account, it appears that most recorded changes in the composition of the Mokokwana *malwapa* are due to movement of children and adults between their respective village *malwapa* and locations outside the village settlement—second dwelling locations in the nearby agricultural zone, urban centers, or farms and mines in South Africa.

Figures 3.1 and 3.2 give a graphic illustration of the complex internal composition of two *malwapa* in Mokokwana. The names enclosed within the circle are of those who resided in the *lolwapa* at the time of the first census I conducted in the village in 1982. Other family members, whose names are indicated on the kinship chart, moved in and out of the village *lolwapa* and contributed money and children to their respective *malwapa*.

As is evident in these figures, the village *lolwapa* is the physical center of a larger, spatially dispersed, economic unit. In the rich literature on South-

FIGURE 3.1   Lolwapa #1

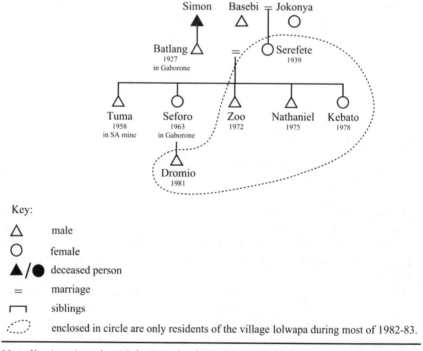

Key:

△   male

○   female

▲/●   deceased person

=   marriage

⊓   siblings

⟨⟩   enclosed in circle are only residents of the village lolwapa during most of 1982-83.

Note: Kay is registered as "Seforo" in this figure because that is her proper given name.

FIGURE 3.2   Lolwapa #2

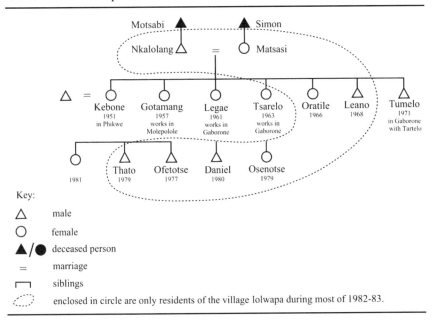

Key:

△   male

○   female

▲/●   deceased person

=   marriage

⌐¬   siblings

⋰⋱   enclosed in circle are only residents of the village lolwapa during most of 1982-83.

ern African households,[11] a distinction is often drawn between what is termed the *de facto* population, which is recorded in the village settlement at any one point in time, and the *de jure* population, which includes all those people who are considered to be members of the village-centered household but who are often absent from the village. The membership of these absent people in the various village *malwapa* is based on social, economic, and kin ties with the dwellers of the coresidential unit observed in the village settlement.

RESIDENTS AND ABSENTEES

In this study, I define an "absentee" man or woman as an individual reported as a member of a village *lolwapa* who has been absent from the village settlement for most or all of the year between December 1982 and December 1983. Based on this definition, by December 1983, there were 87 "absentee members" at the various *malwapa*. The National Migration Study, completed in 1981, relied on a much narrower definition. For the national study an absentee is "a person who normally lives in the *lolwapa* but who did not sleep in the *lolwapa* the night before the day of enumeration" (GOB 1982:851).[12] Ten years later, another nationwide survey, the Household Income and Expenditure Survey of 1991, had expanded this narrow definition to include people who are "not living permanently with the household but expect to be there for at least 15 days of the survey round" (GOB 1997:11).

Based on my definition of what constitutes an absentee, I found that most of the absentees from Mokokwana *malwapa* (63.2 percent) were men. Most of these men were said to be in South Africa engaged in labor employment. More than half of the absentee men were twenty to thirty years old. If one calculates the percentage of absentee men from their specific age and gender category in the village population, one realizes that at any one point in time about 30 percent of the working-age men of the village are absent due to employment in South Africa.[13]

My 1982 complete village census also shows that in addition to the large number of people absent from the village settlement due to long labor contracts in South African mines and farms, an almost equal number who were absent from the village were recorded as living elsewhere within Botswana. In Mokokwana, thirty-one men were reported absent abroad (7.4 percent of the total de jure population). An additional twenty-four men (5.7 percent) who were absent from the village settlement for most of 1982–83 were reported to be "elsewhere in Botswana." Taken together, the category of absentee men and women who were said to be absent from the village but still within Botswana (in towns and in the outlaying rural area) was almost twice as large as that of the absentees working abroad.

Another important statistical distribution concerns the breakdown along gender lines within the group of absentees. In 1982, the number of absentee women was much smaller than that of men. Based on the 1981 national census records for the Tswapong region as a whole, I calculated that absentee men constituted between 4 and 7 percent of the total de facto population of their respective villages, while absentee women rarely accounted for even 1 percent of the total population. Women absent from their respective *malwapa* were most often said to be within Botswana, in urban centers and in the agricultural zone. In 1983, all absent women from Mokokwana were reported to be within Botswana: twenty-eight in urban centers and four in the agricultural zone. All absentee women known to be in urban centers were unmarried mothers. All but one absentee woman from Mokokwana were domestic workers paid between 20 and 60 pula per month (at the time, equivalent to about the same amount of U.S. dollars).[14] This ratio of male to female absence from the village arena dramatically changed during the 1980s, as more and more young women from the village were able to find jobs in the growing urban centers.

In 1993, a complete record of all domestic histories in Mokokwana shows that sixty-three women who were reported as members of the existing eighty-eight *malwapa* were absent from the village for most of that year. All these absentee women were young mothers who left their children behind in their respective rural homes. In other words, there were twice as many young Mokokwana mothers who were absent from their rural homes in 1993 than in 1983. The phenomenon of women absenteeism in 1993 had new characteristics: I recorded twelve absentee mothers who were older women (fifty to seventy years old). These women were the mothers of the young unmarried mothers included in the statistics reported previously. Three of these older women left home and were reported to be employed in urban homes in Palapye. Nine other older women were living in towns with their daughters or employed sons but were not themselves employed. These older women had been the cornerstone of the rural-centered household unit. My records indicate that in five cases (out of a total of twelve cases of absentee "first generation" women), the absence of the first generation woman from her rural *lolwapa* had resulted in the demise of this domestic entity in the village.

The demographic characteristics of the absentee category are clearly reflected in the composition of the de facto resident population. In 1982, the de facto population of most Tswapong villages consisted mainly of women, children, and men more than 40 years old. In Maunatlala, according to the 1981 census, 60 percent of the enumerated population was female, and 40 percent male. Children under the age of fourteen constituted more than half of the village de facto recorded population. Within the resident adult category (twenty years old or older) 70 percent were women, and only 30 percent were adult men. Clearly, as the data presented in this chapter document, a narrow focus on resident population at any one point in time cannot give an accurate representation of the more complex socioeconomic fabric of village life. We are now in a position to turn to an overview of the socioeconomic patterns in Mokokwana. The discussion will make reference to specific numbered household units. These numbers will enable cross-referencing with other facts detailed in various chapters of this book.

MOKOKWANA: SOCIOECONOMIC PROFILES

Wage Employment and Local Sources of Cash Income in Mokokwana

In 1982 and 1983, all but four households in Mokokwana (#3, #26, #35, and #60) included at least one wage-earning member who worked for cash outside the village. The wage-earning members of Mokokwana households included the head of the household, sons, and daughters, as well as other related and unrelated members. Most wage-employed Mokokwana residents were migrant workers. All interviewed Mokokwana wage-earning males held semi-skilled or unskilled positions within the range of mine work occupations and reported earning between P85 and P120 a month. Those Mokokwana residents who worked in urban centers in Botswana held low-paying, service-oriented positions in the government and private sectors. The out-migrating women were most often domestic workers or cleaners in government institutions. They earned between P20 and P60 per month. As noted previously, most of these urban, employed, cash-earning women were unmarried daughters from the village-centered household who supported the children they left behind with their wages.

Local sources of cash earnings in Mokokwana, as elsewhere in small villages in the Tswapong, are extremely limited. In Mokokwana, these sources consisted of one sales position in the local shop divided between two young women who were paid P30 each per month. Both women were related to the shop owner and, like him, were not Mokokwana villagers. The opening of the school in 1982 provided paid employment for two part-time cooks. None of the teachers in the newly opened school was a Mokokwana villager.

The data presented here show that most able-bodied young men and some women in need of cash left the village settlement for employment elsewhere. A large active labor force still remained behind in the village. The extent of this potential labor force within the resident population of Mokokwana became evident during a short-term project implemented in the village during November and December of 1982. Fifty-eight men were recruited from Mokokwana and Moseu to work on the installation of water pipes in the two villages. A few months later, another infrastructure building project recruited fifty-two men and women from Mokokwana alone.

However, aside from such sporadic and short-term projects, local opportunities to raise cash in the village were extremely limited. These included house building, religious and medicinal services, and cattle herding. The frequency of the demand for these various services and the amount of cash paid for them were often not large enough to sustain the people who performed these services. In all cases recorded in Mokokwana, the cash earned for the provision of these services provided only a supplementary income to wage employment outside the village setting. Thus, for example, the traditional medicine man *(ngaka)* was a migrant laborer who provided his services only when in the village between consecutive labor contracts.

Local women generated some cash by selling a beer *(bojalwa)* that they brew from a mixture of sorghum and white corn flour. They also made and sold a stronger alcoholic drink, *kgadi,* made of fermented sugar and wild berries.[15] In 1983, I estimated that a woman made a net profit of about three to five pula from the sale of *bojalwa* produced during three days of intensive labor. Since *bojalwa* must be drunk immediately after it is brewed, and the local market of men with available cash was quite limited in a small village like Mokokwana, the production and sale of *bojalwa* at any one point in time had to be coordinated among the local women. I estimated that during 1982–1983 there was, on average, one *bojalwa*-selling occasion per week in the village. The beer-selling market was further limited to a few "regular" brewing women. These women were often the most needy women in the community—women who had no income from male members of their household. Other, more fortunate women organized a beer-brewing and-selling day only when they wanted to raise cash for a particular occasion, such as the purchase of clothes for church or a trip to a church meeting.

At times, several women joined together and put on a locally publicized *parti* where, to the sound of a battery-operated gramophone, the sale of beer, fried bread *(boroto)* and cooked food took place. On other occasions, more structured collaboration among several women resulted in a kind of local "credit" system. Each of the members of the small self-selected group, known as *motselo,* contributed about three to five pula toward the purchase of staples. In a well-defined sequence, only one designated member of the group received all the intake from the sale.

Important as these local modes of generating cash were for certain women in the village, they were essentially mechanisms of redistribution of cash obtained outside the village. Most consumers of *bojalwa* were young miners who spent their mine wages in the village while on "rest" between work contracts.

Crop Production

The principal crops grown by Mokokwana villagers, as elsewhere in Botswana, were sorghum, maize, and millet. Beans and watermelon seeds were often mixed with the grain seeds and sown broadcast. Ploughing, begun after the first soaking rains, was carried out with a ploughing team of four to six oxen or cows pulling a one- or two-furrow iron plough.

The 1980–81 agricultural season was a drought year. Most Mokokwana households (observed during 1982–83) consumed corn flour purchased from local stores or received small portions of corn flour and oil from the drought relief aid distributed that year. I found that only four households in the village supplemented their purchased corn flour with sorghum that they had cultivated themselves in the previous year. While the vast majority cultivated their land every year, only about five or six households (less than 10 percent) produced enough grain to feed their families without the need to purchase supplemental cornmeal in the course of the year. Sugar, tea, and condensed milk were bought regularly at the local shop.

In 1982, Mokokwana villagers spoke of rain as the only limiting factor to a hoped-for abundant agricultural yield. There seemed to be no perceived shortage of agricultural land among villagers. All applications for arable land, directed since the late 1970s through the land board, had been granted. All but ten households in Mokokwana reported they had their own arable field plot in one of the named land areas belonging to Mokokwana. However, only about 40 percent of the interviewed village dwellers reported that the land they had was sufficient for their needs in terms of size and quality of soil. The majority of the village landholders (almost 60 percent) claimed that their field plots were either too small or too depleted for crop production. Among the ten households that had no arable plot, five were headed by unmarried women (#3, #20, #46, #56, and #81). These women and their children had access to the field of, and shared labor with, relatives who resided in another *lolwapa* in the village. Three other "landless" households were occupied by young couples who had recently constructed their own separate *lolwapa* but continued to share the man's father's field plot. Only two village households had no land of their own and did not have access to, nor cultivate any, land belonging to other villagers, and so produced no crops. The residents of one of these households (#17) relied exclusively on the wage-earning power of its head; the other landless *lolwapa* was occupied by an old childless couple. The old couple was the poorest in the village, since they had no cattle and no children who could contribute their labor to assist their parents in cultivation.

In sum, for the majority of Mokokwana households, crop production provided an important, but rarely sufficient, source of income. This was often the situation in other rural areas in the country. One study concluded that "the mean Botswana farming household on average produces only around half of its [minimum caloric intake] requirements" (Cooper 1982:30). It is interesting to note that even the most affluent households in Mokokwana reported that they had never sold their surplus grain. When available, surplus grain was distributed to less fortunate relatives, brewed into beer, or, at rare times, bartered locally for cattle.

Cattle Raising

Cattle are extremely important for agricultural production, beyond their importance as a source of storable wealth. Ploughing is usually carried out with a team of four to six oxen pulling a plough. To maintain a ploughing team, one's herd must consist of forty animals or more, the optimal size that according to specialists secures self-sufficiency for its owners. Those who own fewer cattle must rely on labor-sharing arrangements with neighbors and relatives. In my estimates, most Mokokwana households owned between one and fifteen head of cattle.[16] Six households in the village owned between sixteen and forty head. None of these households used hired labor for managing their cattle; they all relied on relatives and other arrangements of exchanging services. Only three herds owned by Mokok-wana villagers consisted of more than forty head. These relatively large herds were owned by people who belonged to distinct household units. Often these households were connected through kin ties, and the common herd was seen as a "family herd."[17]

Three households in Mokokwana owned no cattle. Yet these cattleless households, and those who owned too few to maintain a functioning independent ploughing team, often had access to loaned, or *mafisa*, cattle. A *mafisa* arrangement is a common Tswana practice that enables many households without cattle to have access to the draft power and milk of animals placed with them by the cattle owner in exchange for herding services.

Cash employment in the agricultural zone surrounding the clustered village settlement was limited. Cattle were herded in most cases by preadolescent boys supervised by adult members of the household. Very few adults were hired as full-time paid herders. The pay for herding services was extremely low (about a fifth of that of mine work), and in the case of preadolescent herders it often consisted of an animal for the service of several years of herding. Cattle were rarely sold in Mokokwana to meet the daily need for cash. The only case of cattle being sold in the village during the first research period (1982–1984) occurred when expenses of a marriage ceremony had to be met.

Cattle was seldom a source of food. The only occasions when cattle were slaughtered to provide beef were for funerals and weddings. Consumption of milk produced by cattle was also low due to the great distance between the grazing areas and the village settlement. Most people in Mokokwana bought the expensive South African packaged milk in the local shop.[18]

In summary, most Mokokwana households did not own enough cattle for independent timely ploughing operations. The few households who owned no cattle and the majority of cattle owners who owned between one and fifteen head were always dependent on labor-sharing arrangements in carrying out crop production. Such dependency often entailed a delay in the timing of ploughing, which is critical in the fragile ecosystem of this region.

Small stock, most often goats, were kept in the vicinity of the village where they were allowed to forage freely. Every night, goats were brought into a little thorny bush enclosure located near the owner's *lolwapa*. These goat produced little or almost no milk. Like cattle, goats were kept as a potential food source and as storable wealth. Many households kept only a few goats next to their yards. Only one household in Mokokwana owned thirty to forty goats, which were kept at the land area and herded by a hired ten-year-old boy. Small amounts of milk produced by these goats were sold to neighbors and consumed by the members of the household. Most households in the village also kept varying numbers of chickens. Chickens were consumed on occasions of important visits or during meetings of the family group.

If we now place the socioeconomic position of the Mokokwana farmers as recorded in 1982–1983 on the national, four-category, socioeconomic scale outlined previously, we see that no Mokokwana farmer belonged in the upper category of "rich peasantry" or "emergent capitalist farmers," defined as those who practiced regular sale of crop surplus and hired labor to cultivate their land. Most Mokokwana farmers fell within the "poor peasant" or what Cooper (1980) calls a "lumpen peasantry" category, which, unlike the more affluent "middle peasantry," did not "regularly produce enough of their food from their own lands." Most Mokokwana residents fit the "poor peasants" category: they were in a position of absolute dependency on other sources of income, primarily wage income earned by absent members of the household.

The 1993 Record

Aggregate national-based statistics document the remarkable economic growth that has occurred in Botswana since the 1970s. One recent figure records an average rise of around 6 percent per annum in the GDP rate during the past thirty years of the postindependence period: of 1966 to 1996 (National Development Plan 8, GOB 1997:17). In real terms, such growth means an increase from a GDP of P1,682 in 1966 to P7,863 in 1994–5. However, as we have seen, these national growth rates do not reflect variations between urban and rural households, nor can they portray the reality emerging out of multiple links that existed between these two sectors when viewed from the single household perspective. In light of the discussion offered to this point, it becomes particularly interesting to compare the economic profiles of residents in the small village of Mokokwana in the early 1990s with their situation in the early 1980s.

Arriving in Mokokwana a decade after my first extended field research, I was struck by what seemed, at a first blush, to be a dramatic enrichment of the population. The most visible indicator for the change in the overall economic well-being in Mokokwana was the local ownership of three small stores and two bars. A decade earlier, the only shop that offered a small selection of foodstuff (mostly, sugar, tea, soap, candles, distilled milk, matches, and a few bottles of the much desired Heinz ketchup and mayonnaise) was owned by an outsider, a resident of a neighboring large village. This shop, much enlarged, was now owned by a Mokokwana resident. Two other shops, both operating from the *malwapa* of their owners, were also offering services to residents. Two of the three vehicles owned by Mokokwana residents in 1993 (none in 1983) belonged to these local shop owners. Many more people purchased and used donkey-pulled carts for transportation—fourteen in 1993, compared to a single one in 1983.

There were, however, only minor improvements in the village public infrastructure. Water pipes providing clean water in four locations around the village had been in place since 1983. To keep the water clean, cement constructions were built around each water distribution point to keep away cattle and goats. In the course of this decade, two small rooms were built by the District Council for the school teachers, and the family welfare educator had a new mud-brick, cement-plastered, single-room building that she now used as a local clinic (in 1982, she served the public in the shade of a tree). The central *kgotla* arena for the village remained as it had been a decade ago—a shady clear ground adjacent to the local village headman's yard.

The most impressive indicator for the material well-being of Mokokwana residents was the improved quality and style of their domestic construction. In 1993, one kept on hearing about the following four categories of houses: the *tswang, rantafole, polata,* and *gaise.* People made plans to construct a new dwelling unit in their yards, compared existing dwellings, and debated the relative qualities of the various house constructions. A brief description of these domestic construction types is necessary.

Tswang is what is generally known as the "traditional" house that outsiders often refer to as a "hut." The *tswang* is a single room, with a round construction of mud walls and a straw roof. The roof is held on a frame of rough thick tree branches, layered with straw collected in the nearby hills by the women. This straw, locally known as *bojwang ba setswana* (literally, straw according to Tswana way) is distinguished from the better quality straw, collected in selective sites on the hills and arranged in neat bundles. When a roof is made of this better quality straw, called *bojwang ba lefelo* (literally, straw of a broom), the house is known as a *rantafole* (a Setswana way of pronouncing the Afrikaans word). The roof of a *rantafole* is constructed by professional roofers, all men, who use a labor-intensive technique to tie each bundle of straw to the elaborate skeleton of the roof. Despite the reference of the name to a round room, some *rantafole* are square. The walls of the *rantafole,* like those of the *tswang,* are made of mud and plastered with cow dung. At times, the cow dung plaster is painted with store-bought paint. The use of store-bought material distinguishes the more common *tswang* and *rantafole* huts from the *polata* and *gaise.* The *polata* is a single-room construction (often square). The walls of a *polata* are made of cement bricks, and its roof is a flat, corrugated, iron sheet. The roof is known as *senke* (from the word zinc). Finally, *gaise* is a multiroom house made of brick walls and a more solid roof. The roof is placed on a wooden frame and allows for a sliding ceiling space. *Gaise* (literally, a better thing) is also described as "*ntlu e etona*" (a big house).

In 1993, I counted a total of 104 *tswang* houses, 65 *rantafole,* 13 *polata,* and 12 *gaise* buildings. These were found in ninety existing yards, or *malwapa.* In comparison, in 1983 in Mokokwana, all but two domestic constructions (both *rantafole*) were of the *tswang* type. The increase in capital-intensive construction over the decade was dramatic. This was significant in light of the fact that there were no new local paid positions. All the cash invested in these domestic constructions and in the purchase of donkey carts, stores, and and vehicles had originated from earnings outside the village.

Cattle ownership was as hard to assess in 1993 as it had been a decade earlier. It was impossible to observe herds because they roamed freely in the grazing zone outside the village. It was much more difficult to assess the size of a herd "owned" by individuals or domestic units. Cattle that belong to several *malwapa* units were often kept together since they were communally owned by an extended family. Other loan arrangements, known as *mafisa* also complicated any effort of independent assessment. On the whole, 1993 was a drought year and many of the existing cattle had perished. My overall estimates for 1993 were based on fragmented information gleaned from informants and circumstantial evidence. I distinguished between three groups of cattle owners in the village. At the bottom were households who owned no cattle and those who owned up to ten head. More than half (forty-eight of ninety) of Mokokwana households were placed in this category in 1993. The second category consisted of households who, in my multiple examinations,[19] owned between ten and sixty head; thirty-six of the total ninety households in 1993 fell within this category. Only six households fit the most affluent category of households, with more than sixty head of cattle.

To complete the 1993 socioeconomic village profile, it should be noted that ten households in Mokokwana were defined as *batloki*—as destitute—an official classification that qualified these people to receive government food-aid rations. Two of these *batloki* households had no village *malwapa*. They lived permanently in their agricultural lands areas and would come to the village to receive their food rations.

SOCIOECONOMIC IMPACT ON HOUSEHOLDS

Having outlined the socioeconomic profiles in Mokokwana at two specific moments in time, we can now turn to examine the way economic shifts were experienced by individual people. We return to Serefete, her sister Maria Basebi, and to old Basebi's sister—Elisa Lesife—in order to explore the movement of people and resources in and out of these three domestic and family units in the course of a decade.

Lolwapa #1: Batlang and Serefete

In December 1982, *lolwapa* #1 in Mokokwana consisted of five residents: Serefete, in her early forties; her three youngest children who were nine, seven, and four years old; and the son of her daughter Kay (Seforo),[20] who was about two years old. The two older children of Serefete—twenty-year-old Kay and twenty-five-year-old Tuma—did not reside in the village *lolwapa* most of that year. Kay attended secondary school in the capital Gaborone, and Tuma was employed in a South African mine on a yearlong work contract. Batlang, Serefete's husband, lived in Gaborone in a small rented room and worked for the city council in a low-level service position. While attending school, Kay shared her father's room. She cooked and kept house for him.

The family's herd consisted of about ten head of cattle kept at a distance from the village and cared for by Serefete's brother and sister's son. Agricultural land was cultivated by Serefete and a man from a neighboring village with whom Serefete entered into a labor exchange arrangement. Cash income was sent on an irregular basis by Batlang, who visited the village home twice between December 1982 and December 1983. Tuma, the mine worker son, used his cash to construct a nice square dwelling unit in his parents' yard and to purchase a range of furniture (including a battery-operated radio tape player). He also invested some of his earning to purchase three head of cattle, which were kept with the rest of the family's herd.

In 1993, Serefete remained alone in her village yard. For a few months of that year she enjoyed the company of her ten-year old niece who was sent to help her in daily errands. Her husband, Batlang, had died in a car accident in the capital Gaborone. Tuma was married and lived with his wife and three children in a company house in Palapye. Kay was an unmarried mother of three children, who worked as an office cleaner in the same town. Serefete's two younger sons, Zoo and Ishe, also left home in search for work in the urban centers. Zoo, who completed his elementary school education, was hired as a police officer and lived in Gaborone. Ishe, his older brother, looked for work in Palapye and relied on the hospitality of his sister Kay. The youngest daughter of Batlang and Serefete attended secondary school in Palapye. She also shared Kay's urban household.

There is very little evidence of the general enrichment of the previous decade in this shifting household unit's story. The rural residence shrunk into a single-member unit upon the death of the male head of the household and the two younger sons' departure in search for urban employment. Arable production had never sustained this household. In 1993, no agriculture was carried out. The dependency on cash income was therefore acute, and it forced working-age members of the household into urban centers. Indeed, prospects for upward mobility for both men and women coming from families like the Batlang family were grim. Pregnancy, in case of young women like Kay, and limited formal education, as in the case of the two younger Batlang children, meant that they had no marketable skills. Kay entered a cycle of increasing marginalization as a single head of her expanding household, and she supported herself with an insecure and low-paid service job. The two younger sons could barely support themselves and had little or nothing to give to their dependent family members.

The following example illustrates a more complex structure of a four-generational household headed by a widow, Elisa Lesife. The story of this matrifocal household, known in the development literature in Botswana as a "female-headed household," raises for discussion several questions about the changing place of women in the village-based production and consumption unit. By examining the shifting composition of this household during a decade, we also can see the diverse temporal processes that constituted and dissolved such a unit.

Lolwapa #11: Elisa Lesife

Elisa was the younger sister of Basebi (head of #13) and Sebopelo (#27). Her husband, Molesiwa, had gone to South Africa in 1958 and had never returned. All efforts made by his brother (head of #35) to bring Molesiwa back home had failed. In the prolonged absence of her husband, Elisa emerged as the unquestioned head of her independent household. In 1991, Elisa heard that her husband Molesiwa had died in South Africa. She had given birth to five daughters and a son. Her son had died in his youth.

In 1982, the village-based household headed by Elisa was a composite of three clusters of unmarried mothers and their children. The first consisted of Barapedi, a daughter of Elisa's first daughter. Barapedi was born in the neighboring Seolwane village, where her mother lived virilocally (with her husband's relatives). At the death of both her father and her mother, she came back to her mother's natal home and joined her maternal grandmother, Elisa. In 1982, twenty-one-year-old Barapedi was pregnant with her third child. The father was a construction worker employed in Moeng College, located about a forty-minute walk from Mokokwana. The man was also the father of her second child. Barapedi's first son was fathered by a man from Lerala. When asked what happened with the first man, she stated simply that "our love was finished." The father of her second and third children came from a village in the southeastern region, and no effort was made to initiate discussions about a future marriage until January 1984 (when I left Mokokwana). Throughout this time, Barapedi supported her children through sporadic work as a maid in Palapye and in Selebi Phikwe.

The second mother and children fragment in Elisa's household was composed of Kemoto, daughter of Elisa's second daughter, and her four children. Kemoto was born in 1950 in Mokokwana. She was a premarital child and was left in her mother's mother's yard when her mother married a different man from Mosweo. Kemoto's own conjugal union to a man in Lerala came to an abrupt end in 1978, when the man who had fathered her first two children died. Despite more than seven years of virilocal residence at this man's natal home, their conjugal relationship was never established as marriage and upon his death, Kemoto returned to Mokokwana. In Mokokwana, Kemoto had three more daughters (born in 1975, 1977, and 1981). The father of the last two daughters was rumored to be a married man in Mokokwana. This lover (*nyatsi*) provided sporadic and unpredictable financial support to Kemoto and the children. In 1983, Kemoto found a part-time job as a cook for one of the teachers in Moeng. When the position was terminated a few months later, she went to the remote cattle post to help her mother's sister Kumanego by herding Elisa's cattle.

Kumanego, Elisa's youngest daughter, married and lived at her husband's village, Ratholo, for a few years. But when this marriage dissolved, she, too, returned to her natal home. Her three older sons, who were fifteen, seventeen, and twenty-one in 1982, resided in Elisa's yard in the village, while their mother and her four younger children lived in the cattle post. In 1966, Kumanego gave one of her own newly born children to her older sister who was married in Moremi village. The child—a girl—was given, Kumanego explained, because the sister "had only boys."

Elisa's fourth daughter, Anna, also an unmarried mother of seven, headed household #79. She told me in 1982 that until 1979 she, too, was resident in her mother's yard. She moved out of the yard to establish her independent household when the younger women, Barapedi and Kemoto, daughters of her sisters, began to have, as she put it, "too many children."

In 1993, this four-generational household had effectively dissolved. Elisa, the grand matriarch, died in 1991. Barapedi, who left in 1990 for Gaborone, sent for her children after she had secured a job as a cleaner in a small firm. Kumanego, now herself a grandmother, applied for a village plot from the land board, and in 1993 she lived there with her younger son and his two children. Kemoto inherited Elisa's *lolwapa* where she lived with her three younger daughters. Her two older sons, who were twenty-two and twenty years old at the time, lived in Gaborone. They contributed little to their mother's needs. The family's herd, kept in the cattle post and cared for by Kumanego's oldest daughter, was still undivided two years after Elisa's death.

The story of the changing composition of household #11 illustrates several processes that were common in the lives of many rural women in Botswana. At the center of this three-generational household lay the fragile nature of conjugal associations. The parameters of these unstable or never-established conjugal relations were directly linked to specific historical and social circumstances. Indeed, Elisa's own marriage had collapsed and effectively dissolved due to the most obvious strains of prolonged separation caused by labor migration. Elisa was deserted by her husband after several years of marriage, itself characterized by brief, irregular visits during time off between labor contracts. The husband opted to resolve the tensions inherent in this truncated marriage by centering his life in South Africa. Elisa opted not to follow her husband to South Africa, as many women in preindependence time had done, and thus she emerged as the head of her household and manager of the family herd.

Elisa's daughters' conjugal relationships were similarly unstable, but for a different set of circumstances and social realities. For several of her daughters, years of virilocal residence ended with the return of the woman to her natal home upon the death of the man or the breakdown of what had been an inherently unstable conjugal union. But the route to an independent house for a nuclear family of a woman and her children could take many years. The need to support her dependents forces the single-parent woman into a migrant career. Her children, and often the children of nuclear fragments of other, related women (sisters or mother's sister's daughters), remain in the yard of, and are reared by, her mother. The result is the three- or four-generation household. The breakup of such a composite multigenerational household occurs at a point when the family fragments of a woman and children becomes a three-generational segment itself. The move of Kumanego out of her mother's yard was a good example of such a temporal process.

The final example of a rural household and its shifting composition also concerns a matrifocal domestic unit. Here we return to Maria Basebi, whose life story was described in Chapter 2 and explore her strategies for survival as part of her effort to establish an independent household unit.

Lolwapa #45: Maria Basebi

In 1983, *lolwapa* #45 was the newly erected homestead of a three-generational family unit, headed by Maria Basebi. Maria, a forty-three-year-old unmarried mother of seven, had resided in her parent's *lolwapa* (#13) until 1981 soon after her firstborn daughter gave birth to a second child. "I was a grown-up woman, with my own grandchildren," she explained. "I had to move out of my parents' yard, so I applied for this plot from the LB, and I built my own." In 1983, Maria continued to cultivate a field, together with her brother Moses. Her son, twenty-one years old at the time, was on his first mine work contract, and Maria was pleased because "he was helping [financially, by sending some money]." The household was also supported by the man who fathered Maria's daughter's two children. This young man's help was not regular, and Maria made it clear that he had not initiated any formal steps toward establishing the process of marriage. Maria herself was known as a *nyatsi,* a lover of a married man in the village. Her last-born child was known as the son of that *nyatsi.*

Only children lived in *lolwapa* #45 in the summer of 1993. Maria's six older children had all left the village. Modiro, the oldest, now mother of three, lived and worked in Moeng College. Her three children lived in Maria's yard. Maria's second son (born 1962) and her fourth (born 1968) worked in Francistown in a wholesale firm. Their younger brother (born 1973) joined them in 1992 but was still unemployed. The third daughter (born 1964) and the fifth (born 1970) both lived in Gaborone; both had young children who they sent to live in their rural homes. Maria had left the village to support her brother Moses, who was hospitalized at the time in Francistown. She was due to return to the village with her four-year-old granddaughter (her fourth daughter's child).

CONCLUSION

This chapter opened with two moments I shared with two young people, a brother and a sister, in the early 1980s. When I first met Tuma and Kay, during the Christmas season in 1982, they were facing critical turning points in their lives. These two young people were making important decisions that enacted and reshaped their social identities. Tuma made the first step toward building his future family in his natal home. Kay made the decision that led her into a life cycle of a single mother and head of her own expanding family. The young man, Tuma Batlang, was at the point of ending his migrant labor career and beginning a family of his own. The young woman, his sister Kay Batlang, had decided to leave school and raise her second child herself.

I met these two young people a decade later, in 1993, and found in their lived situations two quite common examples of life among the new urban poor in Botswana. Tuma left his village home and supported his wife and three children with his meager wages from his job in the growing urban center of Palapye. His sister, now an unmarried mother of three children, had by then established her own household in which the men who had fathered one or more of her children were marginal. With her wages as a cleaner she supported her children, as well as her unemployed brother, school-aged sister, and widowed mother.

These two individual lives were molded in specific socioeconomic and political settings that unfolded in postcolonial Botswana. In an attempt to shed light on the processes through which these men and women have crafted a sense of home and family, the chapter laid out the larger contexts shaping such processes. It opened with a general overview of the political economy of the country and traced its transformation over the past three decades.

The major features of the transforming political economy of Botswana are easily summarized. Despite staggering economic growth in the country during its three decades of postcolonial history, the majority of the rural population remained poor and patterns of inequality have deepened. Agricultural production, cultivation and cattle husbandry, is widely practiced but does not provide the necessary sustenance for the majority of the population. Most Batswana must migrate out of their rural homes and engage in cash employment in order to make ends meet. A dependence on employment in South African mines as a source of cash has been part of Tswana life since the late nineteenth century and has shaped a life of circular migration. Miners returned to their rural homes to establish their families, contribute their labor to agricultural production and support via their wages dependent members of their families. More recent changes in the policies of labor recruitment by South Africa and the expanding mining sector within Botswana have resulted in an increasing number of migrants, especially young women, in urban centers within the country.

These general, nationwide factors were then viewed from the perspective of life in one small Tswapong village in east-central Botswana, the home village of Tuma and his sister Kay. Here we saw the detailed reality of these wider factors—a rural periphery with almost no local sources for generating cash and an absolute dependency on wages earned by absent members of the household. The general enrichment documented at the national aggregate level touched only a few residents of this village. For the majority of the population, increased cash income, when it did occur, was invested in the upgrading of the quality of housing. Yet, improved domestic construction, as with all other visible signs of economic growth in the village (the purchase of donkey carts, local ownership of stores, etc.), was dependent on earnings gained outside the village. It is significant that women, especially young unmarried mothers, had begun to leave the village in search of cash employment in urban centers.

The three last cases of village-centered households illustrate the way these shifts have been experienced in the domestic level, most critically by women. From this analysis, we learn about the malleability and fluidity of the village-centered household and about the fragility and variability in conjugal relations. The analysis provides the underpinning for the following chapters that explore other sites of identity formation—the village community and its association with larger constructed social units and relations.

NOTES

1. These periods of "rest" between consecutive contracts were dictated by the labor regulation of apartheid South Africa. They guaranteed the temporary position of migrant workers like Tuma.

2. Government of Botswana, Statistics Bulletin, December 1991, Vol. 16, No 3. Data abstracted from Table 6.2, page 37.

3. Source: GOB 1991, Table 6.4, Page 39. Note the changes in the exchange rates of the Botswana currency, the pula, over that period. In 1982, 1 pula equaled 0.94 U.S. dollars; in 1984, 0.64 U.S. dollars; and in 1991, 0.48 U.S. dollars. The South African rand suffered less dramatic shifts. In 1982 1 rand = 1.1 pula; in 1991, 1 rand = 1.3 pula; and in 1993 1 rand = 1.35 pula (source: GOB 1991:67; GOB 1993).

4. Calculated from the following data recorded in GOB, May 1993. The GDP per capita for 1990-91 was P5,307. For that same year, when mining was excluded, the GDP per capita stood at P3,061.

5. Real growth estimated in 1996 at 5 percent.

6. Based on "Household Income and Expenditure Survey, June 1985–August 1986," GOB 1995, pp. 86–89.

7. Gross income includes household income in cash and in kind. Income is stated in pula per month. Source: calculated from data in GOB 1991:87–88.

8. More precise data about the sociopolitical links between village and land residence are offered in Motzafi-Haller 1988:196–215.

9. *Lolwapa* #16 became a *matota*, a ruined space, when the single man who occupied it a decade earlier left it unattended. *Malwapa* #72, #37, and #60 were physically there but with no residents throughout that year.

10. Households #81, #82, #83, #87 and #88 consisted of Mokokwana women and men; #85 had a woman from Lerala; #86 and #91 the women originated from Maunatlala; and in #89 and #90 the women originated from Moseu.

11. For Botswana, see Cooper 1979, 1980; GOB 1982. For Lesotho, see Ferguson 1992; Murray 1981.

12. The need to narrow the definition of "absentees" has to do, of course, with the nature of a census that must rely on a single visit to the rural home and must thus set very strict and common criteria. The result, however, is quite startling. If my focal case is any indication, the resident rural population was greatly underestimated.

13. Detailed data summarized in this paragraph are recorded in Tables 4.4 to 4.6 in Motzafi-Haller 1988.

14. By 1997 the exchange rate stood at P3.6 per one U.S. dollar.

15. While *bojalwa* can be made year round, the production of *kgadi* depends on the season of the availability of the wild berries. I have also seen, in villages neighboring Mokokwana, women making alcoholic drinks from fermented candies and other store-bought syrups. Such drinks were consumed by the "hard-core" drinkers and were not favored by most people.

16. It is extremely difficult to actually assess the herd size belonging to villagers partly because the cattle, as noted previously, are not kept next to the village, and in the agricultural zone herds roam freely. When gathered for watering, cattle are not kept in separate family or household related groups. My estimates are based on informants' reports of their herd size and on crossing these with gossip and estimates made by my research assistant, himself a resident of the village.

17. This shared ownership of herds occurred in Mokokwana among households #15 with #21 and #24, #68 with #7, #12 with #8, #19 with #20, and #82 with #30.

18. A small, half-liter square box of distilled milk cost about 50 tebe. The daily wage on government drought relief work in 1983 was one pula and 50 tebe!

19. By "multiple examination" I refer to the following measures: asking the members of the household directly (rarely do you get a straight answer in this way), making "educated estimates" based on local gossip and other knowledge, and checking such estimates with my research assistant and other trusted local people.

20. Most people have a given name and a name they adopt during their childhood and are known by throughout their life. In the Batlang family, Ishe was named Nathaniel, the name I wrote down in my census records. Ishe was surprised to hear this is his given name. Everyone knew the elder daughter of Batlang as Kay. Seforo is the name given for the census records.

4

Historical Narratives
as Identity Discourses

To articulate the past historically does not mean to recognize it "the way it really was" (Ranke). It means to seize hold of a memory as it flashes up at a moment of danger. . . . The danger affects both the content of the tradition and its receivers. The same threat hangs over both: that of becoming a tool of the ruling classes.

Walter Benjamin, *Illuminations*

In December 1979, a group of twelve history students from the University of Botswana carried out a week of oral interviews in the Tswapong hills region of central Botswana. The aims of the "Tswapong Historical Research Project," their teacher David Kiyaga-Mulindwa wrote (1980:i), were twofold: "to train UBS [University of Botswana] history undergraduates in field methods currently used in African historical research" and "to contribute to the history of the Batswapong through the collection and analysis of oral traditions." The initial products of the research project were three volumes of "raw data," verbatim transcription in Setswana of the recorded interviews with partial English translations.[1] These dialogues between the university students and the interviewed residents of the Tswapong region provide a wealth of material about how people in the region interpret their lives, what conceptual frameworks they employed to make sense of their relations to others, and how their construction of the "self" and the "other" related to shifting relationships of power and domination within and beyond the region.

My first goal in this chapter is to examine these interviews as "identity narratives."[2] In tracing this indigenous discourse, I intend to show how people articulate social boundaries verbally and to outline the system of meaning that is continually contested and re-created in these oral texts. Looking closely at a few, selected, oral interviews, I wish to explore how people define leadership, hierarchy, control over land, and social distance and ultimately to grasp how the subjective significance of ethnic categories is produced.

My second analytical goal is to understand these oral interactions in the context of the shifting relation of power in Botswana over the past three decades or more. I wish to show how ethnic categorization has been altered in accordance with changes in the political economy of the region. To do this, I open the chapter with a review of the political history of the wider region within which the Tswapong hills are situated. Using my own and other published and unpublished oral data, the first segment of the chapter explores the dialectics of space, memory, and collective identities in the region over the long term. It traces the origins, the subsequent changes, and the contemporary expressions of these relations within a chronological framework that distinguishes among three major historical eras: precolonial, colonial, and postindependence. The purpose of this diachronic exposition is first to introduce the main features of settlement and land use patterns in Botswana as historically defined dynamic structures and, second, to provide the larger historical and sociocultural context against which the oral texts recorded at the end of the 1970s might be understood. In progressing in this manner, I challenge conventional historiography in two ways: by treating subject populations and their subjective articulation of events and meanings as central to any account of their history and by refusing to portray these subject populations as a uniform "group." These texts open a way to examine how subversive definitions of identity and hierarchy are articulated.

NINETEENTH-CENTURY TSWANA POLITIES

When British control was established over what came to be known as the Bechuanaland Protectorate in 1885, the local population was organized into several independent polities (*merafe*, sing. *morafe*, often translated as "tribe" or "chiefdom"). Each *morafe* was headed by a monarch (*kgosi*, also translated as "chief" or "king") and occupied its own territory. The population of each polity was ethnically diverse, but the ruling communities of the various polities were all of interrelated Tswana groups (Schapera 1952:8–11, 1984 [1953]:14–16; Sillery 1974:6–10).

The Tswana, who according to linguistic and sociocultural criteria, constitute part of the more inclusive Sotho-Tswana category of Southern Bantu speakers, are believed to have entered central southern Africa sometime before 1600. A process of fission and expansion of these migrating groups produced several *merafe,* which formed and dissolved in the course of the two centuries following entry of these groups into southern Africa. The instability of these early political structures led to constant movement, segmentation, and reconsolidation of groups, which produced an overall cultural unity among these early migrants (Kuper 1975:69). Fission and expansion gave way, toward the early eighteenth century, to a process of amalgamation and, by the end of the century, to the emergence of several centralized state systems (Legassick 1969). These early polities, which thrived on trade with the east coast, were torn apart during the first half of the nineteenth century by revolutionary political and economic changes known in the history of the region as the "Difaqane wars" (Hamilton 1995; Omer-Cooper 1969; Parsons 1982:55 ff.). The newly reconstituted, nineteenth-century states were based on the military power of the core ruling groups, who conquered or incorporated other groups into a centralized political system (Parsons 1977; Schapera 1970; Wilmsen 1989).

According to recorded oral tradition, the ruling communities of the four major polities in the area over which British rule was extended in 1885— the Ngwaketse in the south, Kwena at the center, and Ngwato and Tawana to the north and northwest—had migrated from the Transvaal as a single political unit headed by a Kwena Kgosi during the first half of the eighteenth century (Schapera 1952). The Ngwaketse and Ngwato polities were created when a royal relative of the Kwena king broke away from the main group and, accompanied by a group of followers, started a process of conquest and incorporation of local peoples during his northward expansion. The Ngwato royal line traced the moment of its separation from the Kwena origin at around 1760. Soon after (c. 1795), the Tawana seceded from the Ngwato and established their hegemony over the northwest territories around Lake Ngami. The fifth major polity occupying the area east of the Kwena was that of the Kgatla, whose royal lineage had entered the Protectorate area as late as 1871 (Schapera 1952).

The nineteenth-century Tswana polities varied greatly in size, yet they all shared a similar stratified sociopolitical structure. The ruling community, resident around their king in the clustered town, consisted of a nucleus of kinsmen, members of the royal lineage from which the king came, other related "noble" lineages (*kgosana*), and "commoners" (*batlhanka*) who were incorporated into the group early on. Groups that became part of the expanding political system later on were known as *bafaladi,* "strangers" or "refugees." The status of these strangers varied according to the time of their incorporation into the polity and their ethnic origin. Members of related Tswana groups who broke away from the nucleus ruling group of a neighboring Tswana polity were often granted full political and other rights (e.g., Bangwaketse people among the Bangwato). They were allowed to be governed by their hereditary leaders as long as they acknowledged the sovereignty of the king with whom they sought refuge and presented tribute to him.

Members of non-Tswana groups, like the Basarwa (Bushmen) groups who were the original inhabitants of the area, and others who migrated into the area from the north (e.g., the Shona-related Bakalanga), constituted the lowest social class. In the north, especially among the Ngwato and Tawana, their position was formalized into a separate class of "serfs" (*malata*) (Schapera 1952; Tlou 1977). Serfs were deprived of property rights and were attached, as hereditary servants, to the chiefs and other prominent members of the tribe (Schapera 1938:30–33, 250–253, 1970:86–89). The treatment of "serfs," like that of the "refugees," varied according to their ethnic origin and their mode of incorporation into the polity. For example, among the Bangwato, the Bakalanga and the Baphaleng, who sought refuge with the Ngwato king in the middle of the last century, were treated better than the resident subjugated Basarwa population (Schapera 1970:87). Similarly, the Batswapong among the Bangwato and the Bakoba (Bayei) among the Tawana, both small agricultural groups, were allowed some degree of local self-government, and their respective rulers could keep part of the tribute raised by their subjects (Schapera 1970:87; Parsons 1973).

Toward the end of the nineteenth century, several features of this political and territorial organization underwent considerable change. After a long period (c. 1820–1850) of civil unrest and confusion, the reconstituted polities reached the limits of their outward expansion and began to consolidate their rule over their respective territories. Several improvements in the system of rural administration and tribute extraction from subject people were introduced in the northern polities (Parsons 1973; Schapera 1970). The control over subject groups in the peripheries became more effective as resident, rather than visiting, governors became more common. Several rulers introduced a series of reforms that improved the economic position of their subject population. Schapera reports that the Ngwato king Khama, soon after gaining power in 1875, prohibited the sale of Bushmen or Sarwa serfs.[3] A decade later, he advocated that serfs should be paid for their work and be allowed to own property (Schapera 1970:89–90). Among the Bangwaketse, Gaseitsiwe allowed Kgalagadi serfs to own cattle, and Sebele I, ruler of the Bakwena, renounced his claim to tribute from serfs in his territory (Schapera 1970:46, 90, 183, 225).

Toward the late 1890s, the sociopolitical composition of the outlying population also underwent change. Several groups of Tswana-proper people were sent by the rulers to settle the borders of their respective territories. Between 1892 and 1930, five such "border villages" were created in the Kwena kingdom and twelve in the Ngwaketse (Schapera 1970: 64, 86). Among the Bangwato, Khama introduced another change in the settlement organization of the outlying areas. He created "peripheral towns" by clustering the population of several small villages and placing them under his nominated resident governors (Schapera 1938:10).

These political and administrative changes occurred within the context of a rapidly transforming political economy in the region. Livingstone's "discovery" of Lake Ngami in 1849 and the subsequent development of trade routes along the "road to the north" made crucial control over the outlying areas and the population residing in them. Control over trade routes leading to the northern territories and their wealth of ivory and ostrich feathers secured access to horses, firearms, wagons, ploughs, and other goods supplied in exchange by white traders. Thus, tribute paid by subject people and their hunting services became a source of unprecedented wealth to the ruling group at the center.

Access to horses, firearms, wagons, and ploughs had, in turn, important impact on the military, agricultural, and, subsequently, sociopolitical and spatial organization of these late nineteenth-century systems. Horses and firearms changed the balance of military might among the consolidated state systems in the area. Internally, a standing battalion of several dozen mounted horsemen in the capital provided an immediate check over a vast, previously inaccessible territory. Wagons made more efficient the transportation of grain and hunting spoils, extracted from subjects in the remote peripheries of the state (Parsons 1973, 1977).

A change in the means of production—from hoe to plough cultivation— had further, profound implications for the organization and control over labor in these Tswana polities. The use of ploughs introduced cattle (as draft power) into the production process and thus brought men into what had previously been a predominantly female domain. In the large capital agro-towns this meant that cultivation carried out in remote agricultural fields drew the men away from the court at the center of the village settlement and thus reduced the effective control practiced by the chief over the clustered town population (cf. Jean Comaroff 1985).

The first report of the use of ploughs in agricultural production appeared in the late 1870s (Patterson 1878, quoted in Schapera 1943:133). A decade later, another observer (Hepburn 1896) noted that plough cultivation led to cultivation of "very extensive stretches of land" and "large gardens" around the town. Critically evaluating a range of eyewitness accounts, Forsbrook (1971) demonstrated that the introduction of the plough in the late 1870s led to the gradual distancing of cultivated areas from the clustered settlement of Shoshong, the Ngwato capital. The need for larger fields necessary for plough cultivation resulted in a rapid depletion of available arable land at the outskirts of the town. As land in the immediate vicinity of the town was depleted, a gradual process of "abandonment of fields adjacent to the village in favor of more distant lands" (Forsbrook 1971:184) was set into motion. The demands of plough cultivation (intensive weeding prior to ploughing, caring for draft cattle) and the growing distance between the agricultural fields and the town center necessitated, in turn, longer periods of time spent in the remote fields and, eventually, to the erection of a second dwelling in the arable fields zone.

The gradual extension of cultivated areas and their distancing from the town was facilitated by the use of wagons as modes of transporting people and produce between the town and the fields. When British rule was established after 1885, these remote land areas became safer for prolonged residence because the colonial rulers effectively stopped inter-group warfare and cattle raids.

During these years, the demand for better and larger fields grew also in response to the expanding demand for agricultural products by the settled community of white traders, missionaries, and hunters in the town. This market became more important, since supplies of ivory and feathers dwindled in the late 1880s (Parsons 1977). In response to the demand for agricultural products, those who could afford ploughs, wagons, and the required labor force embarked on extensive and intensive field cultivation. For these affluent farmers, agricultural production changed their predominantly subsistence, female-centered orientation and became a source of wealth accumulation.

It is important to note, however, that while the socioeconomic and territorial organization of the capital town was undergoing major changes, the outlying areas at the peripheries of each polity continued to exhibit largely unaltered agricultural and territorial patterns. Among the subject cultivators in the outlying Tswapong areas, according to a visitor to the area in the late 1890s, for example (Willoughby papers 1898), hoe cultivation carried out largely by women was the main feature of agricultural production well into the twentieth century.

FROM KINGDOM TO "TRIBAL RESERVE": COLONIALISM, POLITICAL HIERARCHIES, AND TERRITORIAL REORGANIZATION, 1885–1965

The extension of British authority over the area of present-day Botswana was initially based on the wish to stop persistent Boer attempts to annex the area from the south and German expansion from the west, rather than interest in the potential resources of the territory. Indeed, the declaration of a Protectorate over the area was avidly sought and, when established, welcomed by the Tswana kings (Colclough and McCarthy 1980:12; Schapera 1970:51–54). One British official encapsulated this initial state of affairs, stating in 1888, "Her Majesty's Government desires nothing better than to see the Bechuana Chiefs continue to govern their respective tribes as at present."[4]

Yet in evaluating the nature of the British rule in Botswana (known as Bechuanaland in preindependence time) and in attempting to assess the impact of almost eighty years of colonial presence on indigenous Tswana structures, one must consider two main points. First, the initial lack of interest expressed by colonial officers in influencing indigenous systems gradually changed and culminated in the late 1930s and 1940s in direct efforts to curtail chiefly powers. A historical exposition of this process is thus necessary. Second, in addition to forces directly connected with the introduction of colonial rule, one must also examine "unintended" forces that accompanied the colonial presence or were set into motion due to colonial interventions. Indeed, the very establishment of British rule over the area implied significant, if at times unintended, effects upon indigenous structures. For example, an end to inter-group warfare brought about by the British presence facilitated the process of distancing the agricultural zone from the residential core in the town center. The following is a discussion of the engagement of three forces associated with the colonial presence with local Tswana structures: the demarcation of "tribal reserves," the imposition of the "hut tax," and the direct effort to curb the power held by indigenous tribal chiefs (former "kings").

In essence, colonial demarcation of the boundaries of each Tswana polity, and the creation of internally self-governed "tribal reserves" under the overarching authority of the colonial administration, was an effort to freeze a hitherto fluid political structure. Prior to colonial imposition of firm boundaries, the size of the respective territories of neighboring kingdoms contracted and expanded according to the relative authority of the rulers at the center of neighboring states. Each polity's political alliance with the center was not territorially defined, and segments seceding from one political unit could easily establish new alliances with the neighboring political center where they were allowed to settle in previously unoccupied land. The commitment made by the British administration "to keep peace and order" greatly limited such population movements. Chiefs were not allowed to welcome incoming groups into their territories, nor were they permitted to send out punitive expeditions to control challenges to their power posited by lesser chiefs (Schapera 1970:64, 225). Citizenship became territorially defined, and chiefs stood at the center of concretized, bounded, political units.

Indeed, the definition of rigid territorial units imposed by the British power had set, for the first time, limits on the ability of land to support a given resident population (Parson 1981). The total area of the "native reserves," the area allotted for the use of indigenous peoples, comprised only 37 percent of the total area of the Protectorate. The rest of the land area was designated "crown land" and was directly controlled by the British administration. The best cultivated land (although a small proportion of the total land area) was appropriated for European settlement (Schapera 1943:5–6).

A second major factor associated with colonial imposition that had dramatic effects on local Tswana structures was colonial taxation. The imposition of a "hut tax" after 1899 was intended by the colonial administration as a means of generating resources sufficient to sustain the cost of administering the territory. Collection of the tax was entrusted to the tribal chiefs, who were allowed to keep one tenth of the revenue for themselves. Unlike "traditional" tribute paid in kind or labor, colonial taxes had to be paid in cash. The burden of the "hut tax" was thus particularly heavy on the poorer segments of the population who could not sell cattle or other goods to obtain the necessary cash. As local employment opportunities were virtually nonexistent, these poor were forced to seek employment abroad—in farms and increasingly in the mines of South Africa (Massey 1978, 1980). Schapera notes: "In tribes like the Ngwato, Tawana and Ngwaketse, hardly any prominent members of the ruling dynasty have ever been abroad to work . . . whereas men of what were formerly servile communities (such as the Koba, Sarwa, Tswapong and Kgalagadi) have gone away in large numbers" (1947:42).

The profound implications of this labor migration on the Tswana indigenous economy, the nature of agricultural production, and the exacerbation of an already unequal pattern of resource allocation in Tswana society has been extensively documented (Colclough and McCarthy 1980; GOB 1982; Massey 1980; Parson 1981; Schapera 1947). There is also evidence (Parson 1980:59) that the rising number of labor migrants into South African mines was encouraged by the British who responded to the need for labor in the mines. Several acts, such as the restriction imposed on the sale of Tswana cattle exported to South Africa, restricted the ability of Batswana to earn cash within the boundaries of the Protectorate, thus forcing more people into labor migration. After 1896, more impoverished people were forced to enter the South African labor market after a devastating cycle of drought years and a severe rinderpest epidemic (Parsons 1973:11).

The third main force of change associated with colonial rule in Bechuanaland concerns the gradual redefinition of the chiefly powers. As noted previously, the initial period during which the colonial administration refrained from intervening in the local government of people in the territory gradually gave way to a more direct supervision and involvement. In the early 1930s a series of major reforms drastically curtailed the official duties and executive powers of the Tswana tribal chiefs (Schapera 1970:58). In 1934, two additional proclamations (numbers 74 and 75) gave colonial officers the power to recognize, designate, or remove chiefs and put limits to chiefly courts by establishing a higher level court system to which appeals could be directed. This series of official curtailments of chiefly executive functions culminated in 1938 with the "Native treasury proclamation." This defined that all income formerly accruing to the chief was to be paid to a "tribal treasury" that paid the chief a regular salary.

The chiefs did not accept these reforms of their executive powers without protest. Nor could the administration ignore the authority the chiefs continued to command among their people. Accepting the limits of their power "the administration," as Schapera phrased it, "preferred to advise rather than order chiefs with regard to the government of their respective territories" (1970:248). The proposal, put forward by the colonial government to dissolve the large capital towns is an illustrative example of the nature of the relationships that have evolved between colonial administrative officers on the one hand and those they called "tribal rulers" on the other hand.

In 1931, in the meeting of the Native Advisory Council, which brought together colonial administrators with the various Tswana chiefs, the medical officer lamented that many of the sanitary and nutritional problems he identified among the Tswana people were directly connected to the practice of living in large settlements. The crude sanitary arrangement in such a large settlement and the lack of access to green vegetables, he suggested, were the cause of the inferior physique of the Batswana. Both problems could be resolved, the officer reasoned, once the large town dissolved and allowed people to live in small communities next to their fields. His argument, however, was not novel to the ears of Tswana tribal chiefs. Tswana chiefs had heard from their resident missionaries since the early 1890s that "the people might do better if allowed to live in smaller communities and nearer their gardens and cattle posts." But they used this mode of reasoning selectively. In 1898, when he sent several groups out of his crowded capital town, Khama, the Ngwato ruler reiterated this medical-based reasoning in explaining his action: "We Bechuana people do not know how to keep large towns healthy as you white people do, though we were formerly obliged to live in large towns for the sake of protection"[5]

However, when the same proposition to dissolve their clustered capital town settlements reemerged in the early 1930s, the chiefs had effectively employed the colonial "reasoning style," only this time "progress" and "development" were invoked in order to support maintaining, rather than dissolving, the large settlement form. In 1931, Tshekedi, the acting chief of the Bangwato (quoted in Schapera 1943:270), maintained that:

The concentration of villages is a custom which has been in practice for ages by the Bechuana tribes . . . [it] has conveniently adapted itself to the progress of the tribe . . . [and] people living together form a better basis for the development of social life and the provision of education and medical facilities is made easier [in a large town].

Another Tswana chief, Bathoen, chief of the Bangwaketse, made clear that he shared the goal of "progress," advocated by the colonial officers, but he directly attacked their analysis that dissolving the centralized settlement would bring about this progress. He reasoned (quoted in Schapera 1943:270):

The Heads of the Veterinary and Agricultural departments always wonder why they do not see any result of their doctrines. They think it is because people live away

from the lands and cattle. I do not agree. I say it is because people are unedu-
cated. . . . In order to be able to understand the principles of cattle management
and agricultural methods, one had to be educated . . . and children cannot be educated unless they live with their parents in the main villages, where the schools are.

The Pim commission studying the conditions within the Protectorate in
the early 1930s heard from another chief: "An absence of village means also
an absence of centers from which industrial and commercial developments
can proceed" (Schapera 1943:270).

Whether convincing in their verbal expression of their objection to the colonial proposal to dissolve their clustered large towns or not, the facts remained
the same: none of the tribal chiefs followed the colonial decree, nor could the
colonial presence induce the desired change in the Tswana socio-spatial organization (Schapera 1943:268). As a matter of fact, recorded cases of actual dispersal of population out of a chiefly clustered town (cf. Ashton 1937; Parsons
1977; Pauw 1960; Werbner 1971) were never caused by, or had been out-
comes of, a colonial decree. The dynamics of centralization and decentraliza-
tion in the Tswana world, as this and the following two chapters will demonstrate, are linked to inherent contradictions within the local systems.

In sum, in spite of a growing number of formal checks and limitations
placed on the powers of local Tswana chiefs, they continued to command
great influence over their subjects. The territorial organization associated
with centralized political power was, to a large extent, preserved throughout colonial rule. Incorporation into the regional market economy and the
onset of labor migration entailed profound changes in the indigenous economy enforcing, rather than transforming, precolonial patterns of socioeconomic differentiation.

POSTINDEPENDENCE: CHIEFS, LAND BOARDS,
AND THE IMPACT OF LAND REFORM

Once it became clear in the late 1950s that the Bechuanaland Protectorate was to be granted political independence rather than the expected
handing over to the Union of South Africa, a political system on the West-
minister model was instituted in the territory. In 1963, a constitution was
drafted. Immediately after independence the newly elected government, in
a series of bills, directly restricted the power of chiefs (Colclough and
McCarthy 1980:37; Proctor 1968). The main bills introduced in these early
years were the Chieftainship Bill of 1965 and the Land Act of 1968. These
were designed to transfer most of the executive powers still held by the traditional chiefs to modern elected bodies at the district level. At the national
level, a House of chiefs was created with a limited advisory role to the government in "matters pertaining to traditional customs and institutions"
(Colclough and McCarthy 1980:37).

The boundaries of the "tribal reserves," established under colonial rule, were by and large kept and constituted the postindependence administrative units, the districts. Three governing bodies collaborated at the district level: District Administration, Tribal Authority, and District Land Board. District Administration is carried out to a large measure along the same lines laid down during colonial times. District commissioners function as the senior representatives at the district level of central government. The technical staff working at the district level are directly responsible to their respective specialized ministries. Councils were introduced into the district scene to take over most of the nonjudicial functions previously carried out by the local chiefs. Councils are elected bodies entrusted with authority to provide a wide range of services, including primary education, health care, sanitation, and water supplies.

Tribal authority in each district consists of a recognized network of salaried chiefs, sub-chiefs, and headmen who are entrusted with the task of administering justice in the rural areas. In 1979, some 119 customary courts throughout the country handled almost 80 percent of all civil cases (Egner 1979). A parallel, yet separate, civil judicial system dealt with cases of more severe criminal nature (e.g., murder). The administration of justice in these customary courts became the main task of local chiefs. They also have some ceremonial duties and serve as ex officio members in the councils and land boards.

The nine district land boards established in the late 1960s are statutory land allocating authorities granted the right to allocate land to citizens within the communal land areas. "State lands" are directly controlled by the Ministry of Local Government and Lands. Privately owned farm land is also excluded from land board jurisdiction. District land boards allocate land to individuals and groups for residential or commercial use. Sub-land boards, established in 1973, assist district land boards in allocation of residential and agricultural, but not commercial, land to individuals.

The introduction of the new district level governing bodies occurred in circumstances of absolute poverty. In 1966, Botswana was emerging out of a devastating sequence of drought years that destroyed about a third of the national herd. After eighty years of colonial rule Botswana was "worse off in terms of both social and directly productive infrastructure than any ex-British territory in Africa" (Colclough and McCarthy 1980:28). At independence, a fifth of the population was receiving famine relief and almost half of the recurrent expenditure of the new government was financed directly by the British Government and other donors (Colclough and McCarthy 1980:54). In these circumstances, it is not surprising that the newly introduced bodies were unable to provide the various social services they were empowered to provide.

Yet, ten years after independence, the parameters of this initial situation were drastically altered. A change in the weather cycle from a succession of drought years to one of good rains resulted in the rapid growth and remarkable revival of the livestock sector. The discovery of diamonds and copper led to a similar rapid expansion of the mining sector. By 1976, the national income per capita had tripled. The annual development expenditure in 1979 was almost identical to the Gross Domestic Product (GDP) of the new nation in 1966 (GOB: 1979).

However, little of this economic growth was channeled to the rural areas, where 80 percent of the population resided. The stated national policy during these years was to make the country a financially viable entity in the shortest possible time, and a strong preference for industrial and urban development was emphasized. On the whole, the rural areas received less than 10 percent of the total capital expenditure throughout the years 1966–1973 (Colclough and McCarthy 1980:85).

A major break in this trend occurred in the early 1970s. A year before a general election, a program aimed to achieve visible results in the shortest time was issued by the Cabinet. Appropriately named the Accelerated Rural Development Program (ARDP), it consisted entirely of physical construction projects and lasted some three years. In its course (1973–1976), a total of some 21 million pula (about the same amount in U.S. dollars) was spent on the construction of roads, primary schools, clinics, and water supplies in 27 major villages and 195 small villages around the country (Egner 1979). After the launch of the program, rural expenditure increased fourfold.

The program marked an important turning point in the extent of state impingement into its rural periphery not only because it directed, for the first time since independence, a substantial amount of resources to the rural areas but also for its role in enlivening and restructuring district and local level bodies. The role they played in planning and managing the construction projects during the ARDP years granted councils and their professional staff credibility among villagers. The relations between the Councils and central government was also strengthened as more professional personnel were introduced into planning and implementation at the district level. The new array of village-based, locally elected committees introduced in the early years of the project or immediately prior to it also gained in stature as the tangible infrastructure of schools, health posts, and offices was put in place.

As the ARDP proceeded, a major land reform, known as the Tribal Grazing Land Policy (TGLP), was introduced to the public in 1975. The TGLP proposed a redefinition of the existing traditional land use pattern as a measure of rectifying the alarming process of overgrazing and deterioration of the environment. Under the traditional land use system every tribesman had the right to graze his cattle in open communally held "tribal lands" (as distinct from "state land" and privately held land). The policy suggested the division of the tribal lands into three zones—commercial, communal, and reserve. It offered inducements to large herd owners to move out of the overgrazed communal zone into further grazing areas where exclusive rights in the form of commercial ranches were to be established. The "reserve zone" was intended to be a future "safeguard for the poorer members of the population" (Chambers and Feldman 1973). Several initial evaluations of the TGLP, written by people who were directly involved with the implementation of the policy, have pointed out that the establishment of commercial ranches was given priority in many districts over the needs of the resident population in the area. These dispossessed people, critics warned, would move into the overcrowded communal zone, thus aggravating rather than relieving the pressure in these areas (cf. Greenhow 1980; Hitchcock 1978; Jenness 1978; Von Kauffmann 1978).

These mounting criticisms against TGLP were not occurring in a social and economic void. The lot of the rural poor was becoming a focus of several influential studies that began to appear in the late 1970s. A major report submitted to the government in 1978 cautioned against the political and social dangers of growing unemployment rates in the rural areas (Lipton 1978). Others (Alverson 1978; GOB 1982; Wilmsen 1989) stated bluntly that still in the mid-1980s a large proportion of the population, particularly the lower 60 percent of rural households, had not yet begun to participate in benefits from the country's rapid economic growth.

A short overview of the regional history is necessary before we turn to the texts and their particular ways of articulating and debating collective identities within the region.

AN OVERVIEW OF REGIONAL HISTORY

The precolonial history of settlement in the Tswapong can be divided into two main periods. The first, characterized by a fluid organization of politically independent small groups, lasted until the early 1800s when the region became a frontier zone separating the two rising state powers of the Ngwato to the southwest and the Ndebele to its northeast. The second period began about 1860, when the last stronghold in the Tswapong region, Lerala, fell under the force of the increasingly powerful Ngwato king, and the area became a tribute-paying periphery of the centralized Ngwato kingdom.

The early political history (of the pre-Ngwato era) was characterized by the migration of several waves of Sotho-Tswana speaking people from the south, who incorporated into their social and kin networks the sparsely populated iron-working communities of the region. By the late 1700s, one migrating group, known as the Moremi-Pedi, established itself as the "spiritual lords" of the hills. Subsequent incoming groups who wished to settle in the region had to receive permission from the leader of the Moremi-Pedi, a man named Mapulana, and pay tribute. Yet Mapulana and his group did not create a centralized power structure in the region. A fluid hierarchy of groups emerged, and order of entry into the region and agnatic relationships among fragments of a single totemic group were the main criteria for relative position in the hierarchy. In oral histories I collected in the hills in the early 1980s and in 1993, the claim of the Moremi-Pedi group to what might be called their "moral dominance" over the hills was widely acknowledged. Regardless of their origin, people who resided in the hills reported that only the Moremi people could bring rain by contacting their ancestral spirits. Villagers also noted that one village was "senior" to another because of a putative agnatic link between their respective ancestors. But such seniority did not entail privileged access to resources or control over other local groups.

The inclusive label Batswapong (often Matswapong[6]) appears for the first time in missionaries' accounts at the critical moment in the history of the region, around 1860, when the regional population came under the crossfire of two rising powers, Amandebele to the northeast and Bangwato to the southwest. In these early accounts (Mackenzie, 1871) and in historical compilations largely based on these accounts (Parsons 1973; Schapera 1952, 1970; Sillery 1952), the population of the hills is described as industrious and defenseless iron workers and cultivators who could not effectively resist the military might of the expanding Ngwato lineage coming from the south. Oral evidence suggests that residents of the hills had never attempted to resist Ngwato domination but in fact invited protection against the more destructive raids of the Ndebele armies.

During the first two or three decades of domination (c. 1840–1870), and while the Ngwato lineage was consolidating control over its expanding territory, the population of the hills was accorded a large measure of local autonomy; tribute in the form of wild animal skins was a symbolic token of deference to a higher remote center of power. The "subject tribe called the Machwapong," writes one missionary in the late 1860s, "renders a certain tribute to the Bamangwato, but are permitted to enjoy, after somewhat precarious fashion, their own flocks and herds and other property" (Mackenzie 1871:366). Control over the trade routes to the north rapidly enriched the emerging Ngwato center in Shoshong, southwest of the Tswapong region, thus transforming the nature of the domination. This subject tribe at the periphery of the expanding Ngwato state supplied the changing needs of the center; when elephants and game had all but disappeared from the region by 1880, Tswapong cultivators paid tribute in grain. The advent of the centralized Ngwato state in the last quarter of the nineteenth century formalized the process of dispossession by extending taxation, limiting access to land, and progressively confining the autonomy of local leadership.

In the historical process that defined relations among Ngwato rulers and the various ruled populations, each developed a new awareness of its distinct collective identity. In the dominant discourse of the ruling Ngwato, the population was divided into free citizens and vassals. Free citizens were members of other Tswana polities who joined the Ngwato core due to agnatic competition and segmentation. These *batlhanka* were integrated into the nesting hierarchy of political units as wards, sections, and age sets. Vassals, like the conquered population of the Tswapong, were kept apart as locally independent yet materially exploited subjects. At the bottom of this differentiated hierarchy of groups were Basarwa (Bushmen). Capturing this dominant discourse of ethnic differentiation, a colonial official reported in 1888:

The Bachwapong and Bakalahari speak a dialect of Sechwana and are of lower and inferior rank; many of their chiefs own flocks and herds and they are to be distinguished from the still lower Masarwa by these possessions and the cultivating of gardens. (Botswana National Archives, HC 24/15)

Toward the last quarter of the nineteenth century, the Ngwato king had established an effective system of administration by positioning his own relatives and trusted commoners as resident governors in the region and by systematizing tribute collection. In 1896, a visitor to the Tswapong region (Willoughby 1898) reported: "all these villages are placed under Bamangwato who collect taxes from them."

Political subjugation also resulted in significant demographic changes in the region. In 1895, as part of his effort to ward off encroachment into the region from Transvaal white farmers, the Ngwato king Khama sent a group of people called Babirwa to settle in Tswapong. Again, in 1898, Khama ordered several groups of people out of his large capital town and sent them to settle in Tswapong. A few years later, in 1903, he ordered the clustering of several local villages into one large "rural town" that was ruled by his appointed governor (Schapera 1970:85).

These recent immigrants contributed not only to growing pressure on land in the region but also to an increasingly elaborate structure of differentiation among groups and social categories within the regional population. Superimposed on the existing local political organization of groups (which was predicated on order of entry into the region and agnatic relationships within totemic groups) was a hierarchy based on rank within the stratified Ngwato political system. The groups sent out of the Ngwato capital were ranked higher than the resident population of the Hills. Thus, for example, the Maunatlala-Birwa sent to reside in Tswapong toward the end of the century were considered equal to the Ngwato core group. Marriage between the Ngwato royal family and the Maunatlala-Birwa core group established and signified such rank. In another example, residents of the hills who belonged to another high-ranking group (the Bakhurutshe) served as tribute collectors, entrusted with delivering such tribute to the Ngwato center. This inter-group hierarchy has continued to structure relationships in the region and underlies, as we shall see in sections that follow, much of the more recent inter-village struggles. On the whole, the few larger villages found in Tswapong were created by, and largely composed of, the higher-ranking groups who entered the region under Ngwato orders, while most of the small villages were composed of various lower ranking "Pedi" groups, who later came to be known as "Batswapong" (or Matswapong; see Motzafi-Haller 1993).

Yet this categorization was inherently ambiguous and open to contestations as groups and individuals were continuously engaged in a process of redefining their sociopolitical status within this hierarchy. It is instructive, for example, that Schapera, who attempted to map out the "ethnic composition" of the Batswapong category, needed to revise his categorization several times (Motzafi-Haller 1988; Schapera 1952). His suggestion that some groups in the region, such as the Bakaa, are now becoming known as Tswapong reveals just how the external definition of collective group identities can and did change according to the political and economic fortunes of a group (Worby 1984:40). What we see in the oral texts that follow is that people in the Tswapong region have resisted and challenged this dominant external discourse that defined them as ethnic subjects.

TEXTS AND CONTEXTS

The oral texts were collected in the course of one week in December 1979. At that time, many villages in the region were beginning to feel the direct effects of state reforms and policies promulgated a decade earlier. The most critical of these was the establishment of locally elected land boards, which assumed the right to allocate land hitherto held by traditional chiefs. But the position of local chiefs, despite these seemingly dramatic legislative reforms, was more affected by another state-induced change, namely, that village chiefs were to be paid by the state. Indeed only one person could be officially recognized and paid by the state as the village head, thus the question of who is *the* village head was not simple in the segmented local political field characterizing many Tswapong villages. Heated struggles and debates ensued in which local groups and segments redefined themselves and articulated their collective right to leadership and resources. The students' oral project was carried out in the midst of this atmosphere. In that context, the questions posed by the students were often imbued with the democratic and modern values they, as the most educated people in their young nation, had come to adopt. They often challenged, half jokingly, the interviewees about traditional practices that involved magic and bantered about old restrictions on choice of mates and relations between the sexes. While they accepted and shared with their interviewees many basic notions regarding rights of groups to land, ideas of hierarchy, and legitimacy of power, the students also questioned such notions and made their elders reflect upon and conceptualize them more concisely.

It is important to realize that the students presented themselves, and were treated, as professional outsiders. The students were hosted by Moeng College, located in the Tswapong region; they met there at the end of each day to discuss what they called "points difficult to put across to informants." The interviews were open-ended and informal, but the students all attempted to cover standardized points of reference in their daily interviews. The twelve-person research team consisted of eight men and four women, in addition to their teacher. The ethnic origin of the students is not known. In their interaction with the Tswapong villagers, the students' own backgrounds were never discussed. But it was clear that none of the interviewing students associated him or herself with the "Tswapong people." The students often used the terms "Batswapong" or "Bapedi" to refer to the main group of Tswapong residents as opposed to the local use of "Matswapong," which has pejorative connotations.[7] The main distinction, however, was between young, eager-to-learn outsiders and knowledgeable elders. Students often addressed the elders with terms like *malome* (my maternal uncle); the interviewees replied with the respectful *rra* (sir) or *mma* (madam), but one also sees playful references to *motshegare* (young woman or maiden) and paternal compliments for the student who "understands well" and proceeds to ask the "appropriate questions."

FIRST INTERVIEW: "I AM RELATING OUR HISTORY"

The village of Lerala, with about 1,800 residents at the time of the interview, was one of the two largest villages in the region on December 11, 1979. Lerala was founded by a group of Pedi people not related to the Bapedi of Mapulane, the man known to be the "owner of the hills." The headman of Lerala, Shaw Moroka, was present at the interview, but the main ward represented that day was of a Khurutshe origin. The four key informants were all of Moatshe ward; their totem is *phofu* (eland), which marked them as members of the Khurutshe group. In this, and the next interview selected for analysis, I follow the text closely as transcribed by the students, weaving in running commentary that intends to clarify or summarize points raised in the oral exchange. By keeping the sequence of events as they were told and by quoting long segments from the recorded interview, I wish to enable the reader to feel how indigenous concepts of time, space, and power were actively used and directly articulated. This interview sheds important light on the way group boundaries were constructed and redefined in the changing political history of the region.

The direct link between the historical narrative recorded in this interview and contemporary politics of intra-village relations in Lerala is articulated in the opening statement of the interviewees. The only history they were willing to relate was that of their own group, *Nna kana ke bua letsho la gaetsho la Bakhurutshe* ("I am relating our history, we the Bakhurutshe"), one speaker said emphatically. "You can ask those of Lerala ward [for their history]." The idea that one can tell only one's own history is central for understanding the unfolding interview and touches at the core of the notion of knowledge, in particular the knowledge of *letsho,* here translated as "history" subsumed within the definition of social and political boundaries. We will return to this issue several times in the course of the interview.

Having established his domain of knowledge (only the history of his group), the speaker opens by carefully mapping out the position of the Bakhurutshe-ba-ga-Moatshe, the particular segment of the Bakhurutshe resident in Lerala, within the larger political geography of groups in the region and beyond.

Q: Where did you live before coming to settle in Lerala?[8]
A: Yes, keep quiet I have understood. We were from Selepeng, which is very far away. We followed the line of rail and finally settled at Palapye in Ngwato country. We came together with Bakhurutshe.[9]

The first point established is how the breakup from the original home of the larger Bakhurutshe group had occurred. The term used is "Bokhurutshe." The prefix *bo* indicates location, while *ba* indicates people; thus Bokhurutshe is the land of Bakhurutshe, like Botswana is the land of Batswana. The student and the speaker share the knowledge of the original Bokhurutshe home, a place called Selepeng.

Q: But what do you say made you leave Selepeng in Bokhurutshe area?
A: Motshweneng had fought with Mongwato.
Q: Were those royals and one did not want to be under the other?
A: No, I am saying that Motshweneng (one who[se] totem is the baboon) who remained at Selepeng had himself and his people beaten for the baboon by Masilo's father, the chief. He then left with his regiment. We came together with Bangwato and Bakwena but split on the way. We then left Bangwato at Shoshong.

The split from the main group that remained at Selepeng occurred between a father and his rebellious son. The son left with his age regiment (*mophato*). The break-away group led by the rebellious son then joins the Bangwato and the Bakwena, two other prominent Tswana groups. A second split within the Khurutshe group occurred soon after. (The speaker says *re etla re kgaogana kgaogana,* "we arrived and we split and split.") This splitting, like the first one, is marked in reference to a place—"we had left Khama [Khama III, the Ngwato ruler] at Shoshong"—and as part of another internal agnatic group rivalry.

The speaker mentions a group called Bakhurutshe-ba-Rauwe. Rauwe, he explains, was junior to his brothers from the senior house, Bakhurutshe-ba-ga-Moatshe. The Moatshe faction of Bakhurutshe sent Rauwe to go and look for *ngaka,* here translated by the student as "a doctor who could make rain." The speaker makes a clear reference to the definition of this role in "older times." He says: *gore a ye go ba batlella dingaka tsa dipula tsa bogologolo*, "they were looking for *dingaka* (plural form of *ngaka*) of rain of long ago." Rauwe, continues the speaker, felt they were not treating him well and so went to look for his own *dingaka*. Here is a vernacular distinction glossed over by the student translation of the term *ngaka* solely as "rain doctor." *Ngaka* is a role that involved a range of supernatural forces. The speaker makes a distinction between the original request by the older brother to search for a particular rain-making *ngaka* when he indicates specifically *dingaka tsa dipula;* the younger Rauwe feels cheated and searches for his own *ngaka*, here in the general meaning of a diviner, not a rain-making specialist.

The student suspects the cultural logic that underlies this second internal breakup and proceeds to ask (I am using the English translation provided in the text):

Q: What was the doctor wanted for?
A: So that he (Rauwe) could kill his brothers and become chief himself.

The result of this common tale of agnatic rivalry is that the losing segment, named after its leader Bakhurutshe (thus the Bakhurutshe of Moatshe are known as *Bakhurutshe-ba-ga-Moatshe*) was forced to leave the main group; it ended up in the Tswapong region.

In referring to the segment left behind, the Bakhurutshe-ba-Rauwe, the speaker uses the term *morafe o mongwe*, "another *morafe*." The term *morafe* is used here, and throughout the interview, to indicate political boundaries. Once two brothers with a large enough group of followers split, they became two separate *merafe* (plural of *morafe*). Yet, in order to establish itself as a distinct *morafe*, a group must be defined in relation to space.

After a detailed account of the dispute between Rauwe and Moatshe, the two founders of each of the Bakhurutshe *merafe*, the speaker continues to lay out the social geography of relations among these and other *morafe* groups:

So they left Rauwe at Shoshong and came to settle here. On their way here they came through Mogapi, but left on account of thirst (lack of water) and went to gooMangadi where there is found the Motemane River. It was here that they (the Bakhurutshe-ba-ga-Moatshe) found Mapulane. Khama was then at Palapye.

The constitution of a new *morafe* is depicted here in relation to other existing *merafe* and with regard to their respective positions in space. The break-away group had remained in Shoshong, at that time the Ngwato capital. The Bakhurutshe-ba-ga-Moatshe then settled in Mogapi in the Tswapong region, but they directly encountered Mapulane, the "owner of these hills" when they moved to gooMangadi. Kgama, the Ngwato ruler had moved his capital town to Palapye at this point in time.

The making of a distinct group history is based on a detailed list of the places where the group resided on its way to the present location. Time, as we shall see, is marked through movement in space. But unlike "wild animals" and people with no political center who are like such "wild animals" because they move around space without clear purpose or direction, the detailed list of place names and the reason for moving out of each place is meticulously traced. However, such a wandering, formative phase does not define the boundaries of the new group in relation to other groups. Only permanent residence defines the newly emergent *morafe* and positions it vis-à-vis existing settled groups and then within a hierarchical order that structures inter-group relations. Understood within this indigenous frame, it becomes clear why the speaker outlines the position of two other key groups at the point of entry of his group into the Tswapong Hills region. The social geography of the Bakhurutshe-ba-ga-Moatshe includes two sets of important relationships—with the local ruling group over the territory into which they had ventured and with the increasingly more powerful Ngwato group, whose control had extended into this hills region. In this narrative, political relations and boundaries are marked in space: upon their entry into the hills region, they "found Mapulane" next to the Motemane river and Khama, leader of the BaNgwato, "was then at Palapye."

Yet the matrix of inter-group relations is depicted as an ongoing, always negotiated process in which boundaries and hierarchies are continually reestablished and newly interpreted. The dynamic, fluid nature of such a process is depicted in the following exchange:

Q: You say they found Mapulane at Motemane. Was he the chief (*A e ne ele ene kgosi foo*)?
A: Yes, he is the owner of these hills (*mong wa lentswe le*).
Q: Do you mean that he was the owner of the Tswapong Hills (. . . *mong wa mantswe a a Tswapong*)?
A: Yes, it is Mapulane's land/country (*Ee, ke lefatshe la ga Mapulane*).

The student's use of the term *kgosi,* which he translates as "chief," produces the more definite term *mong wa lentswe,* "owner of the hills," and finally the most explicitly assertive statement "this *is* Mapulane's land" (in the present tense, almost a century after the moment of entry of this Khurutshe group into the region). Forced as he was, due to the persistent probing by the student to make such a statement, the Khurutshe speaker finds himself in a position of having to justify his group's historical right of residency in these "Mapulane lands." He proceeds without delay to tell the following story. (I first quote the English translation as provided in the text and then return to the Setswana narrative for further analysis.)

Mapulane then ran short of sorghum and men had gone out hunting when they found Bakhurutshe living along the Bolowa River and they went back to tell him about them. Mapulane then went to Khama at Palapye and told him that there were people who had settled in his lands but were foreigners and did not belong there. . . . Then Khama sent out men to see the people Mapulane was talking about and he later told Mapulane that the people were in fact of their stock and he should live side by side with them.

Several key features of the emerging structure of group relations in the region are suggested in this narrative.

1. Mapulane's people were predominantly agriculturalists; hunting was taken on only when the harvest of sorghum was insufficient.
2. The territory over which Mapulane laid claim was large enough to allow a group to settle in the region unnoticed for some time. Within the hunting, open zones the definition of political control was fuzzy.
3. Although Mapulane was known as "the owner of the hills," the remote political center of Bangwato and its leader Khama had been establishing power over the region.

This exchange suggests an important, transient phase when the boundaries of local vs. remote power were not directly set. At this point in time, groups that entered the region could establish their right of residence by playing with the ambiguous power base of the local leader. Outsiders had to report to Mapulane. But Mapulane could not expel those he defined as outsiders. The power of the remote Ngwato ruler was gradually extending and being established over this remote region.

A closer reading of the original transcribed Setswana narrative provides a better understanding of the subjective way group boundaries were drawn and hierarchies contested in this exchange. A direct reading of the text in the vernacular transcription also illuminates several important ideas about the ways in which time, space, and power were linked in this narrative. For example, the hunters reported to Mapulane: *go thibeletse morafe o e seng wa letsho la bone,* "a group of people whose origin was not known has been found." The hunters report that the *letsho* of this *morafe* found in the hunting zone is not known. Recall the opening statement by the speaker who insists that he knows and can recount only his own people's *letsho. Letsho,* as historical narration and as a marker of collective identity, is knowledge. In this context, "not knowing" a *morafe* means the sociopolitical relations of such an entity are uncharted. It is thus the "other" to the expandable boundaries of the self. The term *mongwe morafe,* a "different, distinct morafe," is used by Mapulane when he reports to Khama. This "other morafe," Mapulane reports, was found "at my place," but, he insists, *ga se morafe wa mono*—"it is not a *morafe* of this place."

While the hunters, in their report to Mapulane, articulated the "otherness" of this newly encountered group of people by indicating that the *letsho,* the origin or identity of the incoming group, was not known, Mapulane was only concerned with relations to place—this was not a *morafe* of this place. The issue, for him was right of access to land defined in political terms, not the history or origins of the incoming group.

This ambiguity about group boundaries, about what establishes the "other" to the subjectively defined self of the "Mapulane people" is confusing to the student, who stops the speaker's narrative at this point to inquire: "What tribe were Mapulane's people?" The answer is: "They were Bapedi coming from the south." The Setswana term the student uses in his question about the "tribal" identity of the *batho ba ga Mapulane,* "the people of Mapulane," is *e ne ele bakae,* literally "they were of where," *ba* being a prefix indicating "human" and *kae* being "where."

The narration about negotiated boundaries of groups continues. Khama, the speaker relates, was not satisfied with Mapulane's assertion of *ga se morafe wa mono*—"this is not a *morafe* that belongs here"—and proceeded to check for himself. Khama's independent inspection of the group concluded authoritatively: *ke ba garona*—"they are of us; part of us."

Who is the "us" in Khama's reply? Does such an authoritative statement (as reported, of course, by a Khurutshe speaker) refer to Khama's own group, or perhaps to the wider political entity Khama was creating in these very years—an encompassing *morafe* that included the people of Moatshe, as well as those of Mapulane as subjects? The message sent to Mapulane is clear: what you (Mapulane) define as *mongwe morafe,* "a distinct group of others," is part of a larger group of "us," the boundaries of which are defined by the Ngwato ruler and from his perspective. The instruction is thus not to harass the group and let it reside in the Tswapong region.

Interestingly, the student translates *ba ga rona* as "of their stock." Using the English term "stock," a term used in the extensive writing of the most celebrated Tswana ethnographer Isaac Schapera, misses much of the subtle contestation of meanings revealed in this text. "Stock" connotes much more essentialist ideas about shared dynastic origins and traditions. The definition of inclusion and exclusion contested in this interchange between Mapulana and Khama is based on political relationships and with reference to control over space. I will return to this point in the closing discussion.

Another textual signifier of inter-group relations, especially in reference to the depiction of political hierarchy among groups, is suggested by the speech patterns recorded by the interviewee, who uses direct quotations in reconstructing the putative exchange between Khama and Mapulane. Khama is said to have addressed Mapulane as *monna* (man or chap) rather than as *rra* (sir), the appropriate term of respect. Khama's communication with the subordinate Mapulane appears in cryptic commands and statements, such as "they are of us" or "stay still and don't bother them."

As we follow the narrative, it becomes evident that despite the order from above to accept the presence of the incoming group, the relationships between Mapulane and the Khurutshe group were far from peaceful. Mapulane could not directly challenge the authority of the remote Ngwato power, but he found ways of making life difficult for the newcomers. The speaker describes how, after the settlement of the Bakhurutshe in Mapulane's land, Mapulane's sorghum harvest was meager (*go tlhoka mabele*), while the harvest of the incoming Bakhurutshe was large (*ba bolaya mabele*—literally, "they kill sorghum"). When that happened for the second year, relations between the two groups became tense. Mapulane sent a message to Khama indicating that *morafe oo tileng o o na le mokgwa,* "the group of people who came here has destructive powers" ("they bring bad luck to me," as the student translates). *Mokgwa* is a supernatural power used negatively. The incoming group, imposed on Mapulane, disrupted not only his power in the narrow, political meaning; it disrupted his ability to bring about prosperity, to protect his people from *mokgwa*. Mapulane is reported to be saying: "I plough, but I see no sorghum, only melon" (*ke a lema mme ga ke bone mabele, ke bona marotse fela*). He concluded, "They 'kill me'" (*baa mpolaya*). Mapulane began to make life hard for the Khurutshe group (which he never named), forcing them to migrate away from his agricultural land area, perhaps to reduce the danger of their *mokgwa* power over his crops.

The Khurutshe group was made to migrate from one place to another. But in all its settlements it continued to thrive. In one such location their harvest was so large that "Bangwato would come along for beer and *bogobe*" (porridge).[10] When Mapulane continued to argue that the group was still "too close" (*Mapulane are ba sa ntse ba le gaufi*), Khama intervened and put an end to Mapulane's claims. He evinced (again addressing Mapulane as *monna*) "if you only ploughed you will do better." Mapulane was not heard from after that. This Khurutshe group has remained in the Tswapong hills ever since. The informant ends the story with *ke eme foo,* "I stop here."

Several important points emerge from this oral text. The most crucial is the way social distance between units is constructed. A group of people is defined in reference to two unifying symbols—its totemic emblem and its leader. Thus we hear about *Batho ba ga Mapulane*, the people of Mapulane, and about the Bakhurutshe-ba-ga-Moatshe. The group's totem is often selected by its leader at the point of separation from a larger unit. In the case of the Bakhurutshe-ba-ga-Moatshe, the baboon (*tswene*) was adopted by the break-away unit. A similar story describes the choice of the hare (*kgope/mmutla*) by Mapulane when he broke away from his senior prior to his migration into the hills. The splitting group becomes a *morafe* when it establishes its relations to its own social space. The *letsho*, or story of origin of a *morafe,* begins at the moment of its separation and continues through a detailed social geography of its various locations of residence and the reasons for moving away from each place. The administrative position of such a group—as a ward within a larger village "ruled" by another group, or as an independent village settlement—is a reflection of the social geography of the group within the matrix of group relations in the region.

The second important point that emerges from this text is the way such social geography of groups is constructed. Two key elements define such hierarchy: the order of entry into the region and the group's relations with the remote Ngwato center that had extended its control into this region by the late 1860s. The right of the late-comer Bakhurutshe-ba-ga-Moatshe to their land in Mapulane's land is justified on grounds of their relations with Bangwato, despite the resentment of the original "owner of the hills."

In sum, a *morafe* is both a social unit defined by its *letsho* and a political unit associated with a totemic leader who established his group's right to land in the context of competing claims by other similar units. It is not an "ethnic group" with distinct ways of life or customs. As a result, the boundaries of such *merafe* and relations among them are continuously debated and reconstructed in the context of shifting relations of power within and beyond the region.

SECOND INTERVIEW: THE CHIEFTAINSHIP IS THE CHIEF

The second interview took place in the village of Ratholo on December 22, 1979. The single interviewee was Mr. Hanyo Moso of Mangadi ward. The village of Ratholo was in the midst of a dramatic struggle over the central position of the village head in the aftermath of state reforms of patterns of local leadership. Mr. Moso and his Mangadi ward contested the installation of a village headman from the Ratholo ward, a man of Bakaa origin. It is important to note that the long interview with Mr. Moso (pages 178–200) was carried out five days after another group of students had interviewed several residents of the village, all of Bakaa origin, including the brother and nephew of the installed chief. The articulate, at times passionate, replies of Mr. Moso to the student's questions seem to have these other interviews in mind. Mr. Moso, in other words, was conversing not only with the eager university student, but also with his fellow villagers at a heightened moment of political rivalry.

The explosive nature of the interview is evident from the outset. To the student's standard opening question, "What [do] you mean or understand by chieftainship?" Moso replies:

Our chieftainship is that all the village that you see here belongs to Mapulane.[11] We are his people (*re batho ba ga Mapulane*). We were his juniors (*bomonnawe*) before he dispersed us along these rivers/streams.

The student had evidently not expected that answer. He tells Moso, "It appears that you have not understood me well," and proceeds to explain the generic nature of his question. But Moso persists in his unconventional, and loaded, reply. He says, *Bogosi re raya motshwara—motse o re leng mo go one*,[12] "by chieftainship we understand the 'owner/holder' of the village."

The student exclaims: "In that case do you imply that chieftainship is the chief?" Moso replies calmly: *Ee*, "Yes!"

From the very opening of this oral exchange, it is clear that Moso's historical account is steeped in a tumultuous present. He is continually engaged in a dialogue, an argument with his foes in the village, and with different cultural interpretations of leadership, power, and rights, which he perceives as threatening. Thus, for example, he simplifies his definition of chieftainship by pinning it to the office holder, a comment perhaps on the threat to that position at the time of the interview. His insistence that all the villages in the area "belong to" Mapulane, and that "we are the people of Mapulane" is also, as we shall see shortly, an argument that has particular force at that moment of time.

When the student tries to "explain" to Moso the nature of his inquiry of *bogosi*, the institution of chieftainship, he refers to "ka Setswana," to Tswana custom,[13] to the shared community that "often talks of chieftainship."[14] Moso is not interested in such "ka Setswana" definitions; his formulation is directly linked to the political, economic, and moral distinction between "us" (the people of Mapulane)[15] and "them," in this case the Bakaa and the remote Ngwato rulers. Although the student poses his question in the most hypothetical (and thus ahistorical) form—"If you are a chief, normally your people will expect you to do something for them; what was the chief expected to do for his people?"—Moso's reply is historically specific and pregnant with cultural inflection about the political and moral status of the Mapulane people, whose land this is vis-à-vis the remote ruling Bangwato: "A chief is expected to bring his people messages (*mafoko*, words) from the [Ngwato] chief in Serowe." After several other confusing attempts to get "straight" answers to his question regarding the role of the chief, the student catches on to Moso's underlying message. Addressing Moso as *malome* (my maternal uncle), he finally asks the question in the proper fashion. He acknowledges Moso's historical charter: "According to your information it is quite obvious that the Pedi had ruled themselves before becoming the subjects of the Bangwato. . . . How was chieftainship then before you were under Ngwato authority?"

The distinction between indigenous chieftainship during the times *pele ga le nna kafa tlase ga puso ya Bangwato*, "before you were under the rule of the Bangwato," and those after the political subjugation to the Ngwato is central throughout the subsequent exchange. Moso begins his account with: *Bogosi e ne ele taolo ya kgosi a laola rona*, "Chieftainship is the 'act of governing' by the chief (*kgosi*) who 'governs' us." The duties of the subjects include providing their labor for *masotla* (a special field for the chief) and paying in cattle when fined in court (*fa o dira molato*). When the student asks, only partly jesting, "Is this why you find that most of the chiefs are rich (after 'eating' the cattle paid in fine)," Moso replies serenely, "This refers to the old days (*kwa tshimologong*, 'in the beginnings'), and these were *our* laws (*molao wa rona o ne o ntse jalo*)." Moso makes it clear that unlike this former legitimate indigenous rule, the chieftainship of the Ngwato was, and is, a one-way street.

Q: After becoming the subjects of the Bangwato, what did you do for them?
A: We paid taxes, we gave them the *matimela* [stray] cattle which were not claimed. They also took the fines from the trials at our *kgotla*.
Q: Did the Ngwato chiefs do anything for you in your village?
A: We never saw anything of that nature.
Q: You only carried large sums of money to Serowe without any returns?
A: Yes.

The strong undertones of resistance to Ngwato overrule are developed further in the same interview when the student inquires about the origins of the Mapulane people. He asks, "Where were you from before you settled at GooMangadi?" and receives in answer: "We came from GaMapulane [the place of Mapulane]. Our greatest chief is Leso of Letlhakeng."

Inquiring into the more remote past, the student discovers that all the people under Mapulane's rule came from Bopedi (the country of Bapedi), to the east. He then asks what proves to be an explosive question.

Q: What happened which then made you to become Batswapong (*Go tsamaya jang gore jaanong lo fetoge Batswapong*)?
A: Lestwapo is the name of this hill (*Letswapo ke leina la lentswe le*).
Q: From your description, I get the impression that you found these hills already called Tswapong.
A: It is quite difficult to say (*go thata*).

But the student persists.

Q: My question is whether you named these hills Tswapong or you found it already called Tswapong hills?
A: It was the Bangwato who called it Tswapong as a sign of looking down at [on] us or despising us.

The answer in the vernacular is *Lentswe le le ne le bidiwa Tswapo ke ba Gammangwato, e le tshotlo, fela jaaka Mosarwa*. A close translation is: "The hill was named Tswapo by the Ngwato as a ridicule, an insult, simply like Mosarwa." The student does an honest job of translating the term *tshotlo* to mean "looking down at us or despising us," but he omits the reference to Mosarwa that the speaker includes in his reply. The reference to Mosarwa is a culturally pregnant idiom in contemporary Botswana, referring to people classified as uncultured, uncouth "Bushmen" who have no rights to land and may be enslaved; in this context, it is an insult. It is used again by Moso to refer to the acting village chief, whose right to rule he disputes.

Here the narrative moves to depict the internal struggle unfolding at the time of the interview, between two ward units of the village—Moso's Mangadi ward and the newly installed chief's Ratholo ward. The exchange opens with yet another generic question by the student, "I would like you to explain how a chief is chosen according to your tradition (*ka Setswana sa lona*)." Moso answers, "There is nothing like choosing a chief, but a chief is born. You do not put anybody just like making a bull; Moipei our chief is a born chief."[16]

When asked how the ways of the past (*bogologolo*) are different from the present (*matsatsi ano*), Moso replies bitterly (p. 189): "[There is a difference] because now anybody can become chief irrespective of birth."[17] The student continues:

Q: Do you think that this is acceptable?
A: It is not good because I would not be ruled by a Mosarwa.
Q: Do you not think that even a Mosarwa can rule people as long as he is reasonable and capable?
A: As long as he understands that we are his masters, not for him to do what he likes only because he is capable of being chief.
Q: Have any of your chiefs been chosen on this criterion?
A: Yes, we now find ourselves being ruled by someone we do not even know.
Q: Do you suggest that the present chief is not a chief by birth?
A: Moipei is the only legitimate chief (*Moipei o tsetswe*, "Moipei is born").

When the student asks for a clarification, pointing to the fact that there is another chief of the village, not Moipei, Moso states: *Moipei ke ene mong wa lefatshe*, "Moipei is the 'owner/master' of the land." He adds, *yo o mmolelang yoo ke mohaladi hela*, "the one you are talking about is merely a fugitive." When asked what is the origin (*ke motho wa letsho lefe*) of the installed village chief, Moso answers, "He is of Kaa origin," [adding with no delay] "they [the Bakaa] found us here long ago. They came as fugitives (*bafaladi*) from Shoshong."

The student poses another provocative question: "Do you outnumber the Bakaa?" The answer is a resounding, *Nnyaa lefatshe ke la rona ka botsalo*, "No, [but] the land is ours by birth!" (The student translates "by right").

In describing the relations between the "owners of the land" and the Bakaa "refugees," Moso relates:

because the koodos were disrupting the waters of the stream, Setlhabi [father's father of the present Mokaa village headman] and his people were asked to go there, because they were hunters. They paid tribute to Mangadi in the form of chests of animals. This process was later stopped when Setlhabi married Mangadi's daughter.

This short historical account concludes with an immediate return to the present: "The ruling chief today in Ratholo is hired; he also knows that well. A chief is born." But the relations between the two local groups are framed, much like the situation depicted in the first interview, by their respective associations with the remote Ngwato power center. From the perspective of the Bakaa ward, the issue is simple—they owe their right to reside in this region to the Ngwato rulers. In a separate interview (December 14, 1979), a week before the one recorded here with Moso, people of Bakaa origin (including the brother and the nephew of the acting village chief) told another student, "We have always been under the Bangwato chief."[18] Tension between the two groups is suggested by another terse comment: "The people of the area, the Batswapong, who we met at GooMangadi, did not trust us. They thought we might rule them."[19]

Moso frames this triangle of power and segmented group identities in a much more vivid way, "The Bakaa, who were mere refugees (*bafaladi*), came to rule Ratholo village today because of their relations with the Ngwato. While we kept on saying 'this is our land,' they (the Bakaa) made themselves known to the Ngwato and thus became our rulers. Yet such rule is as ridiculous as that of a 'Mosarwa' who thinks he is smart enough to govern."[20] Being "known" by the ruling Ngwato is contrasted with the situation of those remote from power who are thus described as nonhuman, mere wild animals (*diphologolo fela*).

This oral text brings up and develops several themes evident in the first text. Groups are defined by their totemic leader and in reference to space. A distinction is made between owners of the land, fugitives, and remote rulers. Regardless of their origin, all the interviewees note the historical position of the totemic leader Mapulane as the "owner of these hills." Mapulane, in these historical accounts, entered the hills when they were "empty." He thus established his inalienable right as the *mong wa lefatshe*, "the owner of the land." All his descendants, to this day, have thus the inalienable right not only to the land in the region but to rule themselves. Other groups of later arrivals, like the Bakaa, are forever *bafaladi* (fugitives), and their position upon settling in the region must be one of political subordination. However, far from being dogmatic about group boundaries and inter-group hierarchical ordering, this narrative makes clear that shifts in political relations among groups are possible and have occurred (for example, tribute payment stopped when Setlhabi, the Kaa leader, married Mangadi's daughter).

Again the stress is on political seniority and rights to land as the key criteria distinguishing one named group from the other and not on "cultural" or "social" markers of difference. But the importance of such indigenous political hierarchy, even if debated and continuously shifting, must not be underestimated; held up by a powerful moral code, this political cosmology defines not only relations among groups, but the very definition of what

constitutes a social and political entity. Indeed, if the internal order prescribed in this political cosmology is eclipsed (as when the owners of the
land lose their moral right to rule and *bafaladi* or even Basarwa gain local
power), the very definition of the collective self is in question. Thus, owners of the land who do not rule themselves are *diphologolo fela* (mere wild
animals).

CONCLUSION

The politics of constructing a collective memory is a critical issue in contemporary Botswana. These oral interviews illustrate a great deal about
how people articulate their subjective identities and that of others, what
conceptual frameworks they employ to make sense of their relations with
others, and how they define leadership, hierarchy, control over land, and
social distance. An examination of this indigenous discourse provides an
excellent avenue into understanding the subjective significance of social categories and of the system of meaning that lends legitimacy to (or, to borrow
from Said [1983], "renders natural") notions of self and other.

Taken together, these texts work to define social boundaries and the political rights implied in such entities in several key ways. First, the ethnonyme,
Batswapong, is never used as a self-referent; it is a collective term used by
the dominant Ngwato center to suggest the uniform low status of the inhabitants of the region. Those known as "Batswapong" choose to identify themselves as Bakgopeng, in reference to their totemic emblem, or as Batho-ba-
ga-Mapulane, the people of Mapulane, their totemic leader. Those who fall
outside the owners of the land category construct their partisan collective
identities in a similar fashion. They trace their history to their totemic
leader's entry into the region and to the manner in which their right to land
was established within the hierarchical order within and beyond the region.

Resistance to remote Ngwato rule is depicted here with great intensity.
Unlike the indigenous rulers of the hills, Ngwato rulers did not fulfill the
criteria of mutual responsibilities between a leader and his people. From the
perspective of the Batho-ba-ga-Mapulane, the growing power of those
defined as *bafaladi*, supported by the Ngwato rulers in the past and by the
contemporary state, is a blatant violation of their moral right as owners of
this land.

I have raised several theoretical questions in the introductory segment of
this chapter. We are now in a position to return to these questions and
explore them in light of the analysis presented in this chapter. One of the
key questions that underlies the very structure of exposition of this chapter,
and has been at the center of much postcolonial writing, concerns the epistemic relations between "history from above" and "history from below." A
second, closely related issue concerns the distinction between "native voices
and theories" and analytical frameworks constructed by "outsiders."

At the core of this chapter stand two larger frames that are both concerned with historical processes. In the first part of the chapter, a comprehensive historical overview outlined the changing relation between social hierarchy and control over space. The second part of the chapter presented an analysis of transcribed texts of oral history interviews. In schematic terms, the two segments of the chapter could be seen as representing "history from above" vs. "history from below." Indeed, the first segment relied on historical evidence recorded by observers (missionaries, colonial officers, and anthropologists) who presented the views of those at centers of political power. Ethnographic and historiographic representations of systems of social organization and land use at the core of this segment were constructed from the perspectives of dominant centers of power, both Tswana and non-Tswana. The position of subordinate populations, like that of the people residents in the Tswapong Hills, is presented in these generalized historical accounts from the perspective of Ngwato and then colonial rulers. From this historical account we learn that the residents of the Hills are collectively known as "Batswapong" and that this subjugated population had been raising tribute to the Ngwato dominant group.

How different is the "history from below" presented at the second segment of this chapter? Does the perspective of those remote from power serve as a mere complementary source for historical knowledge not available in dominant accounts emanating from the centers of power? Or does the shift into "history from below" raise theoretical and methodological questions that challenge conventional historiographies based on dominant systems of knowledge?

I propose, based on the foregoing analysis of these Tswapong historical narratives, that the perspectives of subjugated people, when allowed to be articulated in their full complexity and historicity, raise new insights that directly challenge, not merely complement, historiographies based on dominant perspectives. I suggest that people in the Tswapong region—unlike some of the anthropologists who represented them or the colonial and postcolonial administrators who dealt with them—have a more fluid and less essentialist sense of their own subjectivity. Looking closely at the way people constructed, debated, and, in the process, redefined their sense of difference suggests that their historical experience, even when they were waging struggles of empowerment, was constructed of connections and shifting boundaries and not of rigid, separate, abstract categories. Specifically, this "from below" exploration has taught us that the "Batswapong" had never been, in fact, a uniform group with distinct historically rooted ethnic boundaries, as external reports have been suggesting. The analysis of these oral texts enabled an exploration of the way endogenous ideas about historical time, control over space, and the nature of power have been constructed, debated, and used. Understanding the particular ways these conceptual frames of reference are actively used in the region today is critical for the analysis of social behavior presented in the following chapters.

The shift into the perspectives of the subjugated also brings to the center important methodological considerations. Historical knowledge from this perspective is not treated as given, valid regime of truth but as a process, as an outcome of verbal interactions. The analysis presented in this chapter has made use of the idea that knowledge is dialogically produced in specific situations. And the "dialogical situation" as Ricour (1971:546) reminds us, is "based on the immediate reciprocity between speaking and hearing." In staying close to the texts and presenting the dialogues as they unfolded in time, such analysis enabled the reader to hear how people in the region debated, reflected upon, and ultimately crafted anew their own subjectivity.

A focus on narratives of subjugated populations invariably brings up the issue of resistance to domination. Indeed, defiance against the remote Ngwato center has been forcefully articulated in these texts. Yet, as Abu-Lughod (1990:35) suggests, defiance and subversive discourse are fairly common in the world. The interesting question is how such resistance to domination is articulated in specific social and political contexts. I will return to the issue of resistance in the next three chapters. A critical and final point links methodological and theoretical insights brought by this "from below" perspective. It concerns the historicity of these narratives. Historical knowledge, as the analysis offered here demonstrates, is a product of dialogical situations—in our case, a series of speech events that engaged Botswana university students and their elders. But this particular knowledge was produced in specific contexts. Walter Benjamin's observation, quoted in the epitaph to this chapter, captures this idea. Articulating their past the elders had not intended to produce a record of "the way things were"; theirs was a statement made "at a moment of danger." This "moment of danger," I argue, occured in the Tswapong region in the late 1970s. A central feature of these oral texts is their palpable portrayal of tensions in the region during the time of the interviews, tensions resulting from state intervention in local patterns of authority and leadership. It was a particularly critical moment when cultural and ideological instability were produced. The "threat," to continue Benjamin's evocative image, was one of "becoming a tool of the ruling class." The active role played by the Batswapong in reshaping their lives in the shadow of that "threat" has taken, as we shall see in the next two chapters, material and immediate forms. In the process that unfolded not only memories and collective identities have been transformed, but the very definition of space, community, and patterns of power was changing.

NOTES

1. In some cases only the English version was provided. As will be shown later in this chapter, much of the significance of the indigenous discourse is lost in the process of the translation. In fact, some of the more interesting insights about these dialogues emerge from an analysis of how the students chose to translate the Setswana idioms expressed by the interviewed villagers.

2. I borrow the term from Martin (1993), who follows Ricour (1971).

3. Wilmsen argues that the reality of such reforms is far from the picture depicted in these reports. See especially Wilmsen 1989:99–101, 131–132.

4. Deputy commissioner's promise to Lentswe king of the Bakgatla, quoted in Schapera 1970, 51.

5. Willoughby's letter to Thompson, the Foreign Secretary of the London Missionary Court quoted in Schapera 1970, 159.

6. The missionaries here use the designation accepted by the ruling group. From this perspective subjugated groups like the Tswapong or the Sarwa are referred to with the "ma" prefix rather than "ba." "ba" is the proper prefix for people, "ma" is often used for inanimate objects—and for subjugated collectives.

7. The prefix *ma* is pejorative but I found that it was still widely used in the region as self-referent. This had changed by the early 1990s. See footnote 6.

8. In this and following dialogue, **Q** designates a question asked by a student interviewer, and **A** designates the answer.

9. The last sentence is ambiguous. Such translation might suggest a separation from the Bakhurutshe and "us." The Setswana reads *re tlile re le Bakhurutshe,* "we came; we were Bakhurutshe."

10. I am not quite clear what this connotes. My guess is that this statement suggests that Bangwato socialized with their social equals, the prosperous Bakhurutshe. Consuming beer together is different from tribute paying by the low status resident group.

11. He says, *yo motona ke Mapulane,* "the oldest, biggest, most senior is Mapulane."

12. The translation provided by the student is inaccurate. It reads, "By chieftainship we mean the leadership of a people."

13. This is common usage to form a contrast to non-Tswana things.

14. *Ke gore ka Setswana re tlotla go nna re re bogosi.*

15. He uses the possessive form *morafe wa gagwe,* "his" *morafe.*

16. Moso's words are *Go tlhophiwa ga ke go itse fela keitse gore kgosi e a tsalwa* ("I don't know about elections; I only know that a chief is born") and then *Ga e beiwe-beiwe fela jaaka fa e ka re o na le Moipei jaana ba tsetswe,* translated by the student as given in the text.

17. Moso uses the same metaphor of cattle born or installed. The student's translation captures the idea communicated without translating the Setswana idiom used by Moso who says, *Go farologanya ka gore jaanong lo tsaya kgomo ya mmopa lo e dira ee tsetsweng.*

18. Earlier, another informant makes the same statement, "The Bangwato chiefs had always been our rulers ever since our arrival in this territory." These earlier interviews in the village were recorded only in English.

19. It would be interesting to know how the notions of "people of the area" and "the Batswapong" were expressed in the vernacular.

20. This is my own translation of the following Setswana text. *Ke gore Mosarwa a feta a itira botlhale a dire ditiro tsa puso, rona re diilwe ke gore lefatshe ke la rona. Ba tlabatlaba kwa Gammangwato gore Bangwato ba bo ba itse bone rone re le diphologolo fela.*

5

The Politics of Space and Place

The reorganization of space to serve democratic ends challenges dynastic power embedded in place.

David Harvey, *The Condition of Postmodernity*

Space is fundamental in any form of communal life; space is fundamental in any exercise of power.

The Foucault Reader

[T]he combined effects of the recent urbanization patterns, some permanent settlement at the lands/cattle posts, and the new tribal Land Laws, have begun to erode the settlement patterns at least within each District.

National Migration Study, Vol. 3

The main question I pose in this chapter is "how space itself functions as an object of social struggle."[1] For if space, as Foucault has taught us, is always a container of social power, then the reorganization of space, which I document in this and the next chapter, must indicate a transformation in social relationships and in the distribution of social power. My main objective is to examine how change in space relationships over the past two decades in the Tswapong has been structured and how it affected the redistribution of wealth and power in this region.

More specifically, the chapter traces changes in socio-spatial arrangements in east central Botswana through an in-depth examination of four extended cases of what I call "village emergence." In tracing the struggles of people in these four sites to redefine their rights over land, collective identities, and social histories, I explore a critical phase in the social history of group relationships in Botswana. I wish to develop my thesis, presented in Chapter 4, that historical narratives of community and entitlement had emerged as central in a particular set of inherently contradictory circumstances unfolding in the region by the late 1980s. In these shifting settings, the process of struggling to redefine respective group rights to land alter not only visible spatial arrangements but also the key sociopolitical and economic divisions within the regional population. The spatial arrangement that has emerged is thus a product of, and a site for, a wider set of understandings of community, self, and modernity.

This analysis of the intrinsic historicity and fluidity of notions of self and community builds upon and develops further the discussions of such notions offered in previous chapters.

SOCIAL SPACE AS A CONTAINER
OF SOCIAL POWER: TSWANA SCENES

Social and political hierarchies have been directly represented in the spatial organization of the Tswana world. The relatively fertile eastern part of Botswana, which stretches along the catchment basin of the Limpopo River, exhibits a largely uniform settlement and land use pattern. Ideally, this pattern consists of three concentric zones: a clustered village settlement in the center surrounded by arable field plots beyond which lie open grazing areas. This pattern of land use generates a seasonal migration of people between their permanent residence in the village settlement and a second dwelling erected next to the fields in the agricultural zone, often called "the lands." Residence in the agricultural zone (in the lands) usually lasts only as long as necessary to complete all production work in the fields. At the end of the agricultural season, most people return to the village center to socialize, celebrate, and resolve their disputes in the central court arena, or *kgotla*. Unlike the clustered residence in the village, dwellings in the lands area mostly made of less durable materials, are situated next to individual fields and are associated with social isolation. Cattle, which provide draft power, are driven at the end of the ploughing operation away from the unfenced cultivated fields to more distant open grazing zones. In this third zone, herders live in temporary dwellings next to water sources. For most people, herding the family's cattle and living in the cattle post is a phase of life. Herding is carried out by young males of about eight to seventeen years old. People who own large herds hire adult herders, often of Basarwa origin, who live permanently in such distant grazing areas.

Dwelling in the clustered village is strongly associated with full citizenship and membership in the social entity. People who do not keep their house in the village are called "bush people" (Motzafi-Haller 1988). The idiom of the "bush" *(naga)* as the uncontrolled, dangerous, and unbounded zone is contrasted with the public social domain of the village *(motse).* While the clustered village is the hub of social life and the center of political law and order, the open outer bush zone is the residence of adolescent herders, impoverished clients, and serfs.[2] People who do not settle down, like the nomadic Basarwa (Bushmen), are said to be like wild animals *(diphologolo fela)* who "move around the forest."

This ideological distinction between clustered villages and the uncontrolled bush has its spatial representation in the structure of each Tswana residential center. Even the smallest Tswana village has at its center a *kgotla,* a crescent-shaped wall of thick poles facing toward an open cleared arena. The *kgotla* is the nexus of public life and the site of the local court over which the village headman presides. Visitors are led to the *kgotla* arena, and its size and state of repair are often cited as an indication of the "proper order" of the village. One of the first collective actions of residents who wish their settlement to become a village is to build this central arena. The *kgotla* provides the most visible expression of aspirations of settled status.

The roots of this settlement and land use arrangement can be traced back to the sociopolitical structure of the nineteenth-century Tswana polities *(merafe)* in the area. In general, most of the population of each nineteenth-century Tswana polity was clustered in one large agro-town around its ruler. From their residence in town, people walked to their outlying fields. Beyond the fields, cattle were herded in an open grazing zone. Early observers estimated the population of these capital towns to range between 5,000 and more than 20,000 people. Early eyewitness accounts and analysis based on more recent archaeological findings (Maggs 1972, 1976) suggest that during the eighteenth and early nineteenth centuries only hunters and the king's clients resided outside the capital town while all other citizens of the polity were clustered around their ruler in a single central settlement.

Schapera (1952) suggests that the multiplication of small villages outside the capital is a later phenomenon begun during the second quarter of the nineteenth century due to gradual incorporation of indigenous populations into the expanding system. This spatial organization is particularly evident in the large northern territories of the Ngwato and Tawana polities. In both cases the indigenous population was left to reside in its original dispersed settlement around the territory. Among the smaller eastern polities of the Malete, Tlokwa, and Kgatla, the number of outlying villages is much smaller. Schapera (1953:36) records that in 1946 all the Tlokwa were concentrated in a single large village and that the Malete had only two small villages outside their major clustered capital.

Early historical sources describe the internal organization of these large capital towns as a nesting hierarchy of units (Burchell 1853; Campbell 1815). In 1938, Schapera described this hierarchy as follows. At the basis of the hierarchy stood the household, made up of a nuclear family and attached dependents. Several households, ideally patrilineally linked, formed an agnatic cluster often referred to as "the family group." Two or more such agnatic segments formed the core of a ward, the major political and administrative subdivision of the town. All members of the ward resided in one section of the town. Each ward was governed by a hereditary ruler, ideally the most senior man in the dominant agnatic segment, who was accountable for his ward to the king. Wards were internally ranked according to the relative seniority of their core agnatic line and, when created by unrelated segments, according to the order of their incorporation into the political entity.

The spatial organization of residence within a Tswana town, like that of the polity at large, gave an explicit expression to internal sociopolitical ordering. Mackenzie (1871:367) gives a vivid illustration.

In laying out a Bechuana town, the first thing is to ascertain where the chief's court-yard with the public cattle-pen is to be placed. As soon as this is settled the remainder is simple. As, after the tabernacle was placed in the wilderness, each one of the twelve tribes (of Israel) knew on which site he had to take up his position, so in the case of a Bechuana town; as soon as the chief's position is ascertained, one says, "My place is always next to the chief on this side," another adds, "And mine is always next on that side" and so on till the whole town is laid out.

The residential dwelling units of members of each ward created a circle around an open arena where most public life took place. The various ward settlements were situated around the king's council place (lekgotla), the center of political, administrative, and judicial life of the town and the polity at large.

The town as a whole was ritually separated from the "wild" open country that surrounded it. When the town moved, as often occurred during the first half of the nineteenth century due to droughts or enemy attacks, various consecration ceremonies preceded the establishment of a new settlement. These ceremonies were "intended to give the village magical protection from disease and other dangers" (Schapera 1938:66).

This and other ritual practices (cf. Jean Comaroff 1985:54–60) served to separate the social space at the core of the concentric settlement pattern from the bush, or the "wild" naga. Spatial division into three zones— domestic, agricultural, and open grazing—corresponded to a symbolic order that contrasted the town (motse, which also means "home"), associated with order, government, and civilization, with the outer asocial, wild zone, where uncontrollable spirits (badimo) and undomesticated animals roamed (Jean Comaroff 1985; Kuper 1975, 1980). Thus, Kuper writes, "The Sotho-Tswana settlement formula . . . was perceived as not simply right and proper, but also as an arrangement cosmologically validated corresponding to a greater world order" (1980:6).

Residence in the central capital town was a sign of full citizenship. Mackenzie, an astute observer of Tswana life in the late nineteenth century, explains: "It is the mark of a freeman to have a residence in the town, while the vassals are doomed always to live in the open country" (1871:368).

The position of subjugated people who moved around the open country or resided in small dispersed settlements next to their individual fields year round was thus marginal in all respects—politically, spatially, and symbolically. Regarded with contempt by people of the ruling community, these marginal people were often called *dikgokong*—mere wild animals (Schapera 1970:87). During most of the nineteenth century and until the boundaries of the various Tswana polities were defined by the British administration, the position of these subject people in the outlying small communities at the fringes of the territories of each polity put them in a precarious situation. They were the most vulnerable target in the raids on cattle and the military attacks launched periodically by neighboring polities. They were expected to give the ruling center warning about approaching raids or armies and often "spent a most wretched existence, having a difficult task to perform of serving two masters" (Mackenzie 1871:267).

MORE RECENT TRANSFORMATIONS
IN SPATIAL ARRANGEMENTS

Many aspects of the socioeconomic and political organization of the precolonial Tswana polities were transformed toward the latter part of the nineteenth century, first by encapsulation into the market economy and then by the declaration of a British Protectorate over the area.[3] A predominantly independent and self-sufficient local economy became a dependent periphery that supplied cheap labor to the expanding industrial South African center (cf. David Massey 1978, Palmer and Parsons 1977). Despite these dramatic changes, an idealized model of a permanent residence in a clustered village and a temporary one in its surrounding agricultural zone (in agricultural land areas and cattle posts) continues to serve as the basic model for recording the rural population to this day. The most recent census, as previous ones, recorded the rural population as being composed of two categories: the resident population in "clustered villages" and people in "localities associated with" named village settlements.

In 1982, the National Migration Study, a major examination of national migration patterns, concluded that "large clustered towns and the three-tiered concentric land-use system associated with them continues to be basic features of human settlement in contemporary Botswana" (GOB 1982: 836). Referring to the precolonial and colonial roots of this ideal settlement pattern, the study contended that "there is evidence that this precolonial settlement pattern is remarkably well conserved even up to the present" (GOB 1983: 826).

This official classification, as we shall see later in this chapter, had defined not only the structure of census-taking records but also the immediate criteria for gaining access to state resources. The provision of schools, clinics, and well water was directly linked with the official status that defined a rural settlement as a "village," "land area," or a "cattle post." Material considerations stood at the center of competitive contrivance and redefinition in the rural areas. Yet utilitarian motivations, as the following cases demonstrate, cannot provide a complete understanding of the forces that animated the socio-spatial transformation of the 1970s and 1980s. Moreover, evidence of significant variations from the ideal settlement pattern used by census takers and state service providers were becoming more evident toward the early 1980s. Using its working model of settlement that distinguishes between "permanently settled" village dwellers and temporary residents in "non-village localities," the National Migration Study (GOB 1982, 1983) recorded that some 46 percent of the rural population of Botswana resided "more or less permanently" *outside* clustered villages[4] in what was described, for lack of better terms, as "non-village locations" (GOB 1982, Vol. I:26). The national study only confirmed similar findings reported in several micro-studies carried out around the country (Comaroff 1982; Hitchcock 1984; Kooijman 1978; Syson 1972). Taken together, these studies documented a general trend of territorial transformation throughout the country. The main parameters of this territorial change were the dispersal of population out from the clustered village centers and a concurrent emergence of permanent communities in areas which were within the agricultural zone.

The record could not be ignored. "Despite this relative freezing of the precolonial ecological-cum-ethnic settlement patterns into reserves and later Districts," the government-commissioned study noted, "it must be admitted that the combined effects of the recent urbanization patterns, some permanent settlement at the lands/cattle posts, and the new Tribal Land Laws, have begun to erode the settlement patterns at least within each District" (GOB 1983:836).

THE PROBLEM

What is the meaning of this evident spatial transformation over the past three decades, and to what extent does it indicate a more profound shift in the social and political fabric of life in various districts around the country? Why were new settlements emerging to assert their communal identities at that point in time? What was the effect of the emergence of these new settlements on social and economic patterns linked to distribution of and access to land? At the core of each of the three case studies of village emergence described in this chapter (and the fourth case examined in the following chapter) is an attempt to present and establish a unique historical charter, one that repositions the emerging community within existing patterns of group relationships. What collective claims and rights were contested through such historical charters? How were people within and outside these emerging communities explaining, justifying, or resisting these claims?

In developing the analysis of the Tswapong case, I draw on analyses that have explored the unfolding struggles over the use and definition of space in Botswana as part of a wider process of class emergence within specific regional populations (cf. Comaroff 1982, 1991, 1997; Durham 1993; Gulbrandsen 1984, 1994; Peters 1983, 1994; Solway 1980; Werbner 1971, 1982, 1991; Wilmsen 1989).

The broad theoretical aim of such work, as Werbner put it, is "to link the study of state intervention to what are problems of ethnicity, class conflict, and center-periphery relationships in a new nation" (1982:i). Particularly useful is Pauline Peters' work that emphasizes that struggles among different groups and categories are "struggles over meaning as much as struggles over resources" (1994:i). Like Peters, I argue that the struggle is not only over who is to control particular parcels of land and secure services provided by the new state but over the very *definition* of community, leadership, and social hierarchy.

MANALEDI: A RELOCATED VILLAGE COMMUNITY

The hand-painted sign—"Manaledi village"—leads the traveler off the main dirt road that links the village of Gotau with the regional administrative and commercial center, Palapye, and into a narrower winding road. A few miles further down that road, a "typical," post independence, small village scene is revealed. At the center of the settlement one reaches a newly built *kgotla* arena, with an adjacent *kraal*. Next to the open *kgotla*—and clearly part of the central public space—are two square, pink-painted, single-room buildings. Constructed by the district council to house school teachers and other locally employed government officials, these uniform buildings (always painted pink and positioned next to the *kgotla* arena) are rapidly becoming a trademark of every little village in the region. The most critical signifier of Manaledi's "established village" status is a borehole supplying fresh drinking water to several taps located throughout the small settlement. Only ten years earlier, this typical village scene was a dream, a vision fought for by a small group of people. In 1983, when I first visited Manaledi, only two residential units (*malwapa*) could be seen near the small *kgotla* arena. There was nothing else to indicate that a village with a semblance of public life was in existence. In official records, Manaledi was defined as a "lands area" belonging to the village of Ratholo. The 1981 national census recorded seventy-three people who occupied fifteen of the existing twenty-three dwelling units in the Manaledi locality. Indeed, the settlement had the physical characteristics of many lands areas—dispersed residence of family units next to their fields and a lack of public services (school, water, local shops). Still, Manaledi residents in 1983 insisted that they lived in an autonomous village (*motse*), not a peripheral lands area of the larger neighboring village. Their struggle to redefine their relationships to their social space took two main avenues. They actively sought to restructure their spatial organization by moving their dispersed hamlets closer to the central *kgotla,* and they worked hard to secure official recognition of their village as an "established village." They wrote letters to district officials, petitioned the land board, and told the following local history to their visitors.

Their original village was located on the top of the nearby hill at a place called Maboong. Maboong was an old settlement, and its history is linked to a man named Keatoletse, the son of the legendary Mapulane, leader of the Moremi-Pedi group, who, to this day, is known as the "spiritual lord" of the Tswapong hills. In their version of the regional history, people in Manaledi acknowledge that the small village of Moremi, to their northwest, is indeed the place where Mapulane and his son Senwedi made their home. Keatoletse, their founding ancestor, the son of Mapulane (the son of the senior wife, in their version) was left behind in Maboong when the main group continued its migration to the other side of the hills. Since then these descendants of Keatoletse lived in Maboong. Beginning in the late 1950s, however, many chose to remain in their lands' residence located at the foot of the hills because this lands area was closer to the main road. This area is called Manaledi. By the late 1960s and after independence, the old village settlement in Maboong was completely deserted. Permanent settlement in Manaledi lands, however, meant that there had been no effective leadership.[5] For more than a decade, throughout the 1960s and until the mid-1970s, their dispersed residence pattern and lack of leadership worked against any expression of communal or political cohesion.

The first impetus for the reorganization of their community emerged in the mid-1970s, following the establishment of land boards in the country. The democratically elected land boards replaced traditional chiefs as the land allocation bodies in Botswana. However, the local impact of this policy was felt only toward the mid to late 1970s, when subdistrict land boards were elected. A group of affluent farmers from the neighboring Gotau village had applied for a large plot of land from the newly elected land board in order to construct a cattle-watering dam. The area allotted for the dam project was not cultivated at the time, but according to Manaledi people, it fell within the area that "belonged" to their village. The Manaledi headman, now permanently resident in the lands areas himself, began to play a more active role in the locality. As a first step in the fight against the dam project, he suggested that the Manaledi people should elect committees similar to those he had seen emerging in other villages. He was elected chair of the Village Development Committee (VDC). He also encouraged people to rebuild their houses clustered around the new *kgotla* arena. As the chair of the new Village Development Committee, the headman sent a letter to the various district bodies stating that his people wished to be recognized as a village, independent from Ratholo. Official response came only in 1984, when two distinguished visitors—the Tswapong-North Member of Parliament and the Tribal Authority Officer—summoned a public meeting in Manaledi.

The first indication that their claims for independent village status were officially approved was the beginning of a local public project—an access road to their settlement. Manaledi residents hired for that project were paid by state funds. Then the cement, pink-painted rooms were constructed. Although no locally employed government or council workers have made use of these accommodations since they were built, these new symbols of modern village settlements sent a clear message of the established village status of Manaledi. The 1991 national population census recorded 191 residents in the "village of Manaledi."[6] Since 1991, the growing settlement has enjoyed clean drinking water after a borehole was drilled. The expanded infrastructure of the settlement and the stability and public esteem it bestowed on Manaledi attracted many new people to live in the village. In 1993, there were eighty-three residential units in the village, almost double the number I estimated a decade earlier (forty-two), and four times the number recorded by the 1981 census. Although such official recognition had not had the immediate results expected and children of Manaledi in 1993 continued to walk the seven kilometers to the Ratholo school, villagers were confident that their local school would soon be built. The sense of empowerment in their collective claims following such official recognition has also expressed itself in the talk of hiring a lawyer to defend such rights. The lawyer, I was told, will be the best to fight for village rights over the newly completed water dam erected by the small group of Gotau farmers.

The Manaledi case illuminates several important elements in the process of redefinition of space and the concomitant transformation of social relationships in the region. First, it shows that a political history of group relationships rooted in colonial and precolonial times continues to provide a powerful charter for inter-village association in postindependence days. Contemporary claims to communal land and collective definitions of social spaces are argued and gain legitimacy, both locally and among the relevant official bodies, through such historical positioning. Both local and official actors shared the necessary knowledge to establish or contest the claims for the access to and the use of space. Moreover, the position of postcolonial officials in this case was clearly articulated within the sociopolitical and cultural framework. District officials were never seen as impartial, objective, or external to local struggles. On the contrary, they were directly linked to the colonial and precolonial structure of Ngwato centralized hegemony and were thus addressed as the still powerful "people of Serowe"—Serowe being the Ngwato capital town turned into the administrative center of the postcolonial district. Once this is recognized, we can view the struggles and contests over claims to space as attempts to establish new collective rights within a seemingly obsolete "traditional" hierarchical order. Thus, in tracing their communal history back to the founding members of the Moremi-Pedi group, the Manaledi people were arguing for their collective position *above,* rather than as subsidiaries to, the larger village they were considered in the 1980s to "belong to." Significantly, prolonged dispersal and lack of physical existence as a clustered village community had not undermined such collective historical claims. In other words, while the physical, spatial articulation of village communal life may change, the collective rights to land vested in the sociopolitical entity are inalienable.

The Manaledi people were advancing the claim not only to their independent (and higher) position vis-à-vis the neighboring village; they were also arguing against the right of the lower-ranking Gotau people to use their lands. Interestingly, and here is the second point, the Manaledi people had never directly addressed the fact that a small group of rich farmers had proposed a project that was to exclude people, regardless of their village of origin. The objection was to a category of "Gotau people" and to what was considered to be unjustified claims of this village-based communal entity vis-à-vis the historically justified collective right of Manaledi people. "Traditionalist" discourse provided the most powerful and effective way of contesting a *new* kind of threat by exclusive, emerging class-based claims.

A third element stands at the heart of the politics of space unfolding in the Tswapong region. It concerns the unintended outcome of multiple struggles that are material and cultural at the same time. In addition to the competition for land and the intricate manifestation of state power in this local scene, there is evidence for a critical shift in the perception of rights and in the meaning of community. Contradictory interpretations of community and rights are carried out simultaneously.

As we have seen, only after the farmers from Gotau laid claims to a specific parcel of land was the "dormant" communal awareness of Manaledi people "awakened." An external threat acted as the impetus for communal action—the construction of a dam by those defined as "outsiders." Prior to that threat, there was never any question nor need to make explicit (and act upon) the collective right over such land or to articulate the corporate entity that legitimated such claims. A village community became an essentialized, bounded entity. Internal variations, as between various loosely defined ward units, and a fluid process of acquiring membership have been subsumed under an idealized, homogenic collective identity. Such emergent collectivity sets its boundaries in relation to other, similarly essentialized collectivities of neighboring village communities.

The appropriation of space for individual or exclusive small group pur-
poses that have been recognized in this region since the late 1970s has made
incumbent a new understanding. Space became something malleable, dominated through investment and thus alienable and fragmented. Against this
kind of new threat "traditional," historical charters were activated and provided the basic language of discourse. The logic of a traditionalist historical discourse—one that established the corporate rights of a village-
community to adjacent lands—was invoked and used within a new reality
of growing demands of exclusive rights to land. Once the process of fixing
rights to land was set in motion, local knowledge of whose rights to what
land would prevail were fiercely debated. The community that was to
emerge based on such traditionalist justifications was thus a rather novel
organization. New forms of local participation (elected committees) and
access to new resources (public facilities, a dam) gave rise to a very different community, one struggling to maintain and redefine its claims for land
in the face of fierce competition. In the next case, social efforts to attach
meaning to action and communication are played out in a rather different
set of circumstances.

MOKHUNGWANA: REBUILDING THEIR "FATHER'S VILLAGE"

In the 1981 population census, Mokhungwana was recorded as a lands
area associated with the village of Lecheng. The census recorded 141 people who occupied twenty-one of the total twenty-six dwelling units in the
area. Mokhungwana emerged as an officially recognized "established village" only in 1986. The 1991 national census noted that 152 people were
present in the village settlement, 79 males and 73 females (GOB 1992:95).
In 1993, the village boasted a health clinic, a watering dam for cattle, and
clean drinking water from a borehole drilled by the district council. A large
shop next to the *kgotla* public arena was built. The local Village Development Committee was active in lobbying for access to other public resources.
Internally, the village was composed of two wards: Palapye and Maokwe.
The people of Palapye are known as Baseleka. The people of Maokwe are
known as Bangwato.

Why Is Mokhungwana Emerging as a "New" Village Settlement?

As in the case of Manaledi, a local history is presented to explain and justify the dynamics of centralization and dispersal.[7] The story begins with two
men: Seloke and his mother's brother *(malome)* Matuba. Matuba was the
headman of the Maokwe ward in the village of Lecheng. At one point,
Seloke disputed Matuba's power. To resolve the matter, they went to
Khama, the Ngwato ruler. In 1900, following Khama's orders, Seloke and
his followers left Lecheng and built a new village in the area upon which

the village of Mokhungwana now stands. A few years later, Seloke invited his mother's brother, Basele, to join him, saying that he was "lonely" in this new place. Seloke had four wives and many children. But when he died, all his children were "young"[8] and could not become village headman. The settlement scattered and many people left to settle in the villages of Matlakola and Lecheng. By the early 1930s, the clustered village settlement was completely deserted, and the mud houses fell into disrepair. When Seloke's children grew up, they wanted to rebuild "their father's place." The process of their return took many years. They were recognized by the government as an officially established village only in 1986.

The case of Mokhungwana, like that of Manaledi, is one of a formerly established village whose population dispersed. The recent reemergence of the clustered village settlement is justified on the basis of its past. Years of scattered existence do not undermine the communal right of people to rebuild their fathers' place. The interesting element in the Mokhungwana story is the direct involvement and unquestionable authority of Khama, the Ngwato chief, to assign people to land. The contemporary claims of communal rights over that assigned land is based on an original royal Ngwato decree. A generation-long residence in another village[9] has not undermined the basis for the collective right of the descendants of a man whose entitlement was granted by Khama. Here again, as in Manaledi, a "traditionalist" political ideology has provided the basis for contemporary claims. In fact, rather than undermining older channels of authority and influence (like the chief or the *kgotla*), central government reforms and legislation and the introduction of elected district councils, new land boards, and a range of village-level committees have, in fact, invigorated old alliances and rivalries, now played out in new circumstances. The Manaledi and Mokhungwana people were successful, as we have seen, in establishing their moral claims to communal land mainly because district officials shared a political culture that made possible the legitimization of such historical claims. The provision of new resources coveted by these newly emerging village communities—schools, tap water, and roads, not only the control over arable lands—made worthwhile the effort to gain official recognition as an established village. However, the way these reforms were played out locally and the shape the struggle for modern services has taken have been closely implicated with a seemingly traditionalist discourse. The cultural idioms of authority and influence—some drawn from the inter-village alliances and divisions, some focused in the links between the various regional groups with powers in the *morafe*-cum-district center—are brought into play in newly defined, postindependence realities. Chiefly politics and the conflation of chiefs with distinct village-based identities have been reinforced in these novel conditions, giving rise and reinvigorating older factions and divisions.

The question becomes: when, in what newly created conditions, do such cultural idioms of political identity and influence retain efficacy for contemporary struggles and maneuvering, and in what circumstances are they marginalized and ignored? In the next case to be analyzed, on Makgabo, a lands area associated with the village of Lerala, the contemporary struggle of emergence into an independent sociopolitical entity with rights over defined zones of land was fraught with difficulties. The articulation of older alliances and rival factions has played into new administrative structures at the local and district levels in ways that reproduced spatial definitions and identities. Attempts to redefine space and collective rights had not succeeded in gaining the "official" legitimization in this case. Why?

MAKGABO: DENIED AUTONOMY

Makgabo is located at the eastern edge of the Tswapong hills, about eight kilometers north of Lerala and 2 kilometers off the main road (paved in 1993) that connects Maunatlala to Lerala. The 1981 population census lists Makgabo as one of seven lands areas belonging to Lerala. According to this census, the locality consisted of eighty-six dwelling units, fifty-eight occupied by 392 people. The population of Makgabo rose to 557 a decade later, but its classification as a lands area—despite the prolonged struggle of many of its residents—had not changed. In 1988, I described this struggle in the following way.

The spatial layout of Makgabo (in the early 1980s) resembled land residences elsewhere: dispersed household units were located next to agricultural fields. The central *kgotla* arena was in disrepair. While other large named land areas around Lerala had piped water, a small trading store, or even a local church, Makgabo did not contain any public facilities. Its water supply came from a nearby stream, and the only public services enjoyed by Makgabo residents were the periodic visits of the veterinary officer who resided in Lerala. Still, Makgabo dwellers were vocal about their claims that Makgabo was a separate entity not belonging to Lerala. They pointed out that their residence in Makgabo was permanent and that most Makgabo people had no second dwelling in Lerala. They noted that since the source of water in Makgabo was dependable, they did not have to return to Lerala during the dry seasons, even in severe drought years. Most importantly, Makgabo residents presented the nature of their historical association with the Lerala political center as the basis for their demand for a distinct communal identity.[10]

When the village of Lerala was still located at a place called Gale, Makgabo was the land area of the founding royal (*kgosing*) ward. It was shared by the two sons of Mpheu, the Lerala chief, and their families and followers. Rramosoka was the son of the senior wife of Mpheu, and Magosi was the son of the second, junior wife. The two were fierce rivals for the village headmanship, and at one point Rramosoka fled and found refuge with Khama, the Bangwato chief in Serowe. Magosi, the junior but more powerful son, ruled the village until his death, whereupon Rramosoka returned and regained his position.

When Rramosoka returned to power, he allocated new fields for himself and his followers outside the Makgabo area. Magosi's descendants kept their agricultural land in Makgabo. As their position in the village political arena weakened, Magosi's people made Makgabo their center and remained in their lands homes throughout the year. The autonomous nature of their separate permanent residence in Makgabo was acknowledged by colonial tax collectors, who stopped in Makgabo first, before their entry to Lerala.

In 1983, a similar external recognition of Makgabo's separate existence was expressed by the Tswapong Member of Parliament and other officials who made Makgabo a part of their tour in the region. Indeed, when I asked the Tswapong MP to list the villages that fell in his electoral zone, he cited Makgabo as a village unit. Despite such widely acknowledged recognition, Makgabo did not emerge into a separate village. In fact, when Magosi, the Makgabo leader, died in 1982, his son Rralesego, a frail and indecisive man in his early thirties, was said to be "too young" to assume power. Matuba Madikwe, a descendant of a junior line in Magosi's group, acted as the local headman. Since the early 1980s, such a role consisted mainly of signing applications for land that were then submitted to the regional land board and occasional unofficial mediation in local disputes.[11]

When I visited Makgabo in 1993, Matuba Madikwe was adamant that he was not a village headman and that Makgabo was not trying to emerge as a village. All they wanted, he insisted, was for the government to help them dig a borehole so they could water their cattle. He reasoned that the government had refused to do this because it suspected that a permanent water source would only reinforce people's desire to be recognized as a village. "This is not a village," he insisted. "People in Lerala are our seniors," he maintained in an obviously lame effort to lay to rest the generations-long contention by the Magkabo people for an equal and separate status. To convince the listener that this place was merely a land area, he noted that when he was cold, he had to go to his "village home" and fetch a warm blanket; in other words, he kept little in this temporary "land residence."

On the face of it, Makgabo was indeed losing its battle to be recognized and emerge as a distinct socio-spatial entity, a village. Little has changed in the spatial organization of the place over the past decade. A local entrepreneur who sold commercial Chibuku beer out of his unkempt hut in Makgabo told me in 1993 that all his efforts to get a "small dealer" license had failed, "because the government says this is not a village."

How different is the Makgabo case from the two previously described? At the core of this local history, in a manner similar to the other two cases, is a story of an agnatic rivalry between two ruling lines. Yet, unlike that of

Manaledi and Mokhungwana, which were known as separate sociopolitical entities at specific points in their histories, Makgabo was never able to establish its independent sociopolitical existence. The effort of this diverging agnatic line to establish independent control over its social space must therefore be understood within the dynastic rivalry within a single village and its politico-spatial boundaries. Two factors mitigated against such diverging effort: weak leadership and the growing influence of Lerala as an administrative center. Weak, uninspired headmen, often described in the traditionalist discourse as "too young," work against the establishment of cooperative action and the moral claims of the dissenting group. We have seen the effects of a "too young" or absent village headman in the former two cases as well. The rise of Lerala as the administrative center also tipped the balance against Makgabo. The failure to be recognized by the state as a separate village had tangible consequences: Makgabo enjoyed none of the services provided to established villages—schools, reliable drinking water, and roads.

However, Makgabo, unlike the other, successful cases of village emergence in the agricultural zone, was not under any immediate threat to its land. The corporate space publicly known to be "Makgabo lands" would not have been altered by a change in Makgabo's official status. The leadership in Makgabo, not the central leadership in Lerala, retained existing control over postindependence land allocation procedures regulated by the land board. This critical point sheds light on the larger process of spatial transformation in the region. Makgabo, I submit, is a good example of the preindependence dynamics of spatial and political articulations that have continued to the present. Such dynamics concern the inherent rivalry within agnatic segments of the ruling group, and the tendency for splitting and territorial separation of rival segments. Unlike the other two cases, the process of village emergence in Makgabo was not part of current, evolving struggles for control over land, not yet. The generations-long effort to break away from the Lerala center has not been redefined or rekindled in light of the new circumstances of struggle, as in the other cases described.

Why are these cases of village emergence occurring at this particular point in time in the regional history?

CONCLUSION

Social space has been dramatically altered in the Tswapong region over the last two decades. Among the three detailed case studies of village emergence traced here, two have evolved into permanent village communities with a much larger resident population and a significantly expanded institutional base. Roads, schools, health clinics, and trade stores have replaced the makeshift dwellings situated next to individual arable fields and isolated, shifting cattle-watering camps. The emergence of these established, clustered village communities on what had been open arable zones altered not only the visible spatial organization of the region but the key sociopolitical and economic divisions within the regional population as well. Space itself functions as an object of social struggle in all the scenarios outlined.

New laws and legislative reforms enacted in the rural areas since the late 1970s had opened the way for small groups and individuals to apply for exclusive land use rights. The more explicit outcome of such new discourse of exclusive rights has led to privatization of land holding evident in the western region of the Central District, where large areas were fenced in and commercial cattle ranches were established. The dynamics of the cases described here provide ample indications that the key components of such capitalist activities are also played out in this and other regions. Yet along with such exclusivist trends, the very structure of the district and local government has acted as a buffer and played against exclusivist trends. Along with the introduction of elected district councils, land boards and a range of village-level committees, older channels of authority and influence (including the chief, the *kgotla,* and internal rival faction groups within and between villages) have continued to play a role in formal and informal political life.

Taken together, these cases provide a powerful illustration of the many ways in which historical charters are used to consolidate communal identities in the region. In all the cases described, a political ideology was invoked to justify current claims to communal land. Yet two specific observations must be made with regard to this widely known practice of using historical charters to bolster contemporary claims and interests. First, the newly established village communities are not and must not be understood as reproductions of preexisting entities, structured along familiar ("traditional") social institutions and relationships. Rather, these newly established communities are a product of a dramatically shifting reality of land relationships and are themselves an articulation of newly defined ideas about collective identity, communal rights, and subjectivity. Second, the use of village-centered collective history proved to be the most effective strategy to fend off the encroachment of exclusivist claims to land at a particular moment in the history of group relations in this region. Thus in Manaledi, the establishment of corporate rights over communal lands was the best defense against capitalist farmers who wished to build a dam for private use. The rhetoric employed is one of inter-village, rather than anti-exclusivist, claims. In Mokhungwana, too, a village-based communal charter was effective in gaining not only political independence but also in securing state services and resources. In other words, communal historical charters were used not to re-create a "traditionalist order" but as the most effective strategy born of a specific and shifting set of conditions. These particular conditions emerged in this region in the early 1980s.

Before I examine these 1980s circumstances, I wish to return to what might sound like yet another scenario of the "history-invented-as-a-tool-for-present-interests" argument and to amend it as follows. People in these and other instances are never mere instrumentalists. More specifically—and directly linked to my main concern here with space as an object of social struggle—becoming members of a clustered village community (transforming "space" into "place") does not only mean securing public resources or fending off the danger of alienation of arable lands; it also means elevation into a status of social citizenship, membership in the social realm, and a sense of collective and individual well-being. By redefining and transforming the social space, by remaking their living environment into a named place with identity and autonomy, these people at the edges of the Tswana hierarchical world act in a meaningful and interpretive, not only instrumentalist, fashion. In the process of remaking their world, people transform their social space and their lives in irreversible ways, ways no one had intended.

An important transformation in social relationships directly linked with the process of spatial rearrangement has been the shift in inter-village hierarchies (for example, between the Manaledi and Gotau village centers on the one hand and the Lerala and the Makgabo groups on the other). The hierarchical order that has linked these small Tswapong communities with the preindependence Ngwato hegemonic power has also gained new meaning. District-level personnel and official bodies were seen not as representatives of a remote, impartial bureaucratic state, but as part of the hierarchical order of colonial and precolonial times.

Each of the case studies showcases a different constellation of evolving social and spatial patterns. However, common processes can be traced throughout these local scenarios. One of the most obvious transformations in sociopolitical relationships within these emerging communities has been the changing role and definition of village headmanship. Paradoxically, the very legislative reform that undermined the executive powers of village heads and transferred their land allocation powers to elected land boards had, at the same time, granted the position a new significance that has given rise to fierce internal struggles. The very process of dealing with external bodies that could grant official recognition opened the way for a profound redefinition of the role. Service for the community and an active role in gaining the popular support of residents sometimes was congruent with, but at times worked against, criteria of rank and priority of residence. We have seen how in one case (Manaledi) the headman whose rank and placement in the traditional hierarchy were unquestioned found it necessary to act as a head of the local VDC. In another case (Gamotse), the official need to appoint a single village head gave rise to serious internal tensions and to the emergence of a popular, non-Tswana leader. When the state stepped in to impose a new village headman, one who did not enjoy local popular support, the moral power of village headmanship was dramatically curtailed.

Finally, consider those few comments about time and shifts in state-local interactions. My analysis offered an examination of the process of changing socio-spatial relationships at two points in time, the early 1980s and the early 1990s. I argue here that: (1) the 1980s were particularly fertile times for the local creative acts of redefinition of relationships and spaces, and (2) many of these local initiatives were curtailed a decade later when the state acted in a more authoritarian fashion to establish structures and define boundaries. (3) Two factors have combined to define the kind of interactions between state bodies and rural people in the 1980s. The first was the immense growth in the national economy of Botswana, wrought mostly through the late 1960 discovery of diamonds. State development efforts in those years were largely directed toward building rural infrastructure and provision of services for the rural populace. These new investments coincided with a period of great uncertainty in the rural areas in the aftermath of a series of legislative reforms. The combined effects of uncertainty on the one hand and of immediate gains to be secured through official recognition of village status on the other enabled this unique era of active rural redefinitions. However, such articulations of communal aspirations and the shifts in the regional spatial arrangements shaped by them were arrested toward the 1990s. "Dynastic power embedded in place," to paraphrase David Harvey (1992:257), had reestablished itself over attempts at the "reorganization of space to democratic ends."

The next chapter provides a portrait of another local struggle and examines the ways in which state discourses and policies and shifts in political and economic structures are drawn into local experience and practice. We will explore how the combined effects of these forces produce a new reality of space and place.

NOTES

1. Amsden 1979, quoted in Lawrence and Low 1990:484.

2. In Chapter 8 I show how prolonged residence in the bush and prolonged dissociation from the village political center diminish one's social standing and, in extreme cases, might relegate one to the inferior nonsocial "Sarwa" category. Basarwa embody the ultimate exclusion from the social world of the centralized village.

3. For a more complete historical analysis, see Motzafi-Haller 1988:21–23, 60–72.

4. What constitutes "permanent" residence and what is "more or less permanent" is, of course, crucial in this case. The convoluted efforts of definition presented in these official texts make the effort to arrest the inherent ambiguity of residence impossible.

5. Their headman, a direct descendant of Keatoletse, was a young man involved actively in migrant labor and was thus absent from the village arena throughout these years.

6. The classification of a "village" vs. "localities belonging to a village" is explicit in the official record. The index to the August 1992 document published by the

Central Statistics office entitled "Population of towns, villages and associated local-ities" is divided into these two distinct categories. Manaledi statistics are recorded under the "alphabetical index of villages," p. 96.

7. Based on interviews in Mokhungwana on May 5, 1993. Informants were Mokente Nagaesele of the Maokwe ward and Kemoepile Magononong Basele of the Palapye ward.

8. "Young" here might be in reference to the biological age of the chief's descen-dants. But it is also likely that no single son emerged as "senior enough" to become the legitimate heir of the chief.

9. The present-day headman of Mokhungwana, Koketso, is the son of Kenosi. Kenosi's father is Seloke. Koketso was born in Lecheng, but that did not weaken his association with Mokhungwana, his "father's village."

10. This historical account was recorded in Makgabo in 1982 during the course of several visits. I checked several aspects of this account in 1993. It is important to note, however, that my information at both times was provided by Makgabo and not Lerala people. The "view from the center" might be different.

11. I was able to interview Madikwe only in 1993. I cannot say if he changed his views in the course of that decade or if he was always against the transformation of Makgabo to village status.

6

Social Space, Collective Identity, and Moments of Resistance

In every era the attempt must be made anew to wrest tradition away
from a conformism that is about to overpower it.
                                    Walter Benjamin, *Illumination*

Just as technologies of control run the gamut from overt coercion to
implicit persuasion, so modes of resistance may extend across a similarly wide spectrum. At one end is organized protest, explicit moments
and movements of dissent that are easily recognizable as "political" by
western lights. At the other are gestures of tacit refusal and iconoclasm,
gestures that sullenly and silently contest the forms of an existing hegemony. For the most part, however, the ripostes of the colonized hover
in the space between the tacit and the articulate, the direct and the indirect. And far from being a mere reflection—or reflex expression—of
historical consciousness, these acts are practical means of *producing* it.
                    John and Jean Comaroff, *Of Revelation and Revolution*

This chapter describes the emergence of a new village community at the
rural periphery of eastern Botswana. In exploring in great detail the complex struggles that have constituted the local politics in this "out-of-the-way
place"[1] and the engagement of such local struggles with national and
transnational forces, I wish to examine the way collective identities, social
space, and social relations have shifted in the course of the past decade or
more in Botswana.

I argue that the complex relations that have enabled the formation of this
local community and the social forces that shaped it in the early 1980s were

contingent on specific historical conditions. As the discussion in the former two chapters has shown, the early 1980s were the period following the promulgation of a major national land reform, when the implications of the policy were largely unclear. The multiple contestations and partial challenge to existing structures of domination depicted in the first part of this chapter unfolded in a meaningful way, I wish to show here, because they occurred at this particular moment in Botswana's history. At this moment of ambiguity and negotiation, participants were struggling to impose their own interpretation of relations and events. However, a decade later, when the state stepped in to impose a new village headman and reestablish hierarchical relations within and beyond the new village arena, the room for negotiation was critically narrowed and the "open" phase of cultural and ideological instability arrested.

What I propose to explore, then, is the processes and practices that created this local community not as a bounded geographical entity but as a site for the expression of multiple and shifting social relations. What kind of social divisions along gender and other lines of social hierarchies were constructed and rearticulated in this focal place, and how have these divisions and the cultural systems that defined them shifted in the course of the past two decades or more?

But in considering these questions and this focal case study, I also return to the issue of resistance raised in former chapters. This analysis of the struggles for communal emergence in the early 1980s suggests that in the process of imagining their collective future, marginalized people in this rural setting had attempted to alter existing social hierarchical relations. In using mimicry and parody of the language of power, they expressed their challenge to regional, national, and transnational hegemonies. However, the reality of group relations in the early 1990s, depicted in the second part of this chapter, shows that dominant patterns of social arrangements had been firmly reestablished. Was I guilty of a "heavy moralism" (Marcus 1994) in my interpretive analysis of the critical years of the early 1980s? Had I "romanticized" (Abu-Lughod 1990) the reality I observed in the early 1980s only to find out a decade later that the power of the state can and has undermined such subtle ways of resisting? The question, I would like to emphasize, is not only the accuracy of my interpretive analysis of the case at point, but one of the value of using resistance as an analytical and theoretical term. Recent work has questioned the value of the concept "resistance" by arguing that the category is deeply dangerous and should not be used. I would like to draw on two other views that have seen the value in exploring resistance not as an indication for people's wish for freedom but as a useful tool for the analysis of power and the working of hegemony. The first view is developed by Abu-Lughod, who draws on Foucault (1982) to show how "resistance" can tell us "about the working of power" (1990:42). By tracing the transformation of the relations within this local community over a decade from one of partial, incomplete challenge to existing structures of domination to a more "sober" reality in the early 1990s, when resistance is all but a memory, I wish to show, like Abu-Lughod, that resistance is a "diagnostic of power." Local Tswapong discourses of resistance in the 1980s, I will argue using Abu-Lughod (1990) and Roseberry's (1996) insights, might have succeeded only momentarily to rupture the existing structure of domination in this rural periphery. Still, the expression of such encounters with hegemonic patterns provides an important setting for our understanding of the "process of domination" and about how people are caught up in, and continually redefine, structures of power.

BACKGROUND TO THE PROBLEM: GENDER, SOCIAL SPACE, AND COMMUNAL IDENTITY IN RURAL BOTSWANA

The story of Gamotse[2] is the story of the transformation of a cattle post (*moraka*) into a settled village (*motse*). Two larger frames of reference must be clarified before the details of this local transformation are described and analyzed. The first is the cultural meaning and significance of these two patterns of residence. The second is the shifting political economy of group relations within the region. We have already seen how, in the Tswana world, residence in a clustered village, the *motse,* is associated with social order and citizenship, while agricultural production is associated with females, the isolated domestic unit, and politically inactive males. There is a basic symbolic opposition between the social, public, male-centered village (*motse*) domain and that of the wild, natural, unbounded—and thus asocial—bush (*naga*) domain.

There are profound signs that these fundamental categories that distinguish between *motse* and *naga,* between the clustered village and the bush, culture and nature, still inform people's worlds and action in the 1980s and the early 1990s. The land board members made it amply evident when they joked loudly with the young Family Welfare Educator who brought us into Gamotse in the early 1980s. "What is a nice girl like you doing in this *nageng* (this wild bush)?" they teased. I watched them as they walked around the emerging settlement on their first visit to the place in 1983, exclaiming, "No, sir, this is a village. Yes, indeed, a village all right." Their attitude toward the gathered crowd was almost condescending. They reserved their incredulous comments about the Gamotse people and about the foreign accent of the Gamotse popular leader for the privacy of the return car ride. In 1993, when we asked an old woman in Lerala about the whereabouts of her son, she commented with sarcasm that her son was "lost," he was somewhere in "the bush." It turned out that he lived in Gamotse. Other people made similar comments about Gamotse being a *moraka*, a cattle post. The struggle to become officially recognized as a "settled village" and escape their social and cultural designation as a "wild" cattle post, depicted in the following pages, must be understood within this prevalent sociocultural hierarchical map.

But the social hierarchical order, as we have seen in previous chapters, is not limited to the tensions within a single cluster of a village core and its surrounding agricultural domains; it is also embedded in the political relations among groups and settlements within and beyond the Tswapong region. These inter-village hierarchies and the political economy that reproduce them were described at some length in Chapter 3. Suffice it to mention at this juncture that the well-watered Tswapong region has been used by some Ngwato herd owners as a preferred grazing area for their herds for more than a century, ever since the region came under the control of the Ngwato clan. Two other important features are unique to the Tswapong hills region. The first is the relatively small size of its settled villages; the largest clustered village residence in 1984 numbered some 2,000 people, compared with more than 30,000 residents in large villages elsewhere in Botswana. The second feature is the strong correlation between village size and ethnic and economic divisions. Most residents of the small village communities in the Tswapong region keep their few cattle in the vicinity of the village, in the open rocky hills. Only the most affluent herd owners (many from the two larger villages of Lerala and Maunatlala) need to send their herds to be watered in the distant northern grazing areas next to the Elibi stream. In these open grazing areas, in the north and northwestern regions, local cattle owners from Maunatlala and Lerala come in close contact with cattle owners from Serowe. A final introductory comment is that the emergence of Gamotse as an "established village" and the process of struggling to gain official recognition, is one among several other attempts by "non-villages" in the Central District to change their official recognition and emerge as "settled" or "established" villages.[3]

A LOCAL HISTORY

In introducing Gamotse, it is significant to start with the twin facts that the 1981 national population census classified Gamotse as a village and not lands or cattle post area and that Gamotse is not mentioned in earlier national population records.

The 1981 national population census recorded 269 people resident in forty-five dwelling units and the existence of the following public facilities in Gamotse: a borehole, a primary school, a health post, and one church. In 1982, when I first visited Gamotse, I had a much less impressive picture of the place. The health post, built by private funds of "Mr. Smith," a neighboring white farmer, offered only occasional services volunteered by a visiting doctor, a friend of Mr. Smith. The clinic was turned over to the District Council and became part of the rural network of health posts in the country in 1982, a few months before my visit to the place. Officially, the local health post was supposed to provide the resident population with a minimal set of services provided by a woman trained in preventative health care (the role was known as a "Family Welfare Educator"). But the Family Welfare Educator who was to provide these services in Gamotse was seldom there; she resided in a neighboring village some twelve kilometers away and had no dependable mode of transportation to bring her to work in Gamotse. The recorded elementary school consisted of a large mud-walled and thatch-roofed room built by local communal effort. With six years of elementary education to her credit, the most educated woman in Gamotse acted as the teacher of the only class, which children of all ages attended. When the thatched roof collapsed in March 1983, teaching in the "Gamotse school" came to an abrupt end. Finally, the local church was in fact a clearing under a shaded tree. Residents' yards (*malwapa*) were made of mud with roofs mostly thatched with locally collected straw. Very few houses had store-purchased glass windows inserted into the mud walls and fewer still had roofs made of corrugated iron or even of the better-quality, professionally installed thatch. At a distance of some three kilometers from the dispersed settlement surrounded by a wire fence was the house of Mr. Smith, a shop, and a chicken farm. At one edge of the settlement, next to a shade tree, a clearing was enclosed on one side by a crescent of locally gathered dry wood. The definition of space around this open arena suggested that this was the village *kgotla,* the most celebrated sign of village settlement in rural Botswana.

Although the 1981 census classified Gamotse as a village and not as a lands or cattle post, the two other modes of land use and residence in Botswana, a short visit to the place in the early 1980s made clear that this locality was in the midst of the process of "becoming" rather than "being" a village. It is this process of an entity being produced, the multiple meanings attached to it by the various participants in the process, and the emerging power struggle at its core that I would like to examine first.

Gamotse was a cattle post area containing temporary huts of transient herders and a few of their dependents until 1948, when one of the more affluent cattle owners in the area, a Maunatlala man, dug a well in the locality. The secure source of water drew other herders from outlying areas and adjacent cattle posts who began to settle in the vicinity of the well. M. M. K. Molefe, the district officer, describes this process of growing stability of residence in the area of Gamotse in 1984 in the following way: "This man allowed the settlement to take root and it grew with every year without much objection from the neighboring cattle farmers in the surrounding villages."[4] The proximity of Gamotse to the white-owned farms in the Tuli Block[5] and to the South African border were also important factors in the rapid expansion of the settlement. Men who could not continue to work on the farms after a certain age, or those who chose to leave the farms due to other considerations, came to Gamotse. Many of these farm workers were not citizens of Botswana, and some were of non-Tswana origin.[6] In 1968, a further boost to the growing settlement was given when a white South African man opened a small shop and dug a borehole near Gamotse. A poultry farm established in 1977 by the daughter of the shop owner and her husband provided more local work opportunities. In 1983, about 50 residents of Gamotse found daily work in this growing poultry business (by 1993 their number had risen to 120), while others could survive as herders for the large herd owners in the area and by cultivating small adjacent gardens. The owners of the poultry farm also offered residents of the locality clean drinking water from their borehole and privately financed the building of the local health clinic.

In 1975, a resident of Gamotse, a non-Tswana man, a relatively poor man in his mid-forties, began organizing the building of the much needed school in the growing settlement. A year later, in 1976, the residents of Gamotse completed the construction of their single-room school. A second communal project was begun in 1981. A large area in the shade of several trees was cleared and bounded on one side by a crescent wall of logs. This was the central public *kgotla* arena, the most visible and explicit symbol of "villagehood" in Botswana. These efforts of communal self-help were encouraged by various official forms of recognition. As Molefe, the district officer, notes (Molefe 1983): "From time to time, this settlement was visited by Parliamentarians, Councilors, Chiefs and Government officials." And, he adds, "Nobody ever questioned the existence of this settlement until recently when the residents of [Gamotse] appealed to the Bobonong Sub Land-Board to be allocated ploughing fields and lands in that area."

When the Bobonong Sub-Land Board approved, in principle, the request of the Gamotse residents to register their individual ploughing fields in the vicinity of their clustered settlement (many were already cultivating such land but had not secured the official legitimacy for their practice), the local rich cattle owners (or ' "cattle farmers," as Molefe refers to them) made explicit their objection of such desired recognition. Their objection was not only to the allocation of ploughing land in the vicinity of the growing settlement; they made, in Molefe's words, "a very strong case," supported by some "influential tribesmen and Councilors" in the district, "that the whole settlement should be uprooted and transferred to [a neighboring established village]." Using the ambiguous administrative division of the large Central District into several subdistrict land boards, these locally powerful cattle owners questioned the authority of the Bobonong Sub-Land Board to make the decision it had made and recruited the members of another sub-land board (the Maunatlala Sub-Land Board) to their side. The question of which sub-land board had jurisdiction over the emerging village became a key issue in this case. At that point, the "official status" of Gamotse became a disputed case, which the Ngwato Land Board, the district-level official body responsible for such assessment, had to resolve. In 1982, the district land board convened a meeting in the large village neighboring Gamotse in an effort to resolve the dispute. In the resulting settlement, the "operational boundaries" of the two sub-land boards were defined, but "the question of recognition [of the Gamotse settlement] remained unresolved" (Molefe 1983).

There was another important twist to the story. Official village recognition also entails a recognition of a village headman. Village headmen recognized by the Tribal Authorities—a parallel postindependence establishment of tribal courts presided over by recognized village heads—were expected to preside over their local traditional courts, and in the larger villages they were paid by the tribal authorities for performing their role. Moreover, because every application for land had to be signed and approved by a "local headman" prior to its submission to the land board, assessing who is the local headman of Gamotse became an issue of official concern. In November 1982, the Maunatlala Sub-Land Board rushed a letter to the District Tribal Authority in Serowe requesting that it appoint a headman in Gamotse "so that land board will be able to process applications" (Maunatlala Sub-Land Board files, Maunatlala). But the procedure of "appointing" a local headman turned out to be a complex and involved matter. The Maunatlala Land Board members made several visits to Gamotse. On their third visit to Gamotse, on April 28, 1983, they convened a public meeting and explained the new procedures of land allocation to the gathered people. They were well received. The evidence of a local struggle for village headsmanship was evident in the setting of the public meeting with the visiting land board. Two men sat with the visiting land board members behind the long table facing the gathered community. One was a relatively poor man in his forties who spoke Setswana with a foreign accent; the other was an old Ngwato man, one of the richest cattle owners in the area. Both men claimed to hold the right to represent Gamotse to its official visitors. Yet what could have remained a local, parochial power struggle became, through the requirement of the land board and the involvement of other state agencies, an official concern to be publicly resolved without delay.

These, then, are the circumstances, the context in time and space, that render the "local moment" (Moore 1987) I turn now to describe as significant. The event is extremely revealing, not only because it illustrates the way conflicting interests and existing power and social differences were articulated, but also because it was itself a setting where such social divisions and the legitimate forms of discourse that establish them were contested. In this focal event, I contend, history was made—not merely told—as various groups of people questioned, redefined, and, in the process, created their communal identity.

THE EVENT

The public meeting with the land board did not result in any clear resolutions. It was a setting, a public stage for the claims staked by the two contenders for local leadership, and it was an occasion where the fragile reality of village existence was played out. When the land board members left the open-air meeting, the whole gathered group of residents remained seated. None of the approximately fifty adults present at the meeting left the place when the land board members said their closing, polite words and rose to leave the open arena. Most of those present were women (by my count, about thirty-four) who sat in one end of the arena, their feet stretched in front of them, their backs straight. Most sat on a small rug made of an empty sugar sack or a flattened cardboard box they had brought with them. The men, clustered at another end, sat on objects that elevated them from the swept, red earth—a small wooden stool, a chunk of unhewn dry wood, or a rock. A few were standing behind the women. Children were clustered in small groups behind the group of women.

I seized the opportunity and began what I originally thought was going to be an oral history session, one such as I had conducted in many other villages in the region. I began with what I had learned after scores of similar interviews to be the accepted opening question. I asked how their village 'started' and who were the first people to settle here. This usually effective "ice-breaking" question was met with a general embarrassed silence. The young, "aspiring headman," I will call Mpho, was first to speak. He started by saying with great unease that he did not know when the village "started" and who came first. Another man offered some help, hesitantly suggesting that there are "those of Bobonong" (*bone ba Bobonong*) and "those of Lerala," referring to the two large well-established villages to the north and south of Gamotse. Several other comments were equally vague and hesitant. The old Ngwato cattle owner, a man I will name Rrapodi, interrupted these attempts rudely. "They don't know anything," he told me, addressing the younger man. He said, "You have been here only since yesterday" (i.e., too recently to know anything). He then turned toward the gathered crowd and stated: "We are the people of Serowe and we are the *bakgosing*, the royal/ruling people of this place." By emphasizing his origin from Serowe, the old man invokes his rank as a Ngwato "royal" and, hence, his legitimate right for ruling over the community. He attempted to discredit the claims made by his young competitor by invoking another criterion—pioneership. The earliest settlers are known as those who have the rights to the land they occupy.

The initial hesitant efforts by the villagers to describe "those of Bobonong" and "those of Lerala" drew on yet another element in the same political ideology. Two of the largest land owners in Gamotse originate from Bobonong and Lerala, respectively. In the normative, "traditionalist" model, individuals who wish to settle in a community and cultivate fields in its vicinity must approach the village headman, who has the legitimate power to grant such right of use. Membership in the host community is often cast in fictive kinship terms. By referring to the two prominent men— the one from Lerala and the other from Bobonong—as heads of their "wards," the Gamotse residents redefined their individual, haphazard process of settlement in terms of order and hierarchy of units. They engaged with, made use of, and adopted idealized elements of a "traditionalist discourse" (Thomas 1992).

Old Rrapodi's aggressive claims for local leadership were met with strong popular objections. The group of women sitting at the edge of the arena on the ground interrupted his words with their loud cries of disapproval. These women made their objection to Rrapodi's claims and their approval of Mpho's supporters through bursts of loud laughter, through loud exchanges of opinions among themselves, but never in the form of individual speech articulated in front of the whole group. Their catcalls (most often an incredulous "aa . . . aa" sound) had effectively silenced those they wanted to quiet. At one point one man rose up to speak. "All newcomers who joined us recently," he argued, "they are 'under' Lerala and not 'under' Serowe. So how is Serowe the *kgosing?*" Implicit in this man's question was the Tswana norm that newcomers are expected to become part of the chiefly *kgosing* ward. It is one prerogative of the ruling descent group at the core of the *kgosing* ward to absorb new settlers. This man thus posed a challenge to the basis that establishes the seniority of the Serowe group claimed by the old man. The final challenge to the old man's assertions was soon to emerge after a long clamor. A voice surfaced above the general tumult to assert: "It was Letso who came here first, and this man here (pointing to a frail young man in his thirties) is his son."

Letso was a Serowe cattle owner, one of the first residents who made his home in Gamotse. Although a Serowe man, like the powerful Rrapodi, the two are not related. The speaker thus combined two Tswana norms, rank and pioneership, to discredit the specific claims of Rrapodi to seniority. According to this villager, the son of Letso had stronger claims to a position of local leadership than Rrapodi, who came to Gamotse later. However, the challenge posed here was inherently contradictory. For unlike Rrapodi, who was a rich cattle owner, Letso met misfortune, and his son and two daughters were among the poorest in the community and in no position or personal inclination to pose a claim to power in the emerging village. Rrapodi, it became clear, couldn't refute the basis of this claim, and in spite of the implicit ridicule of the proposal posed by the villager, he acknowledged that old Letso was indeed the first man from Serowe to arrive in the locality. Yet he hastened to add, "So I now say, myself and this one (the son of Letso), we both rule (*busa*) here."

At that point, the gathered people became extremely animated. For a long while no single voice or clear statement rose above the crowd's internal exchanges of opinions. While I decided not to intervene and to see who would be the next person to lead the discussion, my assistant Moses Basebi, a Motswana[7] man in his early thirties who followed the whole scene with amused disbelief, began on his own initiative to "sort things out." I quote some of the exact exchanges between Moses and the people because the use of terms and the internal dynamics that unfolded in the interchange are illustrative of the process through which meanings were negotiated and group identities drawn during this crucial event. The exchange is also interesting because it was conducted by an outsider, a Tswana man with no position of power among the gathered people, yet one who comes from a "proper" established village.

> **Moses:** Old man (respectfully addressing Rrapodi, the old man from Serowe), where do you live/stay (*O nna kai*)?
>
> **Rrapodi:** Here, in this place.
>
> **Moses:** And do you have a house there in Serowe?
>
> **Rrapodi:** Yes, But I am the "elder among them" (*motona mogo bone*) here.

In this initial interchange Moses attempted to question the old man's claims by invoking the norm that a headman lives in his village. The fact that the old man maintained a home in Serowe questioned his belonging to, let alone ruling, this locality. When the old man bluntly rejected the challenge, Moses proceeded to use another measure of defining a village headman: he explored who, in fact, performs the main role that defines a village headman—resolution of local disputes. (Turning to the people gathered there, Moses asked, "When you have a dispute (*tseko*) to be resolved, where do you go to settle it?"

It became clear, after some interchanges, that the younger contending headman was fulfilling this role. Mpho, it turned out, was the first to be approached for dispute resolution. If no resolution was reached after such mediation, the case then moved on to the established neighboring village's traditional court.

Satisfied with this, Moses then proceeded to clarify the presence of other social categories of a "proper" settled village life. Moses referred to key components of a settled village structure—ward units with their known heads. He asked, "And these people of Bobonong who you tell me are here, who is their head (*tlhogo*)? And who came first—the one from Bobonong or the man from Lerala?" The answers to these questions, pieced together from several partial accounts and further probing, led Moses to conclude: "So you have here a Bobonong ward, a Lerala ward, and a Serowe one" (he said, *bone ba Bobonong, bone ba Lerala . . .* , literally "those of Bobonong" and "those of Lerala"). The gathered people responded, "Yes, these are our wards."

This exchange between Moses, an articulate Motswana whose questions were clearly formulated by his cultural perception of what "proper" group relations in such village settings *should* be, and the gathered residents of

Gamotse, a newly evolving village community, is a powerful illustration of how social meanings and roles are reaffirmed and at the same time challenged. Moses acted here as the voice of tradition and social order. He attempted to "fit" the reality of this atypical community into the traditionalist discourse of group relations, evoking criteria such as a single central authority in the form of a headman, pioneership, rank, and permanency of residence. Moses tried to force the ambiguous, untidy social reality of this marginal community into an ideal model that is itself replete with inherent contradictions. Theirs was an effort to engage in this discourse and essentialize the attributes of their social relations to fit elements in that discourse.

The Gamotse residents adopted and resisted the traditionalist model at the same time. They made use of the symbolic language of this model: they built a central *kgotla,* the most visible sign of "villagehood" They also made sure to build their own school, which in postindependence days is another sign of settled independent village life. Yet, when it came to village headmanship, they radically departed from the prescribed order of things. In fact, they skillfully played with inherent contradictions embedded in this traditionalist order. Hence, while the old rich cattle owner invoked his rank and origin to legitimize his claims for power over the emerging village, the contesting villager turned such a claim on its head by proposing the competing claim of a now impoverished and powerless son of an equally highly ranked man. The young impoverished son was a weak, uninspiring person and an unlikely candidate for any position of leadership in the community. By posing the rightful claims of such an obviously inappropriate candidate, the villager ridiculed the moral basis of the old man's claims and communicated a subtle message of resistance to his fellow villagers. While playfully undermining the rightful claims to leadership of young Letso (whose father, like old Rrapodi, had been an affluent Ngwato cattle owner), they openly supported the position of the non-Tswana populist leader. The authority and legitimacy of the populist leader was based not on traditional criteria of rank and wealth, but on his performance as a capable mediator of local disputes and organizer of communal projects.

But how effective has this subtle, ironic undermining of the old man's claims and his "language of power" been in transforming the entrenched social hierarchy? Indeed, if we look closely at this local discursive event we cannot ignore the limited scope of its focal act of resistance. The whole event emerged and was defined by the need to comply with the official requirement to be registered as a "settled village." The unfolding struggle was therefore for a *particular kind* of subjectivity—settled villagehood— defined and legitimized by this official requirement. Moreover, throughout the process of constructing a possible future for themselves, these people have never questioned the hierarchical political organization that defines social relations in such "established village" settings; nor at any point did they challenge the gender privilege embedded in such definition of spatial relations. They spoke of village wards "ruled" by affluent cattle owners. They invoked rank, pioneership, and the hierarchical ordering of groups— all key elements in the dominant ideology—in their statements. Moreover, when we turn to look at the women who constituted the majority of those present, it is obvious that they have joined their men in undermining old Rrapodi and what he represented only to support a reconstituted male-centered village domain. Is this another example of Gramscian "ideological consensus," whereby the subalterns adopt and use the "mentality, ideology, and aims" of those in power? Were these marginalized people merely reestablishing dominant frameworks and relationships? I believe not. James Scott has argued repeatedly (1985, 1990) that the dominated might use the forms and language of those in power in order to be heard, but that this use does not indicate they have accepted such ideology.

What we see in this case, I suggest, is only a partial appropriation of the dominant language of power, a fragmentation of this language in ways that redefine its intended aims. These relatively powerless people succeeded in transforming the meaning of the key role of the village chief by exploiting the ambiguities and contradictions of this central role in new circumstances. The leader they supported was not only a relative newcomer, but like many of the people in this marginal community on the border with South Africa, he was, as it turned out a few years later, not a citizen of Botswana. He was known to have started as poor and as destitute as the majority of the local population. He owned no cattle and the small field he was cultivating with his family in 1983 was an important source of food to supplement his irregular wage earning. Clearly, this man fit poorly the criteria of rank, wealth, and priority of residence that qualify a headman in the political ideology contested in the exchange between Moses and the villagers. In supporting this man against the representative of the rich cattle owners, the majority of the poor herders and farm laborers in Gamotse were articulating, although in an indirect way, their collective material interests of securing access to arable land in face of the objections of large herd owners. Turning the language of the powerful to their own ends, they were able to challenge the very definition of village headmanship and, with it, the moral economy that claimed their labor and defined their limited access to resources.

People were clearly not re-creating an existing social order, nor, I wish to argue, were they constructing a coherent, alternative "neotraditional" one. What we see instead is a rather untidy, internally contradictory process of attempts to redefine the bases of power within a small community and through it some signs of an emerging challenge to existing patterns of control over people, land, and the cultural order that maintains these patterns of control over resources in the area. We see how these relatively powerless people recognize and address the system of power and, at the same time, resist it. Their resistance, to use Roseberry's words, has been "shaped by the process, terms, [and] conditions of domination" (1996).

It is important to emphasize, at this point of the analysis, that the potential for change in this and other processes of "ongoing construction and dismantling of symbolic material" (Rebel 1989) is *not* unlimited. The challenge to established forms of power and control over resources and people has occurred in this case, as elsewhere (cf. Abu-Lughod and Lutz 1993, Herzfeld 1991, Vincent 1986 Wolf 1986, Worsley 1984), in the context of unequal social and economic forces. It is to this larger context that we now must turn.

THE POLITICAL ECONOMY
OF A TRANSFORMING GRAZING AREA

On one level of analysis the struggle in Gamotse can be easily framed and understood in terms of the clear distinction between the two main sections of the population: the few rich cattle owners and the many impoverished herders and small subsistence farmers. The interests of these two socioeconomic categories were in direct conflict here. The large herd owners originated from Serowe, the district capital, and from large established villages in the area. Their social identity and their arable fields were linked to these large villages. For many, and especially for the affluent herd owners, Gamotse was only one among several places where their cattle were tended. These people had no interest in improving the infrastructure of Gamotse and saw the growing size of the settlement as a drain on available water and grazing land. In fact, this is how the district officer explains what happens in Gamotse in his official report (Molefe 1983). The rich "cattle farmers," he notes, had done their best, using their powerful connections with district officials, to dismantle the growing settlement and "transfer" it to a neighboring village. He speaks about the interests of this group of powerful "cattle farmers" in no ambiguous terms: their position, he writes, stems from their "land hunger" and, more specifically, their perception of a "lack [of] land for grazing."

The interests of this group opposed the interests of the second, and larger, socioeconomic category, which consisted of poor herders, farm laborers, and small cultivators who made a home in the locality and were interested in improving the conditions of their settled life. These people contributed their labor and limited resources to the erection of their local school and the central *kgotla* arena and welcomed the involvement of the land board in the process of gaining an official established village recognition. While many of these poor households had already been cultivating small plots next to their homes, their use of these plots was dependent on the goodwill of the large cattle owners as long as Gamotse remained a cattle post area. Unfenced and unregistered, such fields could at any moment be reclaimed as grazing

grounds. Such uncertainty of tenure could be greatly reduced if one succeeded in registering one's plot with the land board. Indeed, as the percep-
tive Molefe observed, no one objected to this settlement until an effort to
register arable plots was begun by these people.

Such conflict of interests between affluent cattle owners and the numer-
ous subsistence farmers is not unique to Gamotse. A review of the files in
the offices of the Ngwato District Land Board in Serowe reveals that in
1982, Gamotse was one among six similar cases of struggles by settlements
located in the grazing zone within the large Central District to gain established village status. Several reports submitted by officials who visited these
local sites record the ambivalence and open-endedness of these situations.
As one land board official wrote after his visit to the site, [these people]
"are confused as to whether the village is a cattlepost or what." Another
official reported about this fear articulated by the people he met. Speaking
about the onset of the establishment of commercial farms and private
ranches in the area, he noted that people were afraid that "the ranches
would leave them a small area for fields" (Ngwato Land Board file number
119/82).

The dynamics of the current struggle over land in other regions in eastern Botswana is thoroughly documented by Ornulf Gulbrandsen, a Nor-
wegian anthropologist who was commissioned by the government of
Botswana to study changes in land tenure practices in the country. Gulbrandsen cites two main reasons for growing land scarcity in Botswana: (1)
a greater demand for land by a rapidly growing population with few
options for income and jobs outside the agricultural sector, and (2) the
expansion of commercial arable agriculture encouraged by the national
land reform promulgated in the mid-1970s (1984:4ff).

According to Gulbrandsen, this increasing demand for arable land aggravates the conflict between two categories of the rural population with different interests in land—crop cultivation and grazing. Gulbrandsen
describes several regional variations in what he calls "the arable/grazing
conflict" (1984:10ff). In some cases (e.g., Barolong), the conflict emerges
when people begin to fence in fields in what is known to be grazing areas
and thus bring about "serious reduction of available pasture" (1984:10ff).
In other regions (e.g., Kgatleng and Bangwaketse) the conflict is between
"minor subordinate communities located outside the tribal capital" and an
increasing demand for arable lands by "capital village residents." In this
variation of the arable/grazing conflict, "tribal capital residents, who have
their cattleposts at distant places, complain about pasture degradation
caused by arable expansions from local settlements" (1984:11).

The Gamotse case, as we have seen, has many of the characteristics of the
latter rural conflict scenario. Unfolding, as it did, in the aftermath of the
national land tenure reform that redefined access to land in the communally
held zone, the Gamotse case was indicative of the prevalent uncertainty of

these transitional times. Although large commercial farms and ranching had not made their appearance in this eastern region, the fear that land was about to become scarce informed the actions of all actors in this unfolding event.[8] In fact, the struggle over land in Gamotse might have been more acute precisely because claims to land were not fixed in this outlying area: the greater the uncertainty about rights to land, the fiercer the struggle to redefine such rights by competing groups and interests (Werbner 1991:22).

But the Gamotse case is illustrative of more complex dynamics of rural politics that go beyond such basic opposition between two socioeconomic categories with conflicting vested grazing and arable interests in land. Three critical factors complicated the particular circumstances of rural struggle in Gamotse:

1. The internal divisions within the affluent cattle owner group between those who originated from the remote capital center of Serowe and those who came from established villages within the region
2. The active role played by the white farmers and shop owners who employed Gamotse residents in their farms and small businesses
3. The fact that far from being a uniform group of "resisting subalterns," the impoverished group of herders and farm workers was internally divided along lines of gender, kinship, clientship, tribal/ethnic group, and citizenship

The case of Gamotse illustrates internal conflicts within the affluent group of cattle owners, in this case between those who originate from Serowe, the district capital, and those whose primary home is in large villages in the region—Bobonong, Lerala, or Maunatlala. The conflict within this group, which on the surface shares the same interests in land, helps clarify some of the complexities and regional variations of relations to land and class structure in contemporary Botswana.[9] The division within this group of large cattle owners appears here at two important junctures. It appears first in the ambivalent relationships with the actual and imagined past contested by the participants in the "local moment" described previously. In recalling and rearranging such communal history, the powerless herders and farm workers elect to include affluent herd owners who originate from the regional large villages as "ward headmen," while excluding and delegitimizing the claims for leadership by those who came from Serowe, the remote precolonial ruling capital center. Such internal division within the group of affluent cattle owners is also expressed in a powerful way when the rich cattle owners from Serowe use one sub-land board to represent their objection to the emerging village while the locally based cattle owners support another. The Bobonong Sub-Land Board made a point of defending the aspiration of the villagers to permanent arable land use, while the Maunatlala Sub-Land Board manipulated by the affluent Serowe people, dragged its feet on the issue, awaiting the Ngwato Land

Board decision. The heavy-handed political maneuvering of these official bodies by the powerful elite encroaching from the district center underscores the fact that the events within this little marginal village was a focus, the local arena where larger processes of regional and national scope intersected.

The second critical element in the Gamotse scenario is the vicinity of the emerging village to the white-owned Tuli Block Farms and the South African border. The emergence of this small settled community is closely linked to the labor needs of these capital-intensive private farms. The owners of the "Smith farm," as we have seen, provided employment for a growing number of people in the settlement, supplied clean drinking water, and encouraged the building of a clinic and a local school. But toward the early 1980s, such voluntary acts of goodwill could not keep up with the growing needs of the expanding settlement. In a series of letters, the owners of "Smith Farm" requested that the District Council "take over the supply of water to the village," because "the responsibility of such a large number of families is now getting beyond our small resources."[10] To support his argument that the village should be officially recognized (and not "transferred" en masse to the neighboring settlement), the district officer insisted that such a valued source of employment, "blessed by the Government," should not be disrupted. The dependence of these rural poor on rare private employment opportunities was unquestionable.

The third important element in the formation of this community is the varied makeup of its populace. These poor herders and clients of large cattle owners who made their home in this emerging village originated from various "ethnic" or "tribal" groups. Many belonged to the various totemic groups collectively known, as the discussion in the previous two chapters has shown, as "Batswapong." Others, especially those herding cattle of the Serowe cattle owners, are locally known as "Basarwa" (the Tswana term for Bushmen). A third category of people in this border marginal community is made up of what Molefe, the district officer, calls "foreign nationals." Many of these foreign nationals—people who are technically not citizens of Botswana—are of Tswana origin. They belong to Tswana communities within South Africa. Others, like Mpho, the populist village headman of Gamotse, are South African citizens who belong to other ethnic groups of non-Tswana origin, such as Ndebele or Xhosa.

Although international borders were set in 1966 when Botswana gained its political independence, the rate of migration and the labor needs in the border zones between Botswana and South Africa structured a reality of movement of people across these international borders in both directions. But when this marginal community was to be officially recognized, those defined as "foreign nationals" were constituted as "undesirable elements" who, as Molefe suggested in his report, "should be repatriated to their countries of origin." National citizenship became a criterion for inclusion in the emerging community only when the state reiterated its control over this marginal periphery.

The position of those known as Basarwa in the emerging community was also in flux. The position of Basarwa at the bottom of the hierarchical Tswana social world was powerfully articulated by the Tswapong elders in their oral interviews with the University of Botswana students discussed in Chapter 4. We have seen how the category "Basarwa" is used as an idiom for lack of civil rights within contemporary indigenous discourse. In the next chapter we shall explore in more depth the social process of exclusion of these Basarwa along gender and class lines. This internally complex composition along ethnic, citizenship, and social lines within both categories— the cattle owners and the arable farmers—calls into question any facile analysis that posits rural struggles between two prepostulated groups for narrow material interests. The specific dynamics of this case and the multiple struggles at its core are not mere replica of rural conflicts elsewhere in the country, but a set of shifting social relations that have emerged and are transformed in these specific historical conditions. In these specific settings, why was one set of hierarchies (along ethnic and class lines) openly resisted while another (along gender and clientship) not tackled? What kind of resistance is allowed and what alliances are forged to achieve hoped-for social changes? Before addressing these questions it is instructive to turn to the evolving pattern of social arrangements in Gamotse a decade after the events described previously took place.

THE NEW GAMOTSE, 1983–1993

In a course of the decade between 1983 and 1993, the local population of Gamotse more than doubled.[11] Its public social infrastructure also expanded impressively. In 1993, the local elementary school, once a single mud room, boasted several cement block class and office rooms where thirteen teachers offered a complete elementary school education for the growing community. Two pink painted cement block rooms, built by the local Village Development Committee (VDC), were rented out to school teachers and to a resident nurse. There was also a large store, a butchery, and a bar. The houses, many still made of mud and thatch roofs, were square and not round. The settlement included several long straight lines of square houses, simulating modern streets instead of the more common maze of interconnected paths around a central public arena. The feeling conveyed is that there has been a special effort to construct a "modern" community with whatever limited resources were at hand.

Re tabolotse, we have developed, evolved," declared chief Bonolo Mafoko, the village headman, who, since 1988, has been paid by the government for his duties. The nephew of Rrapodi, the old Serowe man who struggled for headmanship in 1983, Mafoko was born in Serowe but spent much of his childhood herding cattle in Gamotse, which had been his father's cattle post since 1907. He took over the headmanship from his uncle in 1986, because the old man, as Mafoko explained, "could not read" and had an increasingly hard time dealing with government officials and forms. And what of Mpho, the populist contender to the village leadership in 1983? When his popular support threatened Rrapodi,[12] the old Serowe man arranged for the younger populist leader to be arrested for illegal residence in the country. The younger man spent six months in jail in 1985 and had not been heard from since. From his office adjacent to the central *kgotla* arena, the officially nominated and paid Mafoko administered the *kgotla* court proceedings aided by two stationed policemen and a young national service *(tirelo sechaba)* woman.

Most interesting was the structure of the village wards the new village headman outlined in 1993. In this account, the village contained four wards *(kgotlana)*. The largest ward, named Bolomba, was composed of all the people who were "from South Africa."[13] It had no ward chief. As the village headman, Mafoko explained, he was the head of this large ward. The second ward was named RaMerry, after a known ward in the village of Serowe. The headmen for this ward were two affluent Ngwato men from Serowe who used Gamotse as one of their cattle posts. The ward was made up of "their people," mostly Basarwa herders.[14] The other two wards, much smaller in size and with no coherent internal composition, were named Maaloso and New Town. Both are names of existing wards in Serowe, the Ngwato capital town. While the members of these wards were people of various origin, including Babirwa, Batswapong, Bakalanga, and Bangwato, they were all considered to be—unlike the people who made up the two wards described previously—"Batswana." The headmen of these two wards, both absent from the village, originated from the district capital, Serowe.

This depiction of political units within the now established village is significantly different from the one "dreamed up" by the Gamotse residents in 1983. The structure of relations in Gamotse, described by the new headman in 1993 was characterized by: (1) a new division of the resident population into wards that distinguished non-Batswana citizens from "Batswana," and between Basarwa and "proper Batswana" groups and (2) a systematic appointment of Ngwato men from Serowe as heads of all named ward units in the village. This change is particularly significant when one recalls that the model of group relations constructed by the Gamotse residents in 1983 had no place for the Serowe people as ward heads and resisted the claims by the Serowe cattle owners to village leadership. In the process of crafting their communal identity the Gamotse villagers depicted a "Lerala ward" and a "Bobonong ward," thus linking local herd owners to segments of the emerging community. The internal tension between the local elite and the one emanating from Serowe—evident in 1983 when the two sub land boards came to represent the two camps—was apparently resolved in the Gamotse case in favor of the Serowe originating group. Serowe cattle owners, mostly absent from the local scene, were now placed as heads of all newly created ward units. The local elite emanating from the large villages in the area (Lerala, Bobonong, and Maunatlala) was nowhere to be found in this new arrangement. Most significant was the redefined position of village headmanship. The foreign-born populist leader, effectively excluded from the village arena by the state, had been replaced by the Serowe affluent cattle owner Rrapodi, who stepped down a few years later so his young, better educated nephew could take the post, a position now paid by the state.

ON HISTORY, THE LIMITS (AND POTENTIAL) OF RESISTANCE, AND THE RE-CREATION OF THE MALE-CENTERED DOMAIN

What are we to make of these recent developments? Is this a not-so-surprising outcome of the all-pervasive power of the state to silence shortlived "bubbling" from below? Do we have here yet another, less-than-dramatic scenario of a dominant power crushing and effectively dismantling limited, fledgling attempts at counter-hegemonic discourse and action? And why should we concern ourselves with the minutiae, grubby details of this one marginal case? The questions I am posing here are not as provocative as they might sound at a first reading; they are directly linked, in fact, to the key theoretical and analytical issues I have raised in my short introductory section. What do we learn about the nature of power from the study of local resistance? How can such detailed examination of one settlement contribute to our understanding of larger frames of time and space? And how can a feminist perspective be applied to a setting that never directly articulates gender-based hierarchies?

Let us return for a moment to the Gamotse case and offer a short summary of the analysis developed so far, which began with an examination of a single critical event. In this "diagnostic event" (Moore 1987), people were actively engaged in the process of "inventing themselves" by exploiting the ambiguities and contradictions of a traditionalist dominant discourse that defines Tswana "custom." In the community that is imagined, impoverished herders, former serfs, and wanderers who crossed international boundaries are part of a new entity with well-defined claims to land and locally respected leaders. I have outlined how the construction of such a possible future was intimately implicated with an imagined and actual past and argued that, while recalling and partially appropriating elements of dominant patterns of history and community, these marginal people had in fact articulated a challenge to existing patterns of hierarchy and the social arrangements it sanctioned. Specifically, in the course of this fleeting, if critical, moment of encounter with structures of domination, people tried to redefine the role of village headmanship, challenged a political ideology that classified them as "bush" people, and presented their claims to arable land in the vicinity of their growing settlement.

But such process of "explicit cultural debate" (Parkin 1978) and the contest over the meaning of received social categories and positions unfolded in a field of unequal power relations. In placing this analysis of discursive construction and struggle in the context of the political economy within which it unfolded, I was able to examine both the potential for creative play and the constraint on such budding discourse of resistance. Indeed, as Corrigan and Sayer (1985) observe, the power of the state in this and other cases rests not so much on coercion or through the use of its police, courts, or armies, but rather with official routines of licensing and registering procedures that define and legitimize certain kinds of subjects and identities while ruling out other kinds of identities and social practice. As we have seen, these former serfs and impoverished farm workers actively sought the official recognition of their settled life, and in imagining their future, they fashioned a community and identity defined within such dominant images and terms.

Why had these marginalized people adopted such dominant patterns of subjectivity and identity to express their hopes for the future? And how had such dominant patterns limited the kinds of subjectivity they could imagine? In an insightful examination of Gramsci's work on such inherent tension between domination and resistance, Roseberry (1996:81) argues that the "forms and languages of protest or resistance *must* adopt the forms and languages of domination in order to be registered or heard," and that resistance is always shaped by "the process, terms, and condition of domination" (1996:81, his emphasis). In Gamotse, the dominant discourse certainly established the form and limits of the "language of resistance," but it has also made clear the fragility and contingent nature of such forms of domination. The explicit use of ridicule and mimicry succeeded in exposing the internal contradictory nature of dominant "traditionalist" discourses and brought to the surface what Scott (1990) described as "the critical gap" between *understanding* the ideology of those in power and *accepting* it.

In fact, what makes the moment in early 1983 more interesting is not that it was an expression of a seamless, coherent discourse of resistance, but rather because of the evidence it provides of the *possibility* of subsuming and going beyond such internal divisions. In that specific moment of their history, these marginalized people had, in fact, forged an alliance, however fleeting and fragile, that bridged beyond their internal divisions by citizenship, ethnicity, *and gender*. Recall that women were the majority of those present in the public meeting and that they made their objection to the Ngwato headman's claims to leadership clear via "non-discursive" means, their loud "aa . . . aa" calls. Their act of support for the populist leader and their support of the idea of creating a settled community challenged traditionalist frameworks and enabled them to position themselves within the very systems that excluded them. The ambivalent relationship of women to the established traditionalist male-centered Tswana discourses of history and community did not mean in this case a rejection of accepted gender hierarchies. An understanding of these "complex conversions between exclusion and empowerment" (Tsing 1994:280) is key to grasping the nature of this moment of collective struggle.

Let us now return to the unresolved question of understanding the 1993 reality. If indeed one accepts the general premise of the analysis offered here—that in the early 1980s we witnessed a dynamic, emergent moment of resistance and social creativity in this, and perhaps other rural areas in Botswana—the question then becomes: how far can such marginal processes of "creative imagination" go in opposing the fundamental power vested in the modern nation-state? More generally, how effective are such miniature, delicate modes of resistance in altering the fundamentally antagonistic class and gender forces in contemporary societies? In Gamotse, as the stark reality of the 1990s suggests, the incomplete moment of "rebellion," and the long process of subversive acts of communal construction that preceded it, had little success in the long run. Not only was the populist leader effectively excluded from the community and the support for local elites undermined, but internal divisions along citizenship, ethnic, client/class, and gender lines within the emerging community have been effectively reconstituted.

Roseberry, Abu-Lughod, Tsing, and others have seen the value of examining such local moments of resistance not as an indication for the growing freedom of these people but as a useful tool for understanding the way domination is established. Taking my lead from them, I propose that the Gamotse people probably had not profoundly altered the conditions and structures of domination they sought to redefine. What they had succeeded in doing was to reimagine—even for a brief and fleeting moment—a different, new way of being in the world. They had a vision of a future where familiar social divisions and categories of cultural difference are repositioned and rearranged. Perhaps what was at stake in this liminal moment was the awareness it provided—for the marginalized actors and the scholar who attempts to comprehend their actions—of the limits of hegemonic power and the power of subtle social imagination. For the very expression of such alternative, counter-hegemonic vision of subjectivity draws our attention to the tensions that are always there between hegemonic constructions of reality and the stubborn hope for potential change. It makes us aware that categories of power and social imagination are engaged in a continual process of renegotiation and that, ultimately, social categories are inherently unstable.

This parochial story of the transformation of a marginal cattle post community into a permanent village is also suggestive about the wider historical context of the changing relation of people to land and the larger process of nation building in Botswana. It provides a detailed example of the complex, at times contradictory, ways in which the modern nation-state interacts with groups in its rural periphery. While government reforms in Botswana sought to dissolve "traditional" institutions by creating land boards, they also permitted and unwittingly encouraged the rise of a new type of local leadership. Since defined leadership has become the primary marker of group cohesion in these changed contexts, group relations and the local political scene have taken on new meaning. In the early 1980s, a greater uncertainty in the aftermath of the national land reform empowered local people to explore, challenge, and reinvent identities and question existing patterns of social hierarchy. But these shifts and manipulation of meaning, tradition, and history were greatly limited a decade later, when local chiefs were paid, and more tangible resources (land, water, schools, and clinics) were allocated by the state. Attention to the specific divisions within the regional political economy and to the complex positioning of individuals and groups in the grid of networks of clientship, ethnic-cum-political affiliation, and citizenship requires that we acknowledge that the effects of uniform policies enacted by the nation-state cannot be predicted from a simple formula. Instead, the analysis of the formation of this one marginal community forces us to attend to the important conjuncture of power, history, and socioeconomic structures in specific historically contingent circumstances. Collective identities and subjectivities, as the next chapter illustrates, are mutually constituted at the crossroads of gender, class, and sociocultural divisions.

NOTES

1. I borrow this phrase from Anna Lowenhaupt Tsing (1994).

2. Gamotse is a name I had given to the village. Unlike all other names of places and people cited in this book, I felt that the case of Gamotse contains sensitive information that might be used against some people, and I thus opted to conceal the identity of people and the name of their village. All names, but that of Mr. Molefe, are not the real names of people I met.

3. Within the large Central District in 1982, Gamotse was one of six recorded cases (in the Ngwato Land Board files) of emerging communities struggling to gain official recognition of their permanent settlement status. Several unpublished reports by officials sent to examine such local cases pointed to the ambivalence of these situations. As one report phrased it, people "are confused as to whether the village is a cattle post or what." Another official record made explicit the fears of local people directly affected by the establishment of commercial, enclosed farms and ranches that "the ranches would leave them a small area for fields" (Ngwato Land Board 119/82).

4. Molefe sent a copy of his report to Smith with the note, "Please receive two copies which I prepared to fight your case. You are not to worry. All is well." I would like to thank "Mr. Smith" for making this correspondence available to me in 1993.

5. The Tuli Blocks are privately owned farms that lie in the eastern ridge of Botswana along its border with South Africa. The emergence of these farms as private, rather than communally held, land is a result of specific historical developments in the region.

6. In his letter cited earlier, Mr. Molefe refers to these people as "foreign nationals."

7. "Motswana" refers to a person of Tswana origin. *Mo* is a prefix for singular, *Ba* for plural. Thus Batswana are people of Tswana origin. Setswana is the language.

8. Both Gulbrandsen (1984:5) and Werbner make this point. In Werbner's words, there is "a major conceptual as well as practical change in land tenure" (1982:vii).

9. The Gamotse case is suggestive of similar processes that involve internal conflict between the local elite at the periphery and that encroaching from the centers of power of the district (cf. Holm 1989, Parson 1981, Picard 1987, Werbner 1991).

10. Letter dated August 20, 1984 to the District Council in Serowe.

11. The 1981 census recorded 269 residents. The 1992 population census cites 676.

12. As the installed chief of Gamotse put it in a May 6, 1993, interview, the "populist leader" was doing some jobs for Rrapodi, but then people came to old Rrapodi and told him that "this man," (our "populist leader") *o rata stilo,*—literally, "he likes the chair," the position of power. Rrapodi replied: *ga obatla stilo, boela ko ga eno,* "if he likes to rule, [he should] go to his own people."

13. Gamotse's proximity to the South African border and its large population of "foreign nationals" give an excellent insight into questions of forging a national identity in Botswana. The issue of "transnationalism" on this border, especially in the post-apartheid era deserves a more thorough exploration. The relegation of these people to a single ward placed under the direct supervision of a nominated headman and without their own representation attests to Botswana's ambivalent way of dealing with such people in spite of its claims of building a "plural society." The position of these "foreign nationals" as embodied in the fate of the aspiring headman drastically changed over this decade from one of a hope of integration into new communities to one of ambivalence or direct exclusion. Molefe, the district officer, has no problem suggesting that "foreign nationals should be repatriated to their countries of origin" and in defining these people as "undesirable elements." Clearly more work should be done on this subject in ways that problematize the liberal rhetoric of the process of nation building in Botswana.

14. These Basarwa herders, the village chief insisted, plough land and live in houses like everybody else. This point is taken up in greater detail in Chapter 7.

7

Ethnicizing Gender, Engendering the Ethnic Other

Sarwa are still considered inferior to other members of the tribe, who deem it degrading, for instance to intermarry with them.
Isaac Schapera, *The Tswana*

I am a Mosarwa, because my mother is a Mosarwa.
A woman in Tamasane village, July 1993

This chapter investigates the process of production of social difference and hierarchy at the intersection of cultural, socioeconomic, and gender representations and experience. It maps out some of the ways in which a group of women, residents of an established Tswana village, who speak nothing but Setswana and who, to the outsider, look no different from their poor neighbors, come to be known as "Basarwa." Their designation as Basarwa meant that these women and their children have been excluded from access to social networks, legal protection, and economic resources. Sarwa women were marginalized, and their social and economic exclusion was reproduced from one generation to the next. The first part of this chapter explores the shape this process took in the 1980s when I first encountered the Tamasane Basarwa. It lays out the historical process that has produced the social category "Basarwa" and the way in which this marginal positioning was experienced and re-created almost two decades after the establishment of the democratic state. The second part of the chapter investigates how these same women have challenged their marginal position by adopting discursive frameworks provided them by more recent official rhetoric of equality.

In the early 1990s, these women had drawn on the inherent contradictions in the Tswana social order to redefine their position in the community. An analysis of the mix of discursive frameworks intersecting at that historical moment helps us understand the social position the women occupied, negotiated, and resisted.

THE SETTING

Tamasane, laying east of the rail line in the northern regions of the Tswapong hills area, resembled its neighboring small villages of the early 1980s with its new school, small general store, and a central *kgotla* arena where public meetings were held. However, unlike the ethnic composition of other Tswapong villages, and due to unique historical circumstances, the village population included a large number of affluent, cattle-holding people of Ngwato origin, a large presence of people of Kalanga origin, and a smaller group of Basarwa.[1] In fact, until the late 1950s, Tamasane was a cattle post area where Ngwato cattle owners kept their herds. It had evolved into a permanent village residence with public amenities and services only toward independence in the mid-1960s. In the early 1980s, when I first came to Tamasane to record its local history, I learned that a group of Basarwa lived permanently in the village. For six intensive weeks and in more sporadic visits throughout my work in the Tswapong region during 1983, I recorded the life stories of these Basarwa women, who headed their own extremely poor households. My analysis of the social profiles of these locally known Basarwa households shows, however, that a good number of them have no traceable genealogical Sarwa heritage. In fact, the oldest woman who reported that she was brought to Tamasane by a Ngwato family at the turn of the century assured me she speaks no "Sesarwa," the Setswana collective label for the varied languages spoken by those known as Basarwa. In their language, dress, physical features, or any other criteria, these poor women and their children were indistinguishable from others in the village. Yet their lives had been dramatically and adversely affected by their Basarwa identity. They told me how Tswana men refused to acknowledge the children they fathered with them, that their sons were not paid according to local standards for their herding services because "they say we are Basarwa," and that their brothers and fathers did not support them and were not able to represent them in the local *kgotla* court because most of them disappear into the bush, unable to accumulate enough to establish a household in the village arena.

The next segment of this chapter explores the mechanisms of exclusion. It examines the ways in which those designated Basarwa have been systematically cut out from social networks of support and how their extreme poverty and social marginality have been reproduced from one generation to the next. Tracing the life histories of three generations of those known as

Basarwa and placing these stories in the larger political economy of shifting Sarwa-Ngwato relations I shall examine how—despite the rhetoric of equality in postindependent, democratic Botswana—the social stigma associated with Sarwa identity has continued to structure the effective social, political, and economic marginalization of Basarwa in Tamasane.

Ethnicity and Class in Historical Perspectives

Tamasane village is located in the northeast corner of the Tswapong region in the Central District (Map 7.1). The 1981 census recorded 692 persons belonging to 106 residential units in the village. Internally, villagers divided themselves into members of four named wards: three were known as Kalanga wards[2] and one, *kgosing* (chiefly), was a Ngwato ward. In 1983 I recorded forty-four households in the Ngwato ward: three households were of "royal" Ngwato origin, twenty-one of "commoner" Ngwato origin, six households were known as Tswapong, two Herero, one Kwena, and eleven Sarwa.

It is important to note here that these ethnic labels were used by the people to describe themselves in all but the Sarwa case. As we shall see in this chapter, all those known in the community as Basarwa did their best to escape such designation. The particular history of the relations between the royal Ngwato and those designated Sarwa in Tamasane must be situated within the larger history of group relations in the region.

Briefly, the area of today's Central District corresponds to the territory of the precolonial Ngwato kingdom. The nineteenth century Ngwato kingdom was ruled by a Ngwato king, or *kgosi,* and a "royal" core group of his agnates. Members of the Ngwato lineage who were not related to the king were known as "Ngwato commoners," people of other "Tswana proper" stock, like the Bakwena or Bangwaketse, who resided in the Ngwato territory were full citizens. Non-Tswana groups of Kalanga, Herero, or Tswapong origin paid some tribute to the Ngwato king but maintained a large measure of local political and cultural autonomy. At the bottom of the stratified state system stood the *malata* or *balala,* vassals or serfs of Kgalagadi and Bushmen origin. Schapera (1930, 1952) describes the position of this *malata* underclass in the late nineteenth century as one of absolute dependency and exploitation. Serfs had no property or legal rights. They could be transferred at will by their masters, and their children were from birth "hereditary servants." Many Sarwa serfs worked as herders and lived all their lives in remote cattle posts herding the cattle of their masters. Others were domestic servants in affluent Ngwato households.

Tamasane was, since the early 1900s, one of a series of cattle posts belonging to an influential Ngwato family, the Ratshosas. The first generation Basarwa in the three-generation unit I traced in 1983 had been themselves hereditary servants of the Ratshosas. In tracing the transforming

MAP 7.1   Republic of Botswana

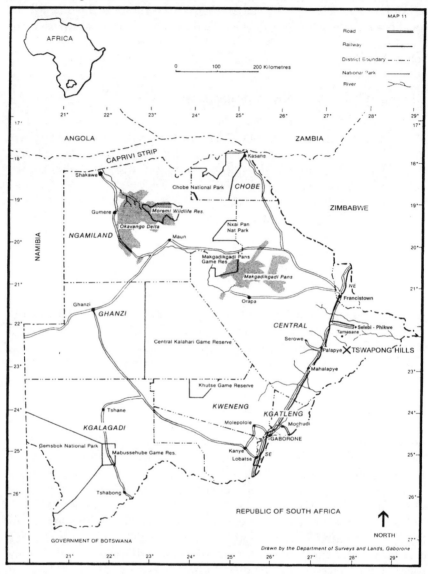

relationship between the progeny of these 1920 Sarwa servants with their former masters and the changing composition of the village that formed around them by the early 1980s, I hope to illustrate how the dominant discourse regarding Sarwa identity had been reproduced and altered as colonial reserves became regions in an independent bureaucratic state.

The Tamasane cattle post was given to Bessie, the oldest daughter of Khama, ruler of the Ngwato, around the turn of the century. Her husband, Ratshosa, was Khama's closest advisor and a powerful man in the royal elite. In 1926, after a prolonged power struggle between the three sons of Ratshosa and Tshekedi, the chief-regent, the cattle of the Ratshosas located in Tamasane were sold, their herders, including many Basarwa, were kept by Tshekedi, and their houses in the village were set on fire. Protesting these drastic measures taken by Tshekedi, one of the Ratshosa brothers, Simon Ratshosa, an educated outspoken man, opened a series of legal cases in which he demanded the restitution of and compensation for this confiscated property.[3] Throughout these court cases and also in letters sent to the press Simon Ratshosa made the allegation that "the Masarwa became slaves" in the Protectorate. Public opinion in Great Britain at the time and, no doubt, Simon Ratshosa's talent at publicity led the administration to intervene directly in this case and launch a series of official inquiries into "slavery" in the Bechuanaland Protectorate. Tshekedi's efforts to respond to these British official reports, which pushed for a general emancipation of all Basarwa, were unsuccessful.[4] When the High Commissioner, Lord Athlone, announced in Serowe in 1927 the official emancipation of all Sarwa serfs, Tshekedi followed suit by freeing only those Basarwa owned by his enemies, the Ratshosas. Tshekedi explained his act, saying:

After Johnny had left this reserve in February 1927, I removed all my people who were in Johnny's, Simon's and Obeditse's cattle post in my reserve who were *not paid servants*, because I could not have *my people* serving them when they had quarreled with me.[5] (emphasis added)

What was the fate of the freed Tamasane Basarwa who were caught in the midst of this affair involving the most powerful men in the polity, the British Administration, and eventually the League of Nations? While at the center of public attention, the Basarwa had no public voice of their own. The court proceedings do not contain any testimony given directly by a Mosarwa herder. We do learn, however, from a Mongwato man named Segoabe, who was questioned by the court, that the regiment sent by Tshekedi collected all of Ratshosa's cattle and paid herders and that "with them were also brought the Mosarwa [sic] herdboys." About a dozen Tswana-sounding names are then listed; all named people are said to be Basarwa. The same Mr. Segoabe also added later that "[t]he Masarwa I have mentioned were brought to Tamasane and were also brought into

Serowe with us. . . . They have not gone back to the cattle post at Shashi." Little else is known about these people. An understanding of the economic and political circumstances of the time when these people were "freed" can fill in the gap.[6]

Throughout the 1930s, and despite Khama's reforms of the late nineteenth century, most Basarwa received no pay and stood largely outside the money economy of the Protectorate. By the late 1920s, scarce employment opportunities in the Protectorate and dwindling hunting grounds turned many of the freed Basarwa into stock thieves. British officials soon changed their rhetoric and what was initially viewed as a growing "spirit of independence on the part of the subservient tribes" was presented, by the mid-1930s, as a "problem" of "disorderly and truculent" Basarwa.[7] Indeed, as Wylie (1990) suggests, regardless of British rhetoric of emancipation, conditions in the Protectorate had, in effect, limited the options of those "freed" servants. While a few, like the Basarwa of Tati, were able to settle in their own villages and maintain a measure of independence by plowing their own fields and securing some access to paid jobs by migration, most freed Basarwa were forced to reenter some relations of patronage with Tswana herd owners.

By the late 1930s, the nature of these patron-client relations were rapidly changing. As more Batswana found employment in South African mines, and many began to send their sons to school, a new labor shortage emerged among the less affluent who had not used Sarwa services in the past. Basarwa were sought after in these new conditions, not only as herders but also as contractual workers to cultivate fields and as domestic servants. In the increasingly commercial economy of cattle rearing, herd owners found it more profitable to pay individual herders than to serve as patrons for entire families.[8] The cumulative outcome of these changes has been a dramatic worsening of the Sarwa condition. Basarwa clients were subject to increasing demands. At the same time, their few rewards as hereditary clients—usufruct right to land and access to the meat and milk of the cattle they herded—were undermined.

Let us now return to the Tamasane case. By the early 1930s, when a new core of Ngwato residence was reestablished in Tamasane, several dozen Sarwa families also established residence there. In 1928 Tshekedi sent a group of Kalanga to settle in the deserted cattle post. Soon after, Ntebogang, the Ngwaketse royal and second wife of Ratshosa, who was not involved in the dispute with Tshekedi, received many of the cattle left behind by the regiment (BNA file 173:110f). Sarwa herders and domestic servants were in need again. In 1945 this core of Ngwato residents was expanded when other members of the Ratshosa family were allowed to leave their exile in Francistown. At independence in 1966, Tamasane was officially recognized as a settled village with prescribed rights to state development resources such as schools and piped water.

In essence, then, the transformation of Sarwa-Ngwato relations, which had begun prior to the 1920s, must be seen as a historical movement from one sociocultural formation to another. The shifting definition of the Basarwa within the dominant structures of relations of production in this historical moment from that of hereditary servants to free contract workers was marked by a radical alteration in the dominant political ideology in the country. The new, democratic, independent state dissociated itself from the ideological underpinnings of the colonial order within which clientship and tribal affiliations were defined. As colonial "reserves" were transformed into administrative districts, an egalitarian ideology was stressed. Yet, the official ethos of equality did not lead to an immediate change in people's perceptions, nor did it shape their actions and the institutional contexts within which the Sarwa category was defined. While the destruction of the customary relations of clientship and growing commercialization had clearly been underway prior to independence, the state now imparted legitimacy to this process of transformation. This, ironically, facilitated the growing polarization in the community and a hierarchy of social relations predicated on the distinction between "Sarwa" and "Tswana."

To understand the continual social, political, and economic marginality of the Sarwa category within Tswana society over more than a century, we must examine the way a set of ideas about Sarwa identity have interacted with the political economy within which these ideas were expressed. I argue that throughout the last century, and in spite of profound changes in the Tswana political economy—absorption into the regional labor market, a significant alteration in the agricultural base, and an increasing commercialization in a capitalist economy—Tswana cultural definition of the Sarwa category has continued to structure the marginality of the group. It is to this Tswana discourse regarding Sarwa identity and its role in structuring relations between the groups that we now must turn.

TSWANA DOMINANT DISCOURSE AND SARWA IDENTITY

The image of Sarwa people in Tswana discourse has some resemblance to their image in European discourse. Without access to dominant discourses themselves, Basarwa became an object, the "others" for both Europeans and the Tswana.[9] In both cases the Bushmen as "others" were associated with nature and low status. To understand the significance of the nature or wild concepts in Tswana society and the position of the Basarwa associated with the nonsocial realm, one must consider the symbolic map of Tswana cosmology and the sociopolitical order within which it is embedded.

At the core of Tswana symbolic order is the distinction between the social, public, male-centered village (*motse*) domain and the wild, natural, unbounded sphere of animal and asocial beings (*naga*) (Comaroff 1984, Schapera 1938a, Silberbauer 1981). This distinction is expressed in the socio-spatial organization of the Tswana settlement and has important political and economic implications. The emergence of this socio-spatial and symbolic order is closely connected to the rise of the Tswana polities (*merafe*) in the nineteenth century reviewed in Chapter 4. Here I would like to trace the lines that link this nineteenth century socio-spatial order to contemporary ideas of clustered village residence, village internal political organization, and the position of Sarwa men and women within Tswana village order.

Nineteenth century Tswana polities centered on the apical office of the chief who resided in a large capital settlement. Residence in these chiefly towns was a sign of one's citizenship in the polity. Members of politically subordinate groups resided in their own smaller outlying centers. This placement in the town was contrasted with the nomadism of the Basarwa who lacked a permanent home and "moved around the bush." In this, Basarwa were similar to wild animals (*diphologolo*) and were excluded from the social realm of government, court, and popular assembly (*kgotla*) centered in the town. An acute observer of this socio-spatial order and its political implications, Mackenzie (1871:368) noted: "It is the mark of freeman to have a residence in the town, while the vassals are doomed always to live in the open country." When brought into the village political center, Basarwa were deprived of any social status. They were domestic servants in the houses of Tswana citizens, an attachment described to this day in terms of social immaturity: they are the "children" of the Tswana head. Their physical presence did not entail social participation or representation in the body politic.

Sarwa marginality was not confined to the symbolic and socio-spatial realms but was deeply embedded in the sociopolitical sphere. Tswana social order was explicitly hierarchical, and inequality was central in both secular and sacred worlds. Another nineteenth-century observer (Smith 1975[1834]:25–26, cited by Peters 1983a:101–102) described this hierarchical order in the following way:

Nearly every tribe is found to consist of three distinct classes of persons. First, the wealthy class. Second, a portion of the poorer class disposed to reside with and serve the former, and third. . . the detached pauper population of the tribe.

The final category, he explained, were termed Bushmen by early Dutch settlers "as indicative of their being men living amongst the bushes."[10] Toward the end of the nineteenth century, this "detached pauper population" composed of Basarwa and other subjugated groups became a vital economic element to Tswana monarchs engaged in consolidating their power and wealth. As Goold-Adams (cited in Chirenje 1978:42) explained in 1899: "It is a well-known fact that the Masarwa are necessary to herd the cattle and collect skins, feathers—the latter forming (an important) income of the chief and his headmen."

Over the past century there have been fundamental changes in the political and social dimensions of this nineteenth-century reality. But, as we shall see later in this chapter, despite some official rhetoric of equality that produced a series of largely ineffective policies, the marginality of the Basarwa within the Tswana social order remains distinctive. In 1971 Bessie Head placed the outcast position of the Basarwa in Tswana society at the center of her moving short novel *Maru*.[11] The story of a Mosarwa girl, adopted by a white woman, who faces prejudice and humiliation once her Sarwa origin is known, enables a sensitive exploration of contemporary Tswana cultural construction of the Sarwa as the despised Other. When love between the Mosarwa woman and the Tswana chief's son (who "still own[s] the Masarwa as slaves" [1971:59]) triumphs over the deep social divide, "a wind of freedom" enters the "small, dark airless room" that enclosed the Sarwa community (1971:126).

In Bessie Head's powerful prose "the horror of being an oddity of the human race, with half the head of a man and half the body of a donkey" comes to an end when the "wind of freedom" reaches the Basarwa of Botswana (1971:126). In her visionary future "it would be no longer possible to treat Masarwa people in an inhuman way" (1971:127). But Head's vision and her allegiance to the Bushmen/Sarwa cause have little parallel in public discourse in Botswana.[12] While some recent works by Tswana scholars (Datta and Murray 1989, Molutsi 1986, Moutle 1986) have begun to examine the historical and political implications of the position of minorities (including Basarwa) in Tswana society, most depictions of "the Bushmen experience" remain ethnographic. Ethnographic studies of the 1980s and 1990s (Barnes 1980, Hitchcock 1988, Motzafi-Haller 2001, Russell 1976, Solway 1980, Solway and Lee 1990:120) echo Schapera's observation made in the late 1920s that Basarwa are "despised" by their Tswana neighbors. In my work in the Tswapong region in 1980 and 1993, I came to learn that the term "Sarwa" was often used not as an ethnic label to refer to people of Sarwa origin but as an insult.[13] For example, in describing their humiliation by their Ngwato rulers, Tswapong people say they were treated *fela jaaka Mosarwa*—"simply like Basarwa" (Kiyaga-Mulindwa 1980:195, Motzafi-Haller 1993). The Sarwa idiom was also used to indicate the lack of any social standing or claim to political rights. In an interview in 1979,[14] a Motswapong man expressed his frustration with the current practice in Botswana whereby, "anybody can become chief, irrespective of birth." The man objected to what he viewed as the potentially absurd outcome of such practice—"I would not be ruled by a Mosarwa," that is, by a person of no publicly recognized rights to rule.

Basarwa continue to be associated with nature and the wild, uncontrolled bush. While their association with nature entails that Sarwa healers are said to be extremely effective and thus sought after by many powerful Tswana men, it also defines their exclusion from the Tswana social sphere. Thus, the

(Setswana) expression *motho wa naga*, which translates "a man of the bush, the wild," was an extreme insult. People who lived permanently in the dispersed agricultural and grazing zone outside the clustered village were ridiculed as "uncivilized."[15]

In Tamasane, Sarwa identity was so despised that it was a downright insult to openly ask a person (known in the community as a Mosarwa), "Are you a Mosarwa?" Such identity was almost always attributed by others and rejected whenever possible by its bearers. Reluctant interviewees were repeatedly assured by the Mongwato royal who acted as my host:[16] *Mosarwa ke motho*, "a Mosarwa is a person, a human being." Yet ambiguity and contradiction permeated this contemporary Tswana discourse. An old, educated Mokalanga man who had been a teacher in the 1930s described the situation of the Tamasane Sarwa in the following way:

There were a lot of Basarwa who were *badisa* (herders). They are inter-mixed but not married. A Mongwato man will take a Mosarwa woman and the children will be only *badisa* [herders]. But since the *nako ya gompieno* [the present times] of Seretse [Khama, the first president of Botswana], there are cases of real marriage. They are Bangwato—but one can still say who is a Mosarwa and who is a Mongwato.[17]

It is this complex and dynamic mix of codes of "proper speaking" and social practice that I seek to analyze here. Why are children born to Sarwa mothers and Ngwato men made to be permanent herders, *badisa?* What are the social implications of considering Sarwa women nonmarriageable? And how has the changing Tswana discourse regarding Sarwa identity structured relations between the groups in the past century? A synthetic work that poses these questions as part of a larger exploration of the transforming relations between Tswana cultural codes and social reality is still lacking.

Here I examine such interaction of cultural codes and social practice in one local setting in contemporary Botswana. My focus is on the relations between two particular forms of Tswana-Sarwa relations—relations between the genders and those pertaining to work contracts—and on how, predicated within the dynamics of the household developmental cycle, this interaction reproduces Sarwa marginality. Sarwa women, as the cases that follow demonstrate, continue to be viewed as nonmarriageable by Tswana men.[18] Supported by social convention, these men dissociate themselves from any social or material responsibility toward these women and the children they father with them. Contract agreements between two individuals, such as the herding services of a youth or keeping a beast in one's herd until a later date, are not respected when one of the sides is a Mosarwa. In both cases Basarwa are not treated as full social persons with rights and obligations that such standing entails.

SARWA WOMEN AND THE DEVELOPMENTAL
CYCLE OF HOUSEHOLDS

Consider the following facts: Among the nineteen adult childbearing women in the eleven Sarwa households in Tamasane, only eleven women were able to point out the fathers of their children. None of the men was a Ngwato royal or commoner man. Four were Kalanga, one was Zulu, one Herero, one Morotsi, one Zezeru, one Kgalagadi, and two Tswapong. The other eight Sarwa women either admitted hesitantly that their children were fathered by "various Tswana men" or simply stated that they did not know who the fathers were.[19] The nature of the liaison between the eleven Sarwa women and the non-Tswana men who fathered their children varies from case to case, yet common to all is the fact that the men themselves are marginal to the local community and lack a given social and kin network that could have been of use to the women. Moreover, the few women (five of nineteen) who had left Tamasane as a result of certain attachments to the fathers of their children seem to have gone to town centers (mostly Selibe Phikwe) and not to the community of origin of their lovers. Finally, all but two Sarwa households in Tamasane are headed by females.

When we draw these observations together, it becomes evident that Sarwa women, both those who left the community and those who stayed, are generally deprived of social links and thus of an expansion of kin and exchange networks through their relationships with the men who father their children. Tswana men dissociate themselves from any public, much less economic, responsibility toward Sarwa women and the children they father with them. In addition, non-Tswana males who are acknowledged as fathers of Sarwa children tend to be themselves socially and economically marginal and are mostly unable to contribute materially to the support of or to provide an accessible social and kin network to these women. Moreover, as the following cases illustrate, this pattern recurs from one generation to the next.

Old Lesedi was not born in Tamasane but came to live there as a young girl. She worked as a domestic servant in the yard of the Ratshosa royal family. She is the only one among the Tamasane Sarwa who could claim, in 1983, that she once spoke "Sesarwa," the Setswana term for the language of all those designated Sarwa.[20] She gave birth to several children, all attributed to a Mosarwa herder who worked for the same Ngwato family. Four of her daughters are today heads of their own yards, and the fifth lives in Selebi Phikwe with a Morotsi man (see Figure 7.1).[21] Lesedi and the Mosarwa herder never established their own yard; all their children were raised in Lesedi's master's yard. When the Mosarwa herder was taken away to another cattle post (presumably after the 1927 events), Lesedi stayed behind in Tamasane. She moved to her own yard only when the Ngwato woman for whom she worked died in the early 1960s.

FIGURE 7.1   The Cluster of Lesedi and Her Five Daughters

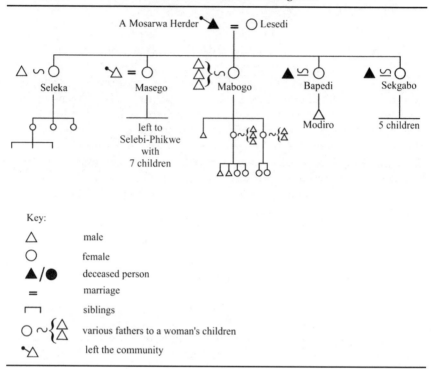

The cases of Lesedi's five daughters exemplify the range of interactions between Sarwa women and their lovers and demonstrate in their various manifestations the general phenomena of social marginality of these women. Seleka, the first born, has three grown-up children who all, she claims, were fathered by a local married Kalanga man. Similar cases of married men fathering children with women other than their wives are not rare in rural Botswana. Often the woman will be known as a *nyatsi*, a concubine, a status that entitles her and her children to some economic support by the man. When a man refuses to support his children, his *nyatsi* can, and often does, resort to legal means to secure her own and her children's rights to such support.

Seleka, and all other Sarwa women in Tamasane, were clearly not part of the social and political system that could secure such support. Seleka gave birth to and raised all her children in her mother's yard. She moved out of her mother's yard to create her own only when her daughter started to bear children.

The second daughter of Lesedi, Masego, followed the Morotsi man who fathered her seven children to Selebi Phikwe, where he is employed. Her younger sister, Mabogo, was not as lucky. Her six children, all born in her mother's yard, were fathered by various local Tswana men, whom she would not, perhaps could not, name. Her own two older daughters have fallen into the same pattern. One has four children, the other has two; neither would name specific men as fathers of their children, but both claimed the fathers were local Tswana men.

The last two daughters of old Lesedi, Bapedi and Sekgabo, head their own households in Tamasane as well. But unlike the other Sarwa households in the village, these two claimed prolonged association with their lovers. In both cases these relationships were terminated upon the death of the men. Bapedi has a son who now works in a South African mine and supports her and the parents of her lover. She is the only one who refers to her Kalanga lover as *nyatsi* (lover/concubine) and maintains an ongoing social and economic interaction with his old parents, even after his death. Significantly though, the old Kalanga couple, parents of her lover, are not part of the larger Kalanga community in Tamasane but are later arrivals. They are poor and lack any social and kin network. Their dependence on her and her son is obvious.

The youngest among the five sisters, Sekgabo, has five children, all attributed to one man whose origin is not clear. She claims he was half Ngwaketse, half Kalanga, while her sister says he was a Mosarwa. Be that as it may, the man arrived in Tamasane alone[22] and established a household with Sekgabo that lasted until his death in 1971. While as poor as her sisters, Sekgabo has the social recognition of "marriage," which they do not. She and her children use the last name of the dead man while all her sisters and her sisters' children carry Lesedi's last name.

The predominant feature in these various cases is systematic social marginality. Local men, Ngwato and Kalanga, do not acknowledge their association with women defined as Basarwa, thus blocking entry of these women into their social and kin networks. Marginal men who create a long association with these women might provide some material support but, upon their disappearance or death, leave the women and their children isolated. The important difference between these Sarwa female heads of households and most of their Tswana counterparts is rooted in this systematic truncation of social ties. A Tswana woman who is an unmarried head of household is not necessarily deprived of social and material ties with the family of her *nyatsi* (see Kerven 1979; Peters 1983b). In many Tswana cases, prolonged residence in the woman's natal home is only a phase in the process of building a new *lolwapa* (literally a yard, but also an independent household). This practice of "marriage as process" has been documented widely in Africa (see, for example, Comaroff 1980). In Botswana, this prolonged process is associated with the recurrent absence of a young immigrant who is expanding his young family while accumulating enough wealth to establish his own independent household (see Motzafi-Haller

1988). In contrast, the liaisons between Tswana men and Sarwa women tend to be, from the outset, of a different nature. Tswana and Kalanga men view Sarwa women as standing outside the social domain within which their responsibility toward their offspring is prescribed. An association with a Sarwa woman, even if it spans many years and results in several children, does not entail an access to the economic resources and social network of the Tswana father.

This discussion suggests that most Sarwa households in Tamasane are headed by females, are socially isolated, and receive no economic support from local men who father children born in these households. In the few cases in which a resident male is part of a Sarwa household, the men are outsiders, of an extremely marginal status both politically and socially. The case of Pirinyana is a good example. Pirinyana was born in a neighboring village to a Sarwa woman and a local Tswana man. She came to Tamasane with her small daughter, whose genitor was a Tswapong man from the village she left. For years she worked as a domestic worker in Pretoria, where she met a Zulu man who fathered her second daughter. Subsequently, the Zulu man came with Pirinyana to her new home in Tamasane. He continued to migrate to South Africa, supporting Pirinyana and her two daughters with his wages. Although lacking any kin network in the community, the couple was able to accumulate enough money to purchase a few head of cattle, and Pirinyana was able to cultivate their field. Pirinyana was more fortunate than the other Sarwa women in Tamasane.

One of the important consequences of the apparent social marginality and isolation of Sarwa households is acute economic disadvantage. In contemporary Botswana a mix of paid work, agriculture, and animal husbandry is the basis of rural household economy. Though most Sarwa households in Tamasane indicated that they have access to agricultural land, they have difficulty acquiring draft animals and adult labor necessary to drive the draft animals. Access to these assets among rural, poor, female-headed households in Botswana is usually achieved through some reliance on the labor of grown-up sons, help from other relatives, or the payment of cash for hired ploughing teams.

Among the Sarwa female-headed households described in this chapter, none of those in the family cluster of Lesedi and her five daughters own any cattle or small stock. While Lesedi and her daughters all indicated the availability of ploughing land, none has an adult male who takes part in the agricultural work. One of the daughters does not plough at all and another hires her labor out and receives some grain in return. The other three households indicated that they do the ploughing themselves with the help of their young children. Cash income for all five households (Lesedi's second daughter, Masego, does not head a household) is generated by the sale of pane worms,[23] thatch grass collected in the hills, and less often, locally brewed beer (*bojalwa*). These limited cash-generating activities are all extremely labor intensive and sporadic. Gathering and drying pane worms and better quality grass for thatching entails long absence from the village by both the women and their children. To brew beer, women need some initial cash to buy sugar and corn meal, and the profit margin is extremely narrow.

Yet, poor as they are, the women heading these eleven Sarwa households stand apart from other Sarwa women who cannot maintain an independent yard and reside in the yard of another Tswana household. I met two such women in Tamasane in 1983. In both cases the Sarwa woman and her very young children resided in the yard of, and provided services for, another household in return for some food and shelter. Older children of these women, in both cases, were sent out to the cattle post. I have also come across several similar situations of absolute economic dependency in the open agricultural areas in the northern Tswapong. Such absolute economic dependence of Basarwa on Batswana appears to be common in the western region of Botswana (Cashdan 1986; Esche 1977; Russell 1976; Solway 1980; Vierich 1979). I have no systematic data to document the extent of such Sarwa-Tswana relations either outside Tamasane or throughout the Tswapong region.[24] The existence of such situations does suggest, in light of the analysis offered here, that the eleven Sarwa households in Tamasane represent only the "lucky few"; that is, they are the few cases that "made it," no matter how impoverished and marginalized, to the village arena. Many other "invisible" Sarwa fragmented units consisting of women and children, or isolated men, had been effectively pushed out of the sociopolitical center and exist in situations of greater dependency outside Tswapong villages. I will return to the significance of this point in the final section of this chapter.

SARWA MALES AND THE RE-CREATION OF MARGINALITY

So far we have seen that Sarwa females are unable to secure the material support and the labor of the men who father their children. The social marginality and acute economic disadvantage of these women is further aggravated when we consider the systematic blockage of two other potential sources of support: from relationships between households through the consanguineal link and from relationships within a mature household between a mother and her adult sons. All but two Sarwa households in Tamasane are deprived of such relationships; brothers of adult female heads of households are dubiously absent from all family records, and most adult sons are said to be away herding others' cattle. The cases in Tamasane demonstrate that the systemic "diffusion" of sons and brothers to the periphery of social life deprives Sarwa women not only of critical access to the earning and labor power of these men but also of legal and political representation in the center. Men are needed to act on behalf of women when access to the *kgotla*, the center of public and local judiciary life, is sought by the latter. Although recourse by aggrieved Basarwa to the *kgotla* arena was made possible at the end of the nineteenth century, Sarwa women in Tamasane have never used such right. The various dimensions of their marginality—social isolation, economic deprivation, and de facto political exclusion—are interconnected.

Sarwa males born into these poor, marginal households, which are unable to guarantee them adequate care, opportunity for education, or inheritance of livestock, start their lives, like many other Tswana poor, in a clearly disadvantaged position. Yet, like their kinswomen, their Sarwa identity aggravates their condition because certain culturally defined Tswana practices are directed toward them. The interaction between the cultural and structural dimensions of this exacerbating spiral carries on throughout the life cycle of a Sarwa male and into an intergenerational reproduction of disadvantage.

In the following discussion, I will compare the life cycles of Sarwa males to those of Tswana males and, more specifically, to poor Tswana male life cycles. The purpose of such comparison is to illuminate the added dimension of disadvantage in cases of attributed Sarwa identity. Analysis of the life histories of Sarwa males is necessary for understanding of the reproduction of marginality of Sarwa households over generations and, ultimately, of the recreation of the Sarwa category and its position outside the sociopolitical arena of the village life.

Born in poor Sarwa woman-headed households, whose main source of livelihood is the local sale of its members' labor, young Sarwa boys are sent early to outlying cattle posts to herd the cattle of Tswana men. The norm in such cases of preadolescent labor is the payment of one beast for the herding services of one year. In Tswana society where cattle are the most general form of wealth accumulation, these beasts earned in preadolescent years can form the core of a poor man's future herd. Sarwa women in Tamasane, however, claimed repeatedly that Tswana men cheat their children of this basic payment "because we are Sarwa." The second important stage in the life cycle of most Tswana men occurs when a youth stops herding cattle to take up paid work, usually in the mines. Mine work earnings are about five to seven times higher than customary payment for herding services. In the course of the ten to fifteen years of active migrant work, a Tswana man sends part of his cash earnings to support his family of origin. Some of this cash is necessary to establish the economic viability of the young man's future family. However, in order to reach that level of accumulation, a man has to balance competing demands: his responsibility to his mother and sisters against that to his own future yard. He also needs some herding services for his accumulating cattle while he is away at his work. The case of Moilwa is an example of the structural difficulties inherent in the position of a young Sarwa man in Tamasane.

Moilwa is the first child born to Mabogo, one of Lesedi's daughters (see Figure 7.1). His father, like those of Mabogo's other five children, never acknowledged his ties with Mabogo or contributed toward his children's material needs. When cattle or cash was paid for Moilwa's herding services, it was "eaten" (consumed) by his mother and younger brothers and sisters. When Moilwa left to work in the mines, his two younger sisters, and subsequently the third, started to bear their own children in the yard. While working in South Africa, Moilwa met a woman and fathered two children with her. In order to resolve the competing demands of his family of origin, with its ever expanding number of sisters' children, and his own future family, Moilwa stopped coming home at the end of his work contracts. His mother says he is a *lekgolwa,* a Tswana concept describing a relative who remains in his work place for extended periods and with whom one has no contact. Moilwa's difficulties were compounded not only by the demands of his poor family of origin but also by its social isolation. Even if he managed to buy a beast with his cash earnings, there was no family herd in which to keep it. Nor was there a mother's brother (*malome*) or any other kin who already owned a herd and could potentially take care of Moilwa's beasts. The possibility of entering an agreement with an unrelated Tswana herd owner has another set of difficulties. Sarwa women complained that Tswana men who were entrusted with cattle belonging to Sarwa sons had "eaten it up." When asked why they did not take such a case to the traditional court (*kgotla*), a right widely practiced by Batswana in similar circumstances, they could not provide a clear answer. Their embarrassed reaction to the question alluded to the implied recognition that a woman alone, and more so a Sarwa woman or a Sarwa youth, without an adult male—husband, father, or brother—to represent her or him does not even approach the public area of the *kgotla* of the central court.

As Moilwa's case illustrates, the path for building an independent yard with a viable economic base by a Mosarwa man tends to be compounded with difficulties. Initial poverty, inability to accumulate wealth due to ever growing demands by unmarried mother and sisters, lack of a supporting network, and inaccessibility to the centers of power and litigation are all factors in this failure. It should be emphasized, however, that this debilitating constellation of factors does not appear in each individual case. For example, Modiro, the only son of the Sarwa woman described previously as the *nyatsi* of a Mokalanga man, was able to support his mother with his salary from his mine work and in 1983 was planning to pay two cattle as bride wealth to consolidate his marriage with a woman with whom he fathered a child. The particulars of his case are less restrictive. The social isolation of his mother was not as acute; Modiro's father had resided with her and established, before his death, a common household. Also, as the only child, Modiro, unlike Moilwa, did not have to support unmarried sisters and an ever increasing number of sisters' children.

Yet despite these structural difficulties the position of Modiro and Moilwa are better than those of most Sarwa males in the community. Mine work, the most common employment and major source of cash income in rural Botswana, is not always part of the life histories of Sarwa males. Among the sixteen Sarwa sons of female-headed households in Tamasane, thirteen were in the age group that is usually involved in active migratory mine work, yet only three among them are miners. Three others continued to herd cattle belonging to other men, four were said to be "doing nothing," and two were described as "looking for work." While mine work, like herding, keeps men away from the village center, the difference in the income generated by these two occupations is significant. When paid in cash, herding services pay about one fifth of what mine work pays. This has important implications for the ability of Sarwa males to accumulate capital. Herding cattle that belong to others as one's only employment means a perpetual economic dependency, an inability to support one's natal family, and clearly no possibility of accumulating capital (in the form of cattle) that could provide the economic basis for an independent yard. Moreover, while poor Tswana herders have at least some kin and social network in the village center and draw their identity from association with one of the wards in the village, a Sarwa herder who resides at the cattle post has no social links or political representation in the village.

Examination of the second generation Sarwa males, the mothers' brothers of the young men like Modiro and Moilwa, tells part of the story about the results of the failure to accumulate capital early in one's life. The most significant fact about this category of adult Sarwa males is that none seems to have established a household in the village center. Tracing family histories of the eleven Sarwa women who head their households in Tamasane and direct inquiries about the fate of these women's brothers yields little verifiable data. Sarwa women tended to answer such inquiries by stating that they were "born alone"—only females—but then "remember" they had brothers who "died" or whom they "did not know."[25] When asked where these brothers are, the women simply said their brothers were *mo nageng* (in the bush). As noted previously, *naga*—the bush, the wild—is the nonsocial category of space in opposition to the hub of social and political life in the village center. By belonging to this "bush" sphere, these Sarwa males are socially "unknown" by, and do not exist for, their sisters. These men might come to the village occasionally to buy locally brewed beer and socialize, but they are not part of the village community. They cannot be counted on to provide material support to their sisters nor, because of their extremely marginal position in the social hierarchy, can they act as social guardians to their own or their sisters' offspring. Economic dependency and socio-spatial marginality resulting from prolonged residence at the periphery of the village create, and in turn are reproduced by, the political proscription of these men. The outcome of this exclusion in communal terms is that the Sarwa group does not constitute a ward, the basic self-ruled unit within the hierarchical organization of the village political structure. Its members do not participate in *kgotla* (the public forum) discussions nor take part in the newly elected democratic institutions of VDC (Village Development Committee) and land board. Deprived of the legal and social guardianship of fathers and adult brothers, Sarwa women are effectively barred from access to social institutions, like the *kgotla*, that could protect their few rights as unmarried mothers.

WHO ARE THE "SARWA" MALES? THE SOCIAL REPRODUCTION OF ETHNIC MARGINALITY

So far I have discussed the way in which ideas associated with one's Sarwa identity feed into an exacerbating spiral of disadvantage and re-create the marginality of the category as a whole. Yet, as some of the case studies presented in this chapter illustrate, at the fringes of this process is a constant movement of individuals who manage to "escape out" or "fall into" the Sarwa category. This movement of individuals must not be seen as a mere exception to a general trend of the "model" presented here. On the contrary, this mobility of individuals across lines alludes to my basic argument that we are dealing here with a *social category* that is defined and redefined in changing historical circumstances, and not with a group of individuals of fixed, biologically distinctive heritage. The case of Boy, who has no Sarwa heritage but is considered a Mosarwa by both Sarwa and Tswana members of the community, provides a specific illustration of this point.

Boy is a loud, constantly drunk man in his mid-forties. He appears in the village whenever he has some cash to buy locally brewed *bojalwa* and sleeps by the courtesy of the beer saleswoman in the corner of her yard. When he appears in the public arena of the *kgotla*, he behaves like and is treated as a jester. He was the only person in Tamasane who stated openly, "I am a Mosarwa," and the only one who was said to be one by both Sarwa women and other Tswana in the community. Yet, Boy's non-Sarwa parentage is known in the community. His mother is a Ngwato commoner and the man who fathered him is a Kalanga. The mother moved on to marry another Ngwato man and left her natal home. Boy stayed behind in his mother's father's yard, but he spent most of his life herding cattle for his mother's father at a remote cattle post. He never left to take on a mine work contract, nor was he paid for his herding services. At various points of his adult life, Boy had several associations with Sarwa women who were economically dependent on, and resided in the yards of, Ngwato families. One of these women bore him three children who grew up in, and in their turn herded the cattle of, the Ngwato man in whose yard their Sarwa mother worked.

The attributed Sarwa identity in this case is a result of several factors. The circumstances of Boy's birth, as an illegitimate son of a woman who moved on to marry another man, set the parameters for his position of social marginality. Boy's initial social marginality was maintained and aggravated by the fact that he never broke out of it in later stages of his life. By remaining in the cattle post beyond the usual age, Boy effectively undermined his chances of creating a viable social and economic basis for an independent household and thus his social standing in the community. His association with socially marginal Sarwa women and his personality structure (a jester and a drunk) contributed to this exacerbating cycle.

Boy's life history is perhaps the best illustration of the way Sarwa identity not only contributes to one's social isolation and marginality but is a label attributed to an individual who had been caught in such debilitating cycles *regardless of one's descent*. In the initial stages of his life Boy lived "like a Mosarwa": he lived at the outlying cattle post and, unlike his mother's brothers, he was not granted the opportunity to attend school. His already dubious social standing was made more vulnerable when he did not develop the potential social links via his mother's kin group but associated himself with Sarwa women. His behavior alienated him from the only link he had with his Tswana heritage and pushed him closer to the Sarwa category. The result was greater economic insecurity and more explicit social marginality. This, in turn, reinforced his inclusion in the Sarwa category and hence his treatment as a nonsocial being expressed in public ridicule and withdrawal from social exchange contracts. Boy thus entered a vicious cycle of disadvantage and social isolation from which he could not, and perhaps did not care to escape. He *became* a "Mosarwa."

Boy's life story contrasts with that of old Lesedi's. Her "Sarwa" origin is not disputed locally—Lesedi came to Tamasane in the 1920s as a "Sarwa servant." Boy's non-Sarwa parentage is publicly known. Yet both Boy and Lesedi are locally known as Basarwa. In fact, it is significant that only in these two extreme cases of an isolated jester and an old woman who had once spoken "Sesarwa," do we find the label Sarwa as self-reference. In all other cases in Tamasane of the early 1980s, Sarwa identity was fiercely rejected and always attributed by others with negative connotations. When we also consider the fact that there are no cultural features or traits, such as language, religion, economic practices, or biogenetic physical features, to distinguish those designated Basarwa from others in the community, it becomes evident that what we have here is not an ethnic group with a subjective self-perception of common identity and unifying cultural or institutional markers but rather a social category.

This social category, Basarwa, could be understood only in terms of the Tswana political and cultural universe within which it is defined. "Sarwa" is a convenient label in Tswana hegemonic discourse that can be applied to people of both Tswana and non-Tswana descent. However, cultural categorization alone is inadequate to relegate a group of people to marginality; we need to analyze the role of social practice in mediating cultural codes.[26] Throughout this analysis I have argued that concepts of Sarwa labor and exclusion from marriage are crucial guiding idioms in the formation and reformulation of the group boundaries and relationships through which resources flow.

What happens when new resources, emanating from outside the local scene, make their way into the small community engaging all poor women regardless of their social/ethnic identification? Such was the case a decade later, in 1993, when I returned to Tamasane to carry out a follow-up study. My 1993 data suggests that most of the older women, the heads of households, gained some cash income through participating in local public works initiated in that year by the central state. Their daughters, like many other poor rural Tswana women, left the village to seek work at the growing urban centers (often leaving behind their young children in their mothers' care). More children of Basarwa households were sent to, and stayed in, public schools. In at least two recorded cases, a "Mosarwa" child made it through the school system to secure a high school diploma and a better paying job.

How significant were these changes in the lives of the women locally known as Basarwa, and how did these changes affect their own sense of Basarwa identity? Had the "Sarwa identity," which had such deleterious effects on their lives only a decade ago, changed meaning? How did the resident Basarwa women and others in the community experience the increasingly powerful national credo that called for equality of all citizens, regardless of ethnic origin? I wish to explore these questions through an interpretive analysis of two key moments in the research encounter that unfolded in Tamasane in 1993.

THE EMERGENCE OF A NEW DISCOURSE: "THERE ARE NO BASARWA IN THIS VILLAGE"

The first was the moment of my reentry into Tamasane. The old village headman who accompanied me in my first visit to the yards of the local Basarwa women had died. I approached his replacement, a young man in his mid-forties (also of Ngwato origin, but not directly related to the old headman), expressing my wish to visit the same women I had met a decade earlier. Through my other local contacts, I had already updated my list of these Basarwa households. The headman was to grant me his official blessing, allowing, as it was, my work in his village. Yet upon hearing my request, the young headman was more than hesitant. "They all have died since," he asserted. "There are no Basarwa here," he objected. When he realized that I knew better and that he could not just wish me away, he scratched his head and giggled. "This is hard. . . . This is hard," he repeated. The difficulty, it turned out in the course of the next few days when his hospitality and friendship toward me were more evident, was not his objection to my work in the village, but rather that the young headman was awkwardly attempting to help me understand and deal with a delicate social reality—a reality that had become more delicate over the last decade. "They will sue you [in the traditional *kgotla* courts] if you walk into their yards saying, 'You are a Mosarwa,' " he exclaimed at one point.

The headman's sincere, if confused, efforts to help me design what might be seen as a socially sensitive "research strategy" tell us a great deal about the changing social and political reality of group relations in rural Botswana and about the ways in which nationalist discourses of equality had been reconsidered and realized. I will deal with three aspects of such transformation: (1) the altered position of traditional village headmanship, (2) the shift in the politics of social categorization and the place of Basarwa identity within it, and (3) the question of who is adopting or defying the nationalist discourse of equality—how and to what local effect.

A decade earlier, the moral authority of the old Ngwato headman who led me into the yards of the poor women locally known as Basarwa was unquestioned. *Mosarwa ke motho*—"a person of Sarwa origin is a human being"—the old man assured the women whose defiance of their inclusion in that social category he felt. Although these women, as I argued previously, had resented their attributed identity and were painfully aware of the constraints and mechanisms of exclusion it structured, they had not attempted to openly defy it, not in front of the old dignified headman. The hesitation and embarrassment that the younger headman had expressed were due in part to his own ambivalent feelings about his position in the community. They asked him to be the official, paid village headman, he told me, but he rejected the offer. "I was simply not interested," said the man who worked as a stable hand in South Africa for most of his adult life and had returned to live permanently in his home village only a few years before I first met him in 1993. "Let them elect their man to sit in the office with a policeman and a court clerk," he explained. "This is not for me."

"They say I am the *kgosi*," he added, "but I am not after such power."

Changes in the nature of village headmanship[27] cannot account for all the differences between the two moments I describe in Tamasane. At issue here, I would like to emphasize, is not that one, more powerful headman could impose his will over the resentful women while the other with less authority would or could not. I propose that a significant shift in the way categories of difference and social distinction were experienced occurred in Tamasane and perhaps in other locations in rural Botswana. To understand the shifts in the local politics of identity, let us turn to the second moment from my 1993 work in Tamasane, a moment that brings in the voices of the very women locally known as Basarwa.

RESISTANCE AND REDEFINITIONS: "SARWA IS MY *SERETO*"

We walked into the front yard of one of the women I had worked with in 1983. His mother would be right with us, said a ten year-old boy; she was washing herself behind the hut after a day of bush clearing at the other end of the village. When the woman appeared, the headman began introducing me as "the woman who writes our traditions," who "walks around the village talking to people."[28] The woman's reaction surprised both of us. She had, indeed, remembered me from long ago when I had talked to her sisters and her mother, she announced directly. She did not need the introductions; she had, in fact, already sent for her sisters. A few minutes later the yard was filled with greetings, loud calls, and laughter as three of the five daughters of old Lesedi, the mother of the core group of Basarwa women I had worked with in 1983, walked into the yard.

The young headman was greeted in proper Tswana manner but without the great deference his predecessor had commanded. They asked about my assistant/translator who had not accompanied me in this visit and complemented my memory of Setswana despite the many years that had elapsed since we last met. For a long while, they exchanged news and gossip with each other. The young headman was ill at ease. The women had interrupted his rehearsed, stiff attempts to introduce me, the *lekgoa* (the white woman) researcher. They had not acted in the serious manner expected in such an occasion. Instead of assuming the respectful posture of answering questions, they had continued to walk about and shout for a long while. The women became even more raucous and at certain points—boldly playful. "Buy our *kgadi* (a local wild berry brew), it's the best in town," they teased the headman. "Don't pretend you don't drink in front of the *lekgoa*," one woman teased. "Look at us, we are dirty. We did not wash up yet," another woman turned to me without much embarrassment. They were clearly having fun; they were spirited and defiant.

When they finally settled down to answer my questions by which I intended to chart changes in the composition of the yards over a decade, they volunteered more than I asked. One woman declared in a voice that was openly aggressive, "I am a Mosarwa, because my mother is a Mosarwa." "Mosarwa is my ethnic/traditional identity" (*ke letsho la me*), explained her sister. But such identity, they made clear, should not be relevant in their daily life: *Ke sereto fela*—"it is my totemic sign only." "Look at him," said one of the women, pointing to the Mongwato headman. "His *sereto* (totemic sign) merely tells you he is a Mongwato, like my *sereto* says I am a Mosarwa." This woman was using *sereto* both to mark her identity as a Mosarwa and to undermine the hierarchical ordering of group identities marked by such a signifier.

Among the Tswana, a *sereto* (also known in other parts of Botswana as *searo* or *seboko*), as Schapera explained almost a generation ago (1984

[1970]:35), is an "object of honour, veneration, avoidance or praise," and "people with the same totem are assumed to have had a common origin." Despite the diminishing relevance of totemic taboos[29] in Botswana, I found that people insisted on holding on to their totemic signifiers in the Tswapong region in the 1980s. In each village where local histories were collected, I was told of the varied totemic signs for the various wards (*kgotlana*) that settled in the village. Wards within each village were known by the geographical space they occupied, their name, their "ward headman," and their *sereto*. The expression was *ba bina mmutla*—"they dance to the hare" (the hare is the totemic signifier of many Tswapong-Pedi people). Yet when the internal structure of each ward was investigated, one often found that fragments, at times as narrow as a single family group consisting of three brothers and their nuclear households, marked their distinction by indicating their own *sereto*, not the one identified with the larger ward. Holding on to a distinctive *sereto* indicates that the group has never lost its distinctive collective identity vis-à-vis the chiefly group. Groups who adopted the chiefly group's *sereto* merged into (in Tswana terms "were eaten up by") the dominant group.

To understand the significance of the statement that "Mosarwa is merely my totemic sign" and what it said about the construction of Sarwa identity in the early 1990s in Tamasane, we must clarify two other points. First, the women knew as well as anyone else in this rural setting that there was no single Basarwa entity marked by a corresponding single *sereto*. Second, totem/*sereto* groups are patrilineal: women, who marry into the group do not change their *sereto* and children who were not rightfully claimed by their father's group inherit their mother's *sereto*. If we bring together these multiple contemporary meanings of *sereto*, we can begin to decipher the subversive play enacted in that short moment in Tamasane. As mothers whose children were not acknowledged by their Tswana fathers, these women and their children were, by force of circumstances, members of the same, three-generation, single-totem group. Instead of lamenting such exclusion and resenting it, as they had a decade ago, the women had made it their weapon and insisted that as a totemic group they should be accorded the same respect for their distinct "origin" as anyone else. By insisting that "his totemic sign merely indicates he is a Mongwato," they went a step further to equalize such distinctly marked groups. *Dilo tsa bogologolo, ga se dilo tsa gompieno,* one of the women concluded: "The things of the remote past are not the way things are today." They acknowledged that social hierarchies and their own exclusion had existed "in the remote past" but that today things were different. Today, one's *sereto* marks one's distinct, not inferior, identity.

If the analysis I propose here is viable, two further questions present themselves. First, what brought about the change from resentment of an attributed (never claimed) Sarwa identity in the 1980s to the defiant adoption and redefinition of such identity in the 1990s? The second question is whether and to what extent the moment I describe here is indicative of larger settings elsewhere in Botswana in the 1990s? What, to use Moore's terms (1987) are some of the "wider processual implications" of this "local moment."

In considering these questions I wish to turn to another string of moments that bring in the voices and action of the Batswapong. Unlike the old Tswapong men who articulated their own collective identity in the late 1970s in the course of an oral history interview (the subject of analysis in Chapter 4), the Batswapong voices we turn to in the following segment are those of children and adults, royalty and commoners who were asked in the 1990s to speak directly about the Basarwa. These people have been exposed to more than two decades of postindependence nationalist discourse promoting the liberal message of equal citizenship. The idea that the Motswana are citizens of a democratic nation where "ethnic roots" are of minor folkloristic interest had clearly filtered into popular discourse and consciousness.[30] Such progressive, unifying national discourse has worked against a deeply stratified and hierarchized Tswana understanding of the world ensconced in a political economy and cosmology that had its roots in nineteenth-century historical realities. What elements of the new liberal discourse had filtered down, and how was this discourse used to structure both perceptions and behavior?

THE SON OF A SARWA WOMAN

A Small Village in the Tswapong Region (Early 1990s)

A woman of Pedi origin told me about the previous season when she and many other people from her village went to collect pane worms in the bush. These worms appear for a short season and are sought after by traders from South Africa who pay in cash or barter in coveted items for these worms. "We lived in the bush," she said. "We were just like Masarwa," she noted, laughing. I followed her lead and asked the group gathered around the evening fire, "Who are these 'Basarwa'? What do you know about them?" A young boy of ten told me, "The Basarwa don't have houses, they live in anthills. I read it in a book." "They don't need cloths or blankets. When they are cold they get closer to the fire. I saw it in the national museum in Gaborone," added a twelve-year-old.

A young man I had known as boy a decade earlier volunteered to describe for me how a "Mosarwa" looks: "Their hair stops here (pointing to the middle of his forehead). Their hair is peppercorn (he says the last word in English). Their eyes are like those of the Chinese, and they are whitish." I had my doubts that my young friend had ever seen a Chinese person, but I also questioned the fact that he had seen a Mosarwa in person. The

Basarwa he saw, he told me proudly, were dancing during the independence day celebration in the national capital, Gaborone. "You should see them," added his mother, "they dance wildly (she illustrated with great animation). They tie beads to their ankles. They are half naked, they sing in funny clicks" (she imitated). *Ga se batho,* concluded another old woman present—"they are not human." As the details of the "nonhuman" attributes of the Basarwa continued to be recounted (they ride donkeys and camels; they eat only meat, no porridge; and so forth), one woman found it necessary to comment in a solemn tone, "No, my people, Basarwa, are also the children of God."

I asked the young woman who was stationed in the village for her national service (a two-year period required of every high school graduate in Botswana) to transcribe the tapes of the interviews I recorded. She came back a few days later with short, creatively edited notes. She tried her best "to fix" the answers she heard in the tapes, she explained, but "these people don't tell you the right things about the Basarwa." She offered to give me a book she had used in her school where all the "correct answers" were written clearly.

I heard these "correct answers" from an educated young village headman in another local site in the Tswapong a few days later. "There are no Basarwa, no Babirwa, no Bangwato," the young village headman assured me in English. "We are all Batswana." But in a neighboring village, another, older village headman (who, unlike his younger counterpart, knew me from the past) elaborated for me (in Setswana) the complicated logic of affinal struggles when the children of a Tswana man reject the claims of their half brother, known to be the son of a Mosarwa woman. The father would be wise, explained the old man, to set aside a few head of cattle for this son before his death, for the share of a Mosarwa woman's son in his father's *boswa* (inheritance) is never secure.

"And what if a young educated man of Mosarwa origin would ask to marry your daughter?" I asked my Motswapong friend who told me about the wild Sarwa dances in Gaborone. "I will be very glad, as long as he is going to have a good job," she answered to the jeering objection of her neighbors.

GENDER, ETHNICITY, AND CLASS
IN SHIFTING CONTEXTS OF POWER

Tamasane of the early 1980s was an emerging village in the Tswapong. Once a cattle post, it had emerged into a settled, officially recognized community with public services and a structure of political administrative order that redefined collective identities and relationships. To grasp the meaning of this spatial transformation and its socioeconomic and symbolic implications, the reader must comprehend Tswana notions of space, memory, and the experience of displacement depicted in earlier chapters of this book. To understand the gendered constitution of "Basarwahood" in Tamasane in the 1980s and the cycle of social isolation and intergenerational poverty it shaped, we need to understand how social hierarchy of groups within the Tswapong defined access to resources and was articulated in spatial arrangements. We also have to explore the experience of daily life in the postcolonial moment, given the critical gap between official national rhetoric of equality and embedded practices of an hierarchical ethnecized and gendered world.

The construction of a gendered identity for the Basarwa households in Tamasane is embedded within these mutually constitutive lines of social difference. The analysis offered in this chapter is therefore not only a detailed exploration of the construction of marginalized gendered identities in contemporary Botswana, it also speaks more generally about similar processes of constitution of gender as one axis among other, mutually defining axes of social difference.

In 1983, more than a decade after national independence with its concomitant official rhetoric of equality of all Batswana citizens, I came across several households, all headed by women, known locally as Basarwa. These female-headed households were the poorest and most marginal in the emerging community. Their ethnic designation as Sarwa at that historical moment was attributed from outside and never claimed by the women themselves. Being identified as a Basarwa woman meant that men did not consider her a legitimate spouse and therefore did not provide such a woman and her children with access to the man's social and kin networks. It also meant that children born to Sarwa women were not paid for their herding services and remained in the outer, herding zones as adults. Sarwa males were unable to build independent households or support their unmarried mothers and sisters.

The combined effect of these two processes has been an intergenerational reproduction of marginality of Basarwa households and an effective exclusion from the village and communal space of Sarwa males. The production of Basarwahood as a social category of impoverished, marginal resident people within the emerging social space of the village arena is therefore inseparable from the feminization of such identity.

One of the conclusions emerging from the detailed domestic histories of this small Basarwa presence in the village is that Basarwahood is constituted as a social category within Tswana discourse and in the context of specific historical settings. There are no distinctive "cultural" features, practices, or body signs that mark this group of poor women and set them apart from their neighbors. Indeed, some of those known in the 1980s as Basarwa were born into families of Ngwato background, and most had Tswana fathers. In other words, the constitution of the ethnic category here, as it is in many other places, is a product of social distinctions drawn in specific settings and not an essentialized, pre-given category.

Yet by the early 1990s, these very women whose ethnicity was imposed on them (an identity that had such deleterious effects in their lives) were affirming their identity using, as we have seen, "traditionalist" discourses. How does such a process of identification occur? And why? Homi Bhabha's notion of *identification* as a process that has agency offers helpful guidelines in our effort to answer these questions. Bhabha proposes that subaltern groups "enunciate" their identity as an active, not passive, act in the space that is created in circumstances of power. The process of identification, Bhabha contends, "occurs precisely in the elliptical *in-between,* where the shadow of the other falls upon the self. From that shadow . . . emerges cultural difference as an *enunciative* category" (Bhabha 1993:60). The women had been defined as Basarwa within the hegemonic Tswana discourse and lived under the shadow of such a powerful definition of identity. In the 1990s, they emerged from that position as active agents. But their act of enunciation did not produce the same meaning attached to "Sarwahood" prevalent up to the 1990s. They articulated a new, redefined identity that included them in the Tswana collectivity without erasing their reclaimed identity. The women's adoption of the totemic sign (the *sereto*) as a collective signifier of their assertive Basarwa identity has reinscribed the meaning of the terms. In the contemporary, openly democratic discourse, the notion of *sereto* becomes a mark of one's distinct, not inferior, identity.

NOTES

1. A more complete description of the village and other elements mentioned in this section can be found in my 1994 essay, "When Bushmen are Known as Basarwa."

2. The history of the Tamasane Kalanga parallels, in many ways, the process of ethnic formation recorded here for the Sarwa. Tracing their roots to a segment of Barolong people with a *tsipi,* iron totem, the group had adopted Sekalanga after years of migrations in the Tonota area. Subjugated by the Ngwato, coming from the south, these people fell into the same low position of other Kalanga. Yet unlike other Kalanga, known to keep their fields and houses together, the Tamasane Kalanga (like their Masojane relatives) have always had their fields away from their clustered villages, Tswana style (Pheko Sebopeng, interviewed at Tamasane, May 17 and 18, 1983).

3. The detailed court proceedings can be found in Botswana National Archives (BNA) file 173, Chief Tshekedi vs. Simon Ratshosa. The correspondence between Tshekedi and the Resident Magistrate and a document entitled "Reports Regarding 'Hereditary Servants' in the Bechuanaland Protectorate," written by Simon Ratshosa, are also contained in this file. Parsons (1978) provides a detailed description of Simon Ratshosa's legal and publicity campaigns against Tshekedi.

4. On November 15, 1926, in a letter to the Resident Magistrate of Serowe (BNA 173), Tshekedi tried patiently to "educate" the British. He placed Sarwa-Ngwato relations in the context of the highly hierarchical order of Tswana society. He wrote: "In order to understand the system under which the Masarwa are governed, it is necessary to first go into the system governing the Bamangwato." After outlining

the hierarchical relations among the Bamangwato as natural and proper, he concluded: "The Mosarwa lives under the same restrictions, he cannot leave his master without his master's consent."

5. Tshekedi's argument skillfully plays with the embedded contradictions of the British position regarding the conditions of Basarwa in "Tswana society." He argued for his right to defend the unpaid Sarwa servants belonging to his enemies on the basis of Khama's reform of the late 19th century. Khama had decreed in 1875 that servants could appeal to their chief if mistreated by their masters. In Tshekedi's view, the Ratshosas had committed a crime by quarreling with their chief (himself), thereby disqualifying themselves from being the rightful owners of their servants.

6. The following section describing the reality in the mid-1920s and 1930s draws extensively on Wylie (1990:86ff). Analyses of the nature of Ngwato-Sarwa relations in specific historical contexts are also included in Tlou (1977), Okihiro (1976), and Parsons (1977). Mabunga Gadibolae (1985) provides a more recent analysis. Miers and Crowder (1988) address more directly the plight of the Basarwa in the Bamangwato Reserve between 1926 and 1940.

7. The official quoted, a Resident Magistrate at Mafeking, seems to have been optimistic about the "emerging spirit of independence among the 'Masarwa.'" He goes on to claim that such spirit of independence is "being recognized and accepted by their so-called 'Masters'" (BNA S 43/7:3, in a letter dated May 12, 1928). Another official (cited by Wylie 1990:88) expressed the opposite view. He was worried about the consequences of "the sudden release of large hordes of more or less savage Masarwa who have been kept under control and authority of their lords and masters, the Bechuana." He predicted that these freed serfs "may wander around the country stealing and killing cattle when they feel inclined" and cautioned that "the Government will have a difficult business at hand" (cited in Wylie 1990: 89).

8. One royal Ngwato woman in Tamasane, for example, reported that she had owned many "Masarwa" who herded her cattle. Only three Sarwa men continued to work for her without cash pay in 1983', the rest of her herders are "babereki," hired people. Her comments regarding those three remaining hereditary herders revealed much disdain toward those "lazy" and "useless" men. The "babereki" who are paid in cash, she maintained, worked better and did not steal.

9. In the eighteenth century, Europeans spoke of the Bushmen as "hordes of wild, bloodthirsty marauders" (Pratt 1986:46). This discourse changed to one in which nature was romantic and the "children of nature" were peace loving and egalitarian when, only a century later, the Bushmen were clearly losing out to colonial encroachment, facing a real threat of extermination. See also Wilmsen (1990) on the Frisch-Passarge debate.

10. Citing other evidence from nineteenth century sources, Peters (1983a:103) suggests that not all stockless people who lived in the open veld were Bushmen. She argues, much along similar lines to what I propose here for the 1980s, that the use of the ethnocultural label "Bushmen" as indicator of economic and political exclusion was convenient for the Tswana elite but that many impoverished people of various ethnic stocks were also part of this category.

11. Text on the back cover reads, "In Botswana, they have a race of untouchables called the Masarwa or Bushmen. Masarwa means the same as 'nigger.'" These are indeed strong and somewhat overstated words. The novel does a much better job of portraying the complex social reality of Sarwa exclusion. The use of the term

"Masarwa," as I pointed out previously, *is* pejorative. Thus, Bessie Head's reference to the "people of the Masarwa tribe" (1971:126) is also out of place.

12. Voss (1990) provides an excellent analysis of the image of the Bushmen in twentieth-century African writers' work. Head is, like most writers Voss discusses, a black South African writer. However, she made Botswana her home and the focus of her work.

13. Schapera records (1965:201, 207, cited by Voss 1990:61) that the term "Bushman" is used as an insult applied in a praise-poem to one of Chief Khama's enemies.

14. The interview of Mr. Hanya Moso on December 22, 1979, is recorded in Setswana and translated into English in Kiyaga-Mulindwa (1980:177–178). Mr. Moso is evidently angry about the imposition of a man with no proper ancestry to the leadership of his village. The new chief, he claims, is a *mohaladi hela*—"merely a fugitive." The chief is of clear Tswana ancestry. Mr. Moso uses the idiom "Mosarwa" to indicate the absurd nature of nominating a man of no clear heritage to the political office.

15. After spending a few days in the outer zone separating the small clustered villages, I was often asked by my friends in the village if those living in the "bush" (*mo nageng*) had not fled from my car. The implication was that my car, a sign of "things foreign," would scare those "uncivilized" bush people.

16. My host, a respectable man in his seventies, spoke no English. At that point of my research, I had enough knowledge of Setswana to carry out these interviews without my assistant/translator, Moses Basebi. I believe strongly that the fact that I was led to these households by this royal Mongwato, and not by my Motswapong assistant who was an outsider to the village scene, made a great difference. The inclusion of a given household into the Sarwa category was based on the authoritative view of my Ngwato host.

17. Pheko Sebopeng, born 1901, was a teacher in Tamasane from 1931 to 1934. Interview, May 18, 1983.

18. Schapera wrote, "Sarwa are still considered inferior to other members of the tribe, who deem it degrading, for instance, to intermarry with them" (1984 [1953]: 37). In 1938, he wrote, "The Tswana also generally refrain from marrying women of inferior stocks, especially Sarwa and other serfs. It is not actually forbidden, but a man who marries such a woman would be greatly despised" (1977 [1938]: 127).

19. The Tswana expression "*ga ke mo itshe*" often implies not the lack of knowledge, per se, but the fact that no social ties can be claimed. Tswana mothers will say "I don't know him" about their son who had left for the mines and had sent no monetary help.

20. There is no single "Sarwa" language, or Sesarwa, as Tswana speakers assume, but many, often mutually unintelligible group languages. The use of the term by the old Sarwa woman is indicative of her complete transformation into the Tswana mode of thought. Lesedi insisted that she forgot how to speak "Sesarwa"; she illustrated the point by drawing the distinction between herself, the owner of a yard, and the itinerant Sarwa men who occasionally come to Tamasane to sell charms and medicine. When these men try to talk to her "beyond the fence," she simply cannot understand their language. While the interview was going on, Lesedi's many grandchildren were giggling and requesting in a jestful way, "Speak Sesarwa, grandma." Her embarrassment over the questioned/forgotten knowledge of "Sesarwa" and the

Tswana-only-speaking grandchildren were strong indications of how remote was this small group of Basarwa from anything non-Tswana.

21. Note that there is no mention of sons. At the time, I did not think to probe further into this issue, assuming that five girls were simply all she bore. In light of much of what is described in the following sections, I tend to think that her sons might have been removed at a young age from the village arena to the remote cattle herding posts and that, as a result of losing all social contact with them, she chose to "forget" about their existence.

22. Here again, we encounter the practice of attributing Sarwa identity to an individual of clearly non-Sarwa origin, but one who is poor and isolated, with no social or political standing in the community.

23. These worms eat the green leaves of the maple tree. They are abundant for only a short season. Sun-dried pane worms make a nutritious snack and are sold by the capful.

24. In systematically recording the population of three lands areas around the village of Mokokwana and in several trips I made to the open grazing zones beyond it (see Motzafi-Haller 1988, 1998), I came across several cases of such Basarwa presence. The "invisibility" of these people was a key issue. For example, I would ask, "Who are the people who live in this yard?" After recording the names, I would proceed to ask how they relate to one another. When individuals known as Basarwa were concerned, this simple question produced much embarrassment, because my hosts needed to state explicitly that these people were not related and that they did not receive any pay for their work. Often I was told they "simply live here." I believe that, in many cases, when resident Basarwa were absent during the interview, their names were not reported as members of the yard. More research needs to be carried out in the Tswapong, and elsewhere, to record the existence of these "invisible" people.

25. See note 19.

26. The role of "practice" in construction of social realities and its relations to systems of domination has been a growing concern in anthropology since the late 1970s (c.f. Bourdieu 1977, Giddens 1979, Ortner 1984).

27. Elsewhere, I described the struggles for local leadership in several sites in central Botswana that might place the crisis in leadership this man experiences in a larger context (Motzafi-Haller 1996)

28. The headman suggested in our long discussions preceding this moment that this was the way I should be introduced in order not to alarm them about the Basarwa issue. The "writing of traditions" is an accepted practice in Botswana. Throughout my work in the Tswapong region I was introduced as "the woman who writes our tradition." The second description about "walking around the village" to emphasize my extensive village, and not Basarwa-specific, focus. I had, in fact, spent several days in the village visiting with people and collecting several household profiles before I walked into this yard.

29. One of the taboos is that people should not eat their own group's totemic animal.

30. See my 1994 analysis of school textbooks where I develop this issue of nationalist rhetoric and its daily uses.

8

Conclusions

Dear Dr. P. M. Haller

Pnina, I am very sorry to tell you that I am sick. I have been admitted to Nyangabgwe hospital on 12-3-93 and discharged on 15-3.93. I have got left leg problem. The leg is very painful, but not swelling, no wound nor any injury. I think problem is nerves, blood is not function accordingly. And now as I am writing this letter, I am from the hospital. . . .

Pnina, I felt very happy when I see the letter DR. behind your name, I mean Dr. which stands for (Doctor). Its sond very nice to me. . . .

Really about my sickness, do not worry, I will try my best to meet you. I will try by many ways to over come this problem. And please do not forget to bring me one of book you wrote.

Greeting to your famely, your husband and children. I have now two sons. I am with them here in Francistown. I am married to the daughter of Magawe.

Moses Basebi, a letter dated March 31, 1993

This is the universe of the marginalized of the modern world system, in some respects a latterday sequel to the making of the European working classes. The logic of this process does not reproduce the structures of proletarianization in any simple sense, however, and its hybrid product, the peasant-worker, poses a complex challenge to established sociohistorical analysis.

Jean Comaroff, *Body of Power, Spirit of Resistance*

Stephen Tyler writes that "every ethnographer is a child of her time and comes to the field informed by contemporary significances; the meaningful events of her generation and the consensus of theory and practice are the landmarks and boundaries of her imagination" (1987:101). Two ethnographic fieldwork experiences, separated by a decade, frame the narrative and analysis of this book. Social theory has shifted in dramatic ways since I first began working in Botswana in 1981. However, more than two decades after the initial entry of critical discourses into anthropology and social theory, it becomes evident that contemporary discourses—in their various "post" articulations, including postmodernism, post-structuralism, and postcolonialism—did not produce a "consensus of theory and practice" that I could adopt and comfortably inhabit when I turned to analyze my ethnographic evidence. This ethnography, in its final shape, is a product of my attempt to take on the challenge of writing in the absence of a guiding "consensus of theory and practice." Writing ethnography at the turn of the twenty-first century must be an act of pastiche, of making use of several theoretical perspectives in order to comprehend a specific ethno-historical process. There is a lesson—not only a necessity—in such an act of theoretical bricolage. I wish to argue that the best way of advancing social theory and enlarging our analytical imagination at this point of postmodernist crisis is by exploring a range of theoretical tools in order to comprehend a specific ethnographic reality rather than by engaging in abstract theoretical debates. By making explicit my struggles to write an ethnography that is informed by more than one theoretical perspective, I wish to make a modest contribution to recent attempts to reach beyond the barren divide and link "modernist" with "postmodernist," subjective and objective sensibilities. In this, my final chapter, I wish to trace the way I have molded this ethnography at the intersections of multiple theoretical and epistemic perspectives.

There is a second challenge in writing an ethnography based on work carried out over more than a decade. When such an account is not reduced to a realist sequence of "ethnographic base" and "postscript" (when the second period of research is not treated as a simple outcome of processes and events described at one point in time), a new interpretive challenge emerges. The challenge I have taken in each of the chapters of this book has been to ask how what I learned in the 1990s has called for a reinterpretation of the reality that I examined in the 1980s. I will discuss the theoretical implications of this question first. I will then return to examine the second issue concerning the multiple theoretical frames employed in this ethnography.

CULTURAL HYPOTHESIS AND A THEORY OF EXPERIENCE

When I first came to Botswana in 1981 to explore the possibility of carrying out ethnographic research in the country, I was informed by the questions that were meaningful to me and to my generation. I was interested in "development" processes and the effects planned social change ("development") have on local communities. I linked these questions of "development" to larger theoretical and epistemic questions. These included the concern with bridging macro and micro analytical perspectives on social processes, the issue of "agency," and the question of integrating history into contemporary realities. Specifically, I was keenly interested in the ways in which people used historical narratives in contemporary struggles. I raised the question of the relationships between local settings and larger national and global forces and structures. And I wanted to explore the manner in which powerless people shaped their lives in circumstances of reforms and regulations directed from above (the question of "agency"). The timing of my research in Botswana in the early 1980s was ideal for these kinds of questions. The Tswapong region was in the throes of dramatic changes in the aftermath of several national reforms. Patterns of local leadership, and the hierarchical order of groups on which it rested, were questioned and redefined when regional land boards began to act as land allocation bodies. Headmen of larger village settlements, and gradually headmen of villages 400 residents strong, were nominated by the state and received payment for their public services. New communities were struggling to gain official recognition as established villages in order to secure state-provided services.

I recorded the parameters of this general process of transformation as I saw them unfold between 1982 and 1984. I identified deep tensions in the region by recording oral histories. I documented the composition of one village community and traced changes in the complex relationships between members of the clustered community who resided in the village and those resident in its surrounding agricultural areas. I observed the working of ethnic and gender exclusion of a group known as Basarwa. And I recorded several public events in which I saw signs of a challenge to received categories of difference and social hierarchy. Based on these empirical data, I proposed that the meanings and values associated with access to land, the nature of community, and the definition of leadership were shifting. The earlier moments I described in Chapters 5, 6, and 7 are examples for the interpretive analysis I developed after I left Botswana in 1984. My analysis depicted several events that articulated resistance to received categories and traditions. I argued that these were moments of emergence, processes in which people were only beginning to imagine an alternative social order.

I returned to the Tswapong in 1993, a decade after my first field research. The second field research provided an invaluable perspective for comprehending the 1980s reality. On the most immediate level, it provided a "solution" to my original "cultural hypothesis." A cultural hypothesis, Raymond Williams observes, is based on attempts to understand emerging social elements and their connections "in a generation or a period" (1977: 132). Williams calls the emerging, not yet formulated, reality I portrayed (based on my early 1980s data) a "structure of feelings" (1977: 132ff). Williams's notion of a "structure of feelings" and his more elaborate theory of social change are useful conceptual tools in articulating the kind of analytical reframing my 1993 data required.

Williams draws a distinction between fixed social forms and institutions and the active, lived experience of the present. There is always tension between received interpretation and practical experience. The "actual alternative to the received and produced fixed forms," he emphasizes, is not silence, "it is a kind of feeling and thinking which is indeed social and material but . . . in an embryonic phase before it can become fully articulate and defined exchange" (1977:131). The processes I describe throughout this book were emerging; they were often not even articulated as social by the actors themselves. When, in the early 1980s, the people of Manaledi (Chapter 5) struggled to establish their communal rights to head off the threat to their land reserves posed by neighboring affluent farmers, they were not yet conscious of their position in a larger social process of class struggle and land alienation. They viewed their struggle as private, idiosyncratic, even isolating. Similarly, when the Gamotse populist leader (Chapter 6) galvanized local support to object to claims by the Ngwato cattle owner for local leadership, he and his fellow villagers were not articulating a coherent alternative order.

My return to the region in 1993, and the ethnographic evidence it yielded, has provided an opportunity to examine my cultural hypothesis. The 1993 data demanded a new interpretive framework and a new analysis of the reality I depicted in the 1980s. For example, when it became obvious that Gamotse had become an established village in 1993, but one that reproduced patterns of social difference along ethnic, clientship, and gender lines, it was necessary to reevaluate my earlier analysis that had noted seeds of resistance in the emerging community. Similarly, the analysis presented in Chapter 7 involves two points of time and two emerging realities for the Tamasane women. The celebration of Basarwa identity by these women in the early 1990s is comprehensible only when one realizes the nature of their identification as Basarwa in the early 1980s.

From the perspective of the 1990s, it became evident that the 1980s were ambivalent and complex years when social structures and conventions were in flux. It was a time of contradictions, fracture, and emergence. By the early 1990s, to return to Williams's notion, a new "structure of feelings" had emerged. The embryonic phase of the social struggles of the 1980s had fully developed into a new set of fixed relationships of class, gender, and communal identities. The direction of the emerging period was not uniform. Some elements in the emerging reality of the early 1980s were dramatically arrested, at least on the surface of social life. In Gamotse, the populist leader was effectively excluded and a new fixed local hierarchy of groups was reestablished. Together with this process of fixing of relationships and hierarchies, the residents also gained their coveted "established village" status and with it, legitimate rights to cultivate arable lands.

THEORETICAL BRICOLAGE: WRITING IN THE POST "POSTMODERNIST" MOMENT

I began my work within a strictly political economy theoretical frame. The height of critical postmodernist theory had not influenced my first, complete ethnographic narrative written in 1988. This book is clearly not a postmodernist essay. What I sought to do here is to draw, retrospectively, on the best of what the postmodernist critique had to offer anthropology and combine it with other theoretical perspectives that are often seen as antithetical. At the most general level, this ethnography seeks to bridge the gap between studies that have placed narrativity, personal histories, and the way the world is experienced by social actors at the center and studies that have analyzed the hybrid world of these marginalized people in Southern Africa in terms of world historical, political economy models.

I have attempted to understand how this fragmented world was experienced and acted upon from the perspectives of the men and women who inhabited this impoverished margin of the global economy. Yet, I worked to do this without losing sight of the political and material conditions that shape these life-worlds. I thus opened my analysis with examining how individuals crafted the stories of their own experience of movement across international borders and among several residential sites within the postindependence state. I then proceeded to examine the setting within which these stories were produced before turning to analyze the subjective frames developed in these personal stories. I proposed that these individual stories and the construction of the larger social framework of conjugality, family, and household within which they were embedded were shaped by specific political and economic conditions emerging in this region in the mid-1970s. These larger economic and political frames were examined at the national, regional, and village levels.

I returned to subjective constructions of the world using oral data recorded in the region by Batswana students. These records challenge historical depictions of the region that were based on external sources and raise the question of resistance to domination by subjugated populations.

The question of resistance runs through the two other theoretical frames used to understand the emerging reality. The first is composed of theories that link struggles over social spaces with communal and social definitions. The second theory is a contemporary brand of critical feminism that insists on including several mutually constitutive lines of social difference in the same analytical frame. Gendered identities are understood in this book only in relation to the construction of other hierarchies and realities of power.

Bibliography

Abu-Lughod, Lila. 1990. "The Romance of Resistance: Tracing Transformations of Power through Bedouin Women." *American Ethnologist* 17(1):41–55.

———. 1991. "Writing Against Culture." In Richard Fox (ed.), *Recapturing Anthropology*. Santa Fe, NM: School of American Research Press, pp. 137–163.

———. 1993. "Shifting Politics in Bedouin Love Poetry." In L. Abu-Lughod and C. Lutz (eds.), *Language and the Politics of Emotion*. Cambridge, England: Cambridge University Press, pp. 24–46.

Abu-Lughod, Lila, and Lutz, Catherine. 1993. "Introduction." In L. Abu-Lughod and C. Lutz (eds.), *Language and the Politics of Emotion*. Cambridge, England: Cambridge University Press, pp. 1–24.

Alverson, Hoyt. 1978. *Agricultural Development in Botswana: Targets and Constraints*. Gaborone, Botswana: Institute of Development Management.

Amsden, J. 1979. "The Spatial Dimension of History." *Radical Historical Review* 1:3–247.

Anthias, F. M., and Yuval-Davis, Nira. 1990. "Contextualizing Feminism—Gender, Ethnic and Class Divisions." In T. Lovell (ed.), *British Feminist Thought: A Reader*. Oxford, England: Basil Blackwell, pp. 103–118.

Ashton, E. H. 1937. "Notes on the Political and Judicial Organization of the Tawana." *Bantu Studies* 11: 67–83.

Baerends, A. Els. 1994. *The One Legged Chicken in the Shadow of Indebtedness*. Groningen, The Netherlands: Rijksuniversiteit Groningen.

Barnard, Alan. 1979. "Kalahari Settlement Patterns." In P. Burnham and R. Ellen (eds.), *Social and Ecological Systems*. New York: Academic Press.

———. 1992a. *Hunters and Herders of Southern Africa: A Comparative Ethnography of the Khoisan Peoples*. Cambridge, England: Cambridge University Press.

————. 1992b. "The Kalahari Debate: A Bibliographic Essay." Center for African Studies. Occasional paper No. 35. Edinburgh, Scotland: Edinburgh University.

Barnes, J. M. 1980. "Economic Status of the Basarwa Population of the Letlakhane Region." Gaborone: Government of Botswana, Ministry of Local Government and Lands.

Behar, Ruth. 1993. *Translated Woman: Crossing the Border with Esperanza's Story.* Boston: Beacon Press.

Beinart, W., and Bundy, C. 1986. *Hidden Struggles in Rural South Africa.* Johannesburg, South Africa: Ravan Press.

Benjamin, Walter. 1969. *Illuminations.* Harry Zohn (trans.). New York: Schocken Books.

Berry, Sara. 1985. *Fathers Work for Their Sons: Accumulation, Mobility and Class Formation in an Extended Yoruba Community.* Berkeley: University of California Press.

————. 1988. "Property Rights and Rural Resource Management: The Case of Tree Crops in West Africa." *Cahiers de Sciences Humaines* 24(1):3–16.

————. 1990. "Hegemony on a Shoestring: Indirect Rule and Access to Agricultural Land." *Africa* 62(3): 327–55.

Bhabha, Homi. 1993. *The Location of Culture.* London and New York: Routledge.

Biesele, Megan; Guenther, Mathias; Hitchcock, Robert; Lee, Richard; and Macgregor, Jean. 1989. "Hunters, Clients, and Squatters: The Contemporary Socioeconomic Status of Botswana Basarwa." *African Studies Monographs* 9:109–51.

Bird-David, Nurit. 1992. "Beyond 'The Hunting and Gathering Mode of Subsistence': Culture-Sensitive Observations on the Nayaka and Other Modern Hunter-Gatherers." *Man* (N.S.) 27:17–44.

Borofsky, Robert. 1987. *Making History: Pukapukan and Anthropological Constructions of Knowledge.* New York: Cambridge University Press.

Botswana National Archives (BNA), Gaborone, Botswana.

————. BNA File 173. Magistrate's court proceedings, "Chief Tshekedi vs. Simon Ratshosa," pp. 21–24, 32, 42, 56–57, 94, 97–98, 111.

————. BNA File HC 24/15.

————. BNA File S 43/7. Report regarding "Hereditary Servants" in the Bechuanaland Protectorate. Forwarded by the Resident Commissioner to the High Commissioner, December 5, 1928; a two-page letter sent to the Resident Magistrate in Serowe dated November 15, 1926, signed by Tshekedi Khama (also included in this file).

Bourdieu, Pierre. 1971. "The Berber House or The World Reversed." In *échanges et communications: Mélanges offerts á Claude Lévi-Strauss á l'occasion de son 60 anniversaire.* Hague, The Netherlands: Mouton, pp. 151–161.

————. 1977. *Outline of a Theory of Practice,* R. Nice (trans.). Cambridge, England: Cambridge University Press.

————. 1987. "The Biographical Illusion." Working papers and proceedings of the Center for Psychosocial Studies, no. 14. Chicago: Center for Psychosocial Studies.

Bourgois, Philippe. 1988. "Conjugated Oppression: Class and Ethnicity among Guaymi and Kuna Banana Workers." *American Ethnologist* 15:328–349.

Bower, Bruce. 1989. "A World That Never Existed." *Science News* 135:264–266.

Brown, Barbara. 1983. "The Impact of Male Labour Migration on Women in Botswana." *African Affairs* 82:328.

Burchell, W. C. 1853. *Travels in the Interior of South Africa.* London: Longman.

Butler, Judith. 1989. *Gender Trouble: Feminism and the Subversion of Identity.* New York: Routledge.

Campbell, John. 1815. *Travel in South Africa.* London: Black and Parry.

Cashdan, Elizabeth A. 1986. "Competition between Foragers and Food Producers on the Botletli River, Botswana." *Africa* 56:299–318.

———. 1987. "Trade and Its Origins on the Botletli River, Botswana." *Journal of Anthropological Research* 43:121–38.

Chambers, R., and Feldman, D. 1973. *Report of Rural Development.* Gaborone, Botswana: Ministry of Finance and Development Planning.

Chase, Susan. 1995. "Taking Narratives Seriously." In Ruthellen Josselson and Amia Lieblich (eds.), *Interpreting Experience: The Narrative Study.* Thousand Oaks, CA: Sage, pp. 1–26.

Chirenje, Mutero J. 1978. *Chief Kgama and His Times. c. 1835–1923.* London: Rex Collings.

Clifford, James. 1988. "Histories of the Tribal and the Modern." In James Clifford (ed.), *The Predicament of Culture.* Cambridge, MA: Harvard University Press, pp. 189–214.

Colclough, Christopher, and McCarthy, Stephen. 1980. *The Political Economy of Botswana.* Oxford, England: Oxford University Press.

Collins, Patricia. 1990. *Black Feminist Thought: Knowledge, Consciousness, and the Politics of Empowerment.* Boston: Unwin Hyman.

Comaroff, Jean. 1985. *Body of Power, Spirit of Resistance: The Culture and History of a South African People.* Chicago: University of Chicago Press.

Comaroff, John. 1980. "Bridewealth and the Control of Ambiguity in a Tswana Chiefdom." In J. Comaroff (ed.), *The Meaning of Marriage Payments.* London: Academic Press, pp. 161–196.

———. 1981. "Preface." In Eileen Krige and John Comaroff (eds.), *Essays on African Marriage in Southern Africa.* Cape Town and Johannesburg, South Africa: Juta and Company.

———. 1982. "Class and Culture in a Peasant Economy: The Transformation of Land Tenure in Barolong." In R. Werbner (ed.), *Land Reform in the Making.* London: Rex Collings.

———. 1984. "Tswana Transformations, 1953–1975." Supplementary chapter to the 1970 edition of I. Schapera's *The Tswana* (1953). London: Routledge & Kegan Paul.

———. 1987. "Of Totemism and Ethnicity: Consciousness, Practice and the Signs of Inequality." *Ethnos* 52(3):301–323.

Comaroff, John, and Comaroff, Jean. 1987. "The Madman and the Migrant: Work and Labor in the Historical Consciousness of a South African People." *American Ethnologist* 14: 191–209.

———. 1991. *Of Revelation and Revolution: Christianity, Colonialism and Consciousness in South Africa, Volume 1.* Chicago: The University of Chicago Press.

———. 1992. *Ethnography and the Historical Imagination.* Boulder, CO: Westview Press.

———. 1997. *Of Revelation and Revolution: The Dialectics of Modernity on a South African Frontier Vol. 2.* Chicago: The University of Chicago Press.

Comaroff, John, and Roberts, Simon A. 1977. "Marriage and Extra-Marital Sexuality. The Dialectics of Legal Change among the Kgatla. *Journal of African Law* 20:92–123.

Cooper, David. 1979. "Migration to Botswana Towns: Patterns of Migration of Selebi-Phikwe Mine Workers prior to and Including Coming to Phikwe." National Migration Study. Working Paper No 3. Gaborone, Botswana: Central Statistics Office.

———. 1980. "How Urban Workers in Botswana Manage Their Cattle and Lands: Selebi-Phikwe Case Studies." National Migration Study. Working Paper No. 4. Gaborone, Botswana: Central Statistics Office.

———. 1982. "An Interpretation of the Emergent Class Structure in Botswana: A Case Study of Selebi-Phikwe Miners." Ph.D. dissertation, Birmingham University, U.K.

Corrigan, P., and Sayer, D. 1985. *The Great Arch: English State Formation as Cultural Revolution.* Oxford, England: Basil Blackwell.

Datta, K., and Murray, A. 1989. "The Rights of Minorities and Subject Peoples in Botswana: A Historical Evaluation." In John Holm and Patrick Molutsi (eds.), *Democracy in Botswana.* Ohio University Press.

DeLauretis, Teresa. 1986. *Feminist Studies/Critical Studies.* Bloomington, IN: Indiana University Press.

Denbow, James R. 1983. "Iron Age Economics: Herding, Wealth and Politics along the Fringes of the Kalahari Desert during the Early Iron Age." Ph.D. dissertation, Indiana University, Bloomington.

Durham, Deborah. 1993. *Images of Culture: Being Herero in a Liberal Democracy.* Ph.D. dissertation, University of Chicago.

Egner, Brian. 1979. *District Development in Botswana.* Unpublished report submitted to the Swedish International Development Agency.

Emberley, J. V. 1993. *Thresholds of Difference: Feminist Critique, Native Women's Writings, Postcolonial Theory.* Toronto: University of Toronto Press.

Esche, H. 1977. Interim Report on Survey of Basarwa in Kweneng. Gaborone: Government of Botswana, Ministry of Local Government and Lands.

Fajans, Jane. 1997. *They Make Themselves: Work and Play Among the Baining of Papua* Chicago: University of Chicago Press.

Ferguson, James. 1992. "The Cultural Topography of Wealth: Commodity Paths and the Structure of Property in Rural Lesotho." *American Anthropologist* 94(1):55–74.

Forsbrook, H. A. 1971. "Land and Population." *Botswana Notes and Records* 3: 172–186.

Foucault, Michel. 1970. *The Order of Things: An Archaeology of the Human Sciences.* New York: Random House.

———. 1975. *Discipline and Punishment: The Birth of the Prison.* New York: Vintage Books.

———. 1982. "The Subject and Power." In H. Dreyfus and P. Rabinow (eds.), *Michel Foucault Beyond Structuralism and Hermeneutics.* Chicago: Chicago University Press, pp. 208–226.

———. 1984. "Des espace autres." *Architectura, Mouvement, Continuité* October:46–49.

Fox-Genovese, Elizabeth. 1994. "Difference, Diversity, and Divisions in an Agenda for the Women's Movement." In Gay Young and Bette J. Dickerson (eds.), *Color, Class and Country: Experiences of Gender*. London and Atlantic Highlands, NJ: Zed Books, pp. 232–249.

Gadibolae, Mabunga N. 1985. "Serfdom (bolata) in the Nata Area, 1926–1960." *Botswana Notes and Records* 17:25–32.

Geertz, Clifford. 1988. *Works and Lives*. Stanford, CA: Stanford University Press.

Gewertz, Deborah, and Errington, Frederick. 1991. *Twisted Histories, Altered Contexts: Representing the Chambri in a World System*. New York: Cambridge University Press.

Giddens, Anthony. 1979. *Central Problems in Social Theory: Action, Structure and Contradiction in Social Analysis*. Berkeley: University of California Press.

———. 1984. *The Constitution of Society: Outline of the Theory of Structuration*. Berkeley: University of California Press.

Gilligan, Carol. 1982. *In a Different Voice*. Cambridge, MA: Harvard University Press.

Gladney, Dru. 1991. *Muslim Chinese: Ethnic Nationalism in the People's Republic*. Cambridge, MA: Harvard University Press.

Gordon, Robert J. 1986. "Once Again: How Many Bushmen Are There?" In M. Biesele with R. Gordon and R. Lee (eds.), *The Past and Future of !Kung Ethnography: Critical Reflections and Symbolic Perspectives, Essays in Honor of Lorna Marshall*. Hamburg, Germany: Helmut Baske Verlag, pp. 53–69.

———. 1991. *The Bushmen Myth: The Making of A Namibian Underclass*. Boulder, CO: Westview Press.

Gottdiener, M. 1985. *The Social Production of Urban Space*. Austin: University of Texas Press.

———. 1987. "Space as a Force of Production: Contribution to the Debate on Realism, Capitalism and Space." *International Journal of Urban and Regional Research* 11(3): 405–416.

Government of Botswana (GOB). Gaborone: Government Printer. 1975. "Rural Income Distribution Survey (RIDS)."

———. 1977. "Central District Development Plan."

———. 1981. "National Population Census."

———. 1982. National Migration Study (NMS) 1982–1983, Vol. 1 and Vol. 2. C. Kerven (ed.), *Migration in Botswana: Patterns, Causes and Consequences*. Central Statistics Office.

———. 1983. National Migration Study, Vol. 3. C. Kerven (ed.), *Migration in Botswana: Patterns, Causes and Consequences*. Central Statistics Office.

———. 1991. Statistics Bulletin, December 1991. Vol. 16, No. 3.

———. 1992. Population of Towns, Villages and Associated Localities. Central Statistics Office.

———. 1993. Stats Update, May 12, 1993. Central Statistics Office.

———. 1995. Household Income and Expenditure Survey. Central Statistics Office.

———. 1997. National Development Plan 8: 1997/8–2002/3. The Ministry of Finance and Development Planning.

Greenhow, T. 1980. "The Tribal Grazing Land Policy and Integrated Land Use Planning: A District View." *Botswana Notes and Records* 10: 159–168.

Guenther, Mathias G. 1977. "More on Khoisan Classification." *International African Institute Bulletin,* Supplement to Africa 47:2–3.

———. 1979. *The Farm Bushmen of the Ghanzi District, Botswana.* Stuttgart, Germany: Hochschul Verlag.

———. 1986. "Acculturation and Assimilation of the Bushmen." In I. R. Vossen and K. Keuthmann (eds.), *Contemporary Studies on Khoisan.* Hamburg, Germany: Helmut Buske Verlag, pp. 347–373.

Gulbrandsen, Ornulf. 1984. *When Land Becomes Scarce.* Bergen Studies in Social Anthropology 33. Bergen, Norway: University of Bergen Printer.

———. 1994. *Poverty in the Midst of Plenty.* Bergen, Norway: Norse Publications.

Guyer, Jane. 1984. "Gender and Agricultural Change in Modern Africa." *Current Anthropology* 20(3):247–272.

Hamilton, C. 1995. *The Mfecane Aftermath: Reconstructing Debates in Southern African History.* Johannesburg, South Africa: University Witwatersrand Press.

Haraway, Donna. 1988. "Situated Knowledge: The Science Question in Feminism and the Privilege of Partial Perspective." *Feminist Studies* 14:3.

Harding, Sandra. 1991. *Whose Science? Whose Knowledge? Thinking from Women's Lives.* Ithaca, NY: Cornell University Press.

———.1992. "Subjectivity, Experience, and Knowledge." *Development and Change* 23(3):175–94.

Harvey, David. 1992. *The Condition of Postmodernity.* Cambridge, MA & Oxford U.K.: Blackwell.

———. 1994. "Subjects and Agents: The Question for Feminism." In Judith Kegan Gardiner (ed.), *Provoking Agents.* Urbana/Champaign: University of Illinois Press, pp. 370–395.

Head, Bessie. 1971. *Maru.* London: Heinemann.

Headland, Thomas N., and Reid, Lawrence A. 1989. "Hunter-Gatherers and Their Neighbors from Prehistory to the Present." *Current Anthropology* 30:43–66.

Hepburn, James D. 1896. *Twenty Years in Khama's Country.* London: Hodder and Stoughton.

Herzfeld, Michael. 1985. *The Poetics of Manhood: Contest and Identity in a Cretan Mountain Village.* Princeton, NJ: Princeton University Press.

———. 1987. *Anthropology through the Looking-Glass: Critical Ethnography in the Margins of Europe.* New York: Cambridge University Press.

———. 1991. *A Place in History: Social and Monumental Time in a Cretan Town.* Princeton, NJ: Princeton University Press.

Hitchcock, Robert. 1978. *Kalahari Cattleposts: A Regional Study of Hunter-Gatherers, Pastoralists and Agriculturalists in the Western Sandveld Region, Central District, Botswana.* Gaborone, Botswana: Government Printer.

———. 1982. Patterns of Sedentism among the Basarwa of Eastern Botswana." In Eleanor Leacock and Richard Lee (eds.), *Politics and History in Band Societies.* Cambridge, England: Cambridge University Press, pp. 223–268.

———. 1984. "Tradition, Social Justice and Land Reform in Central Botswana." In R. Werbner (ed.), *Land Reform in the Making.* London: Rex Collins, pp. 1–35.

———. 1987. "Socioeconomic Change among the Basarwa in Botswana: An Ethnohistorical Analysis." *Ethnohistory* 34:220–255.

———. 1988. "Monitoring, Research, and Development in the Remote Areas of Botswana." Gaborone, Botswana: Government Printer.

Hitchcock, Robert, and Nkwe, T. 1986. "Social and Environmental Impacts of Agrarian Reform in Rural Botswana." In J. Arntzen, L. Negonego, and S. Turner (eds.), *Land Policy and Agriculture in Eastern and Southern Africa.* Tokyo: United Nations University, pp. 93–99.

Holm, John. 1989. "Botswana: A Paternalistic Democracy." In L. Diamond, J. Linz, and M. Lipset (eds.), *Democracy in Developing Countries.* Vol. 2. Boulder, CO: Westview Press, pp. 179–217.

hooks, bell. 1990. *Yearning: Race, Gender and Cultural Politics.* Boston: South End Press.

Hutterer, K. 1990. "Comments on Ed Wilmsen and James Denbow's Paradigmatic History of San-Speaking People and Current Attempts at Revisions: History of San-Speaking Peoples." *Current Anthropology* 31:489–525.

Jackson, Jean. 1989. "Is There a Way to Talk about Making Culture without Making Enemies?" *Dialectical Anthropology* 14:127–145.

Jenness, J. 1978. "Rethinking the TGLP in Light of the Land Use Planning Exercise." Gaborone, Botswana: Government Printer.

Josselson, Ruthellen, and Lieblich, Amia (eds.). 1995. *Interpreting Experience: The Narrative Study of Lives.* London: Sage Publications.

Kent, Susan. 1992. "The Current Forager Controversy: Real Versus Ideal Views of Hunter-Gatherers." *Man* (n.s.) 27:45–70.

Kerven, Carol. 1979. "Urban and Rural Female-Headed Households' Dependence on Agriculture." Gaborone: Government of Botswana, Central Statistics Office.

———. 1984. "Academics, Practitioners and All Kinds of Women in Development: A Reply to Peters. *Journal of Southern African Studies* 10(2): 259–268.

Kiyaga-Mulindwa, David. 1980. "Politics and Society in Letswapo." Tswapong Historical Texts 2. Unpublished manuscript. Department of History, University of Botswana; compiled and edited by D. Kiyaga-Mulindwa, on file in University of Botswana Library.

Kondo, Dorinne. 1990. *Crafting Selves: Power, Gender, and Discourses of Identity in a Japanese Workplace.* Chicago: The University of Chicago Press.

Kooijman, Kristin. 1978. *Social and Economic Change in a Tswana Village.* Leiden, Netherlands: Afrika-Studie Centre.

Kuper, Adam. 1975. "Preferential Marriage and Poligyny among the Tswana." In M. Fortes and S. Patterson (eds.), *Studies in African Social Anthropology.* London, New York, and San Francisco: Academic Press.

———. 1980. "Symbolic Dimensions of the Southern Bantu Homestead." *Africa* 50(1).

———. 1982. *Wives for Cattle: Bridewealth and Marriage in Southern Africa.* London: Routledge and Kegan Paul.

Lawrence, D., and Low, S. 1990. "The Built Environment and Spatial Form." *Annual Reviews of Anthropology* 19:453–505.

Lee, Richard B. 1992. "Science, or Politics? The Crisis in Hunter-Gatherer Studies." *American Anthropologist* 94:31–54.

Lee, Richard B., and Guenther, Mathias. 1991. "Oxen or Onions? The Search for Trade (and Truth) in the Kalahari." *Current Anthropology* 32: 592–601.

Lefebvre, Henry. 1991. *The Production of Space.* Oxford: Blackwell.

Legasick, Martin C. 1969. "The Sotho-Tswana peoples before 1800." In Leonard Thompson (ed.), *African Societies in Southern Africa: Historical Studies.* Berkeley: University of California Press & London: Heinemann, pp. 86–125.

Lewin, Roger. 1988. "New Views Emerge on Hunters and Gatherers." *Science* 240:1146–1148.

Limon, Jose. 1994. *Dancing with the Devil*. Madison: University of Wisconsin Press.

Lipton, Michael. 1978. "Botswana: Employment and Labor Use in Botswana." Gaborone, Botswana: Government Printer.

Lutz, Catherine. 1988. *Unnatural Emotions*. Chicago: University of Chicago Press.

Mackenzie, John. 1871. *Ten Years North of the Orange River: A Story of the Everyday Life and Work among the South African Tribes from 1856–1869*. Edinburgh, Scotland: Edmonston and Douglas.

Maggs, T. 1972. "Bilobial Dwellings: A Persistent Feature of Southern Tswana Settlements." South African Archaeological Society: Goodwin Series No 1.

————. 1976. "The Type Z Sites and Their Cultural Affinities." Gaborone Botswana, unpublished manuscript.

Marcus, George. 1994. "General Comments." *Cultural Anthropology* 9(3):423–428.

Marcus, George, and Fischer, Michael. 1986. *Anthropology as Cultural Critique: An Experimental Moment in the Human Science*. Chicago: University of Chicago Press.

Martin, Denis-Constant. 1993. "The Choices of Identity." Paper presented to the Conference on Ethnicity, Identity and Nationalism in South Africa: Comparative Perspectives. Grahamstown, South Africa.

Mascia-Lees, Frances; Sharpe, Patricia; and Cohen, Colleen. 1989. "The Postmodernist Turn in Anthropology: Cautions from a Feminist Perspective." *Signs* 15:394–408.

Massey, David. 1978. "A Case of Colonial Collaboration: The Hut Tax and Migrant Labour." *Botswana Notes and Records* 10:95–98.

————. 1980. The Development of a Labor Reserve: The Impact of Colonial Rule on Botswana. Boston: African Studies Center, Working Paper No. 34.

Miers, Suzanne, and Crowder, Michael. 1988. "The Politics of Slavery in Bechuanaland: Power Struggles and the Plight of the Basarwa on the Bamangwato Reserve, 1926–1940." In Suzanne Miers and Richard Roberts (eds.), *The End of Slavery in Africa*. Madison: University of Wisconsin Press.

Mitchel, Tim. 1991. *Colonizing Egypt*. Berkeley: University of California Press.

Mogwe, Alice. 1992. "Who Was Here First? An Assessment of the Human Rights Situation of Basarwa in Selected Communities in the Gantsi District, Botswana." Gaborone: Botswana Christian Council.

Molefe, M. M. K. 1983. "A Report to the Central District Council" (memo).

Molutsi, Patrick P. 1986. *Social Stratification and Inequality in Botswana. Issues in Development 1950–1985*. Oxford, England: Oxford University Press.

Moore, Sally F. 1986. *Social Facts and Fabrications: "Customary" Law on Kilimanjaro, 1880–1980*. Cambridge, England: Cambridge University Press.

————. 1987. "Explaining the Present: Theoretical Dilemmas in Processual Ethnography." *American Ethnologist* 14(4):727–737.

Motzafi-Haller, Pnina. 1988. *Transformations in the Tswapong Region, Central Botswana: National Policies and Local Realities*. Ph.D. dissertation, Brandeis University, Waltham, MA.

————. 1990. "Comments on Lee and Solway's Foragers, Genuine or Spurious?" *Current Anthropology* 31:132–133.

————. 1993a. "The Duiker and the Hare: Tswapong Subjects and Ngwato Rulers in Precolonial Botswana." *Botswana Notes and Records* 25:59–72.

———. 1993b. "Beyond the 'True Bushmen': The Politics of Ethnic Categorization in Botswana." Paper presented at the 13th International Congress of Anthropological and Ethnological Sciences, Mexico City, Mexico.

———. 1994. "When Bushmen are Known as Basarwa: Gender, Ethnicity and Differentiation in Rural Botswana." *American Ethnologist* 21(3):539–563.

———. 1995. "Liberal Discourses of Cultural Diversity and Hegemonic Constructions of Difference: Basarwa in Contemporary Botswana." *Political and Legal Anthropology Review* 18(2):91–104.

———. 1996. "Power, Identity and History in Central Botswana." *Identities: Global Studies in Culture and Power* 2(40):325–350.

———. 1997. "Native Anthropologists and the Politics of Representation." In D. Reed-Danahay (ed.), *Auto/ethnography: Rewriting the Self and the Social.* Oxford, England: Berg Publishers, pp. 169–195.

———. 1998. "Beyond Textual Analysis: Practice, Interacting Discourse, and the Experience of Distinction in Botswana." *Cultural Anthropology* 13:522–548.

———. 2001a. "Scholarship, Identity and Power: Mizrahi Women in Israel." *Signs: Journal of Women in Culture and Society.* 26(3):697–734.

———. 2001b. "The Bushmen of the Kalahari." *National Geographic* 33:132–134 (Hebrew Edition).

Moutle, Gadibolae. 1986. "Bakgalagadi-Bakwena Relationships: A Case of Slavery, c. 1840–c.1930." *Botswana Notes and Records* 18:95–106.

Murray, Colin. 1981. *Families Divided: The Impact of Migrant Labor in Lesotho.* Cambridge, England: Cambridge University Press.

———. 1987. "Class, Gender and the Household: The Developmental Cycle in Southern Africa." *Development and Change* 18:235–249.

Nash, June. 1981. "Ethnographic Aspects of the World Capitalist System." *Annual Review in Anthropology* 10:393–423.

National Development Plan 8 1997/8–2002/03. 1997. Ministry of Finance and Development Planning. Gaborone, Botswana: Government Printer.

Ngwato Land Board. 1982. Memo kept in the Maunatlala Land Board Office, file number 119/82.

Okihiro, Gary. 1976. *Hunters, Herders, Cultivators and Traders: Interaction and Change in the Kalagadi, Nineteenth Century.* Ph.D. dissertation, University of California at Los Angeles.

Omer-Cooper, J. 1969. "Aspects of Political Change in the Nineteenth Century Mfecane." In L. Thompson (ed.), *African Societies in Southern Africa.* London: Heineman.

Ortner, Sherry B. 1984. "Theory in Anthropology since the Sixties." *Comparative Studies in Society and History* 26:126–166.

Palmer, Robin, and Parsons, Neil (eds.). 1977. *The Roots of Rural Poverty in Central and Southern Africa.* London and Lusaka: Heinemann.

Parkin, David. 1978. *The Cultural Definition of Political Response.* London: Academic Press.

Parkington, John. 1984. "Saoqua and Bushmen: Hunters and Robbers." In Carmel Schrire (ed.), *Past and Present in Hunter-Gatherer Studies.* Orlando, FL: Academic Press, pp. 151–74.

Parson, Jack. 1981. "Cattle, Class and the State in Rural Botswana." *Journal of Southern African Studies* 7(2):236–255.

———. 1984. *Botswana: Liberal Democracy and the Labor Reserve in Southern Africa.* Boulder, CO: Westview Press.

Parsons, Neil. 1973. "The Economic History of Khama's Country in Southern Africa." *African Social Research* 18:643–675.

———. 1977. "The Economic History of Khama's Country in Botswana." In R. Palmer and N. Parsons (eds.), *The Roots of Rural Poverty in Central and Southern Africa*. Berkeley: University of California Press, pp. 113–142.

———. 1978. "Shots for a Black Republic: Simon Ratshosa and Botswana Nationalism." *African Affairs* 73:449–458.

———. 1982. *A New History of Southern Africa*. London: Macmilllan

Pauw, B. A. 1960. "Some Changes in the Social Structure of the Tlhaping of the Ruling Taung Reserve." *African Studies* 19(2):49–76.

Peel, John. 1995. "For Who Hath Despised the Day of Small Things? Missionary Narratives and Historical Anthropology." *Comparative Studies in Society and History* 37(3):581–607.

Peters, E. Pauline. 1983a. *Cattlemen, Borehole Syndicates and Privatization in the Kgatleng District of Botswana: An Anthropological History of the Transformation of a Commons*. Ph.D. dissertation, Boston University.

———. 1983b. "Gender, Developmental Cycles, and Historical Process: A Critique on Recent Research on Women in Botswana." *Journal of Southern African Studies* 10:100–122.

———. 1984. "Struggles over Water, Struggles over Meaning: Cattle, Water, and the State in Botswana." *Africa* 54:29–49.

———. 1994. *Dividing the Commons: Politics, Policy, and Culture in Botswana*. Charlottesville: University Press of Virginia.

Peters, E. Pauline, and Guyer, Jane (eds.). 1984. *Conceptualizing the Household: Issues of Theory, Method and Application*. Proceedings of a workshop held at Harvard University, Cambridge, MA.

Picard, Louis. 1987. *The Politics of Development in Botswana*. Boulder, CO: Rienner.

Polanyi, Livia. 1985. *Telling the American Story: A Structural and Cultural Analysis of Conversational Storytelling*. Norwood, NJ: Ablex.

Pratt, Mary Louise. 1986. "Fieldwork in Common Places." In James Clifford and George Marcus (eds.), *Writing Cultures*. Berkeley: University of California Press, pp. 27–51.

Proctor, J. 1968. "The House of Chiefs and the Political Development of Botswana." *Journal of Modern African Studies* 6(1).

Rabinow, Paul, ed. 1984. *The Foucault Reader*. New York: Pantheon Books.

———. 1986. "Representations Are Social Facts: Modernity and Post-Modernity in Anthropology." In James Clifford and George Marcus (eds.), *Writing Culture*. Berkeley: University of California Press, pp. 234–262.

Rebel, Herman. 1989. "Cultural Hegemony and Class Experience: A Critical Reading of Recent Ethnonological-Historical Approaches." *American Ethnologist* 16:117–137.

Reed-Danahay, Deborah. 1993. "Talking about Resistance: Ethnography and Theory in Rural France." *Anthropological Quarterly* 66(4): 221–229.

Ricour, Paul. 1971. "The Model of the Text: Meaningful Action Considered as a Text." *Social Research* 38:529–562.

Ritchie, Claire. 1986. "The Ju/wasi of Nyae Nyae—Thirty Years On." In Megan Biesele (ed.), *The Past and the Future of !Kung Ethnography*. Hamburg, Germany: Helmut Buske Verlag, pp. 311–327.

Roberts, Simon. 1977. "The Kgatla Marriage: Concepts of Validity." In Simon Roberts (ed.), *Law and Family in Africa*. The Hague, Netherlands: Mouton.

Rosaldo, Renato. 1976. "The Story of Tukbaw: 'They Listen as He Orates.'" In Frank Reynold and Donald Capps (eds.), *The Biographical Process: Studies in the History and Psychology of Religion*. The Hague, Netherlands: Mouton.

Roseberry, William. 1988. "Political Economy." *Annual Review of Anthropology* 17:161–185.

———. 1996. "Hegemony, Power, and Languages of Contention." In Edwin Wilmsen and Paul McAllister (eds.), *The Politics of Difference: Ethnic Premises in a World of Power*. Chicago: University of Chicago Press, pp. 71–85.

Rushton, Annie. 1992. "The Lore and Oral History of the Tswapong Hills and the Bobirwa People." Recorded by Tjako Mpulubusi, edited by Annie Rushton. Gaborone, Botswana: The National Museum, Monuments and Art Gallery.

Russell, Margo. 1976. "Slaves or Workers? Relations between Bushmen, Tswana, and Boers in the Kalahari." *Journal of Southern African Studies* 2:178–197.

Sahlins, Marshall. 1985. *Islands of History*. Chicago: University of Chicago Press.

Said, Edward. 1983. *The World, The Text, and the Critic*. Cambridge, MA: Harvard University Press.

Saugestad, Sidsel. 1993. "Main Trends in Remote Area Development Studies 1989–1992." Unpublished report to the Remote Area Development Programme Task Group. Gaborone, Botswana: The National Institute of Development Research and Documentation.

Schapera, Isaac. 1930. *The Khoisan Peoples of South Africa: Bushmen and Hottentots*. London: Routledge & Kegan Paul.

———. 1933. "Premarital Pregnancy and Native Opinion: A Note on Social Change." *Africa* 6:59–89.

———. 1938a. *A Handbook of Tswana Law and Custom*. Oxford, England: Oxford University Press.

———. 1938b. "A Survey of the Bushmen Question." *Race Relations* 6:68–82.

———. 1940. *Married Life in an African Tribe*. London: Faber.

———. 1943. *Native Land Tenure in the Bechuanaland Protectorate*. Alice, South Africa: Lovedale Press.

———. 1947. *Migrant Labour and Tribal Life: A Study of Conditions in the Bechuanaland Protectorate*. Oxford, England: Oxford University Press.

———. 1950. Kinship and Marriage among the Tswana. In A. R. Radcliff-Brown and D. Forde (eds.), *African Systems of Kinship and Marriage*. London: Oxford University Press.

———. 1952. *The Ethnic Composition of Tswana Tribes*. Monographs on Social Anthropology 11. London: London School of Economics and Political Sciences.

———. 1957. "Marriage of Near Kin among the Tswana. *Africa* 27:139–159.

———. 1963. "Agnatic Marriage in Tswana Royal Families." In I. Schapera (ed.), *Studies in Kinship and Marriage*. London: Royal Anthropological Institute Occasional Paper, No. 16.

———. 1965. *Praise-poems of Tswana Chiefs*. London: Oxford University Press.

———. 1970. *Tribal Innovators: Tswana Chiefs and Social Change 1795–1940*. London: The Athlone Press.

———. 1977 [1938]. *A Handbook of Tswana Law and Custom*. London: Frank Cass.

——. 1984 [1953]. *The Tswana*. London: Kegan Paul International.

Schrire, Carmel. 1984. "Wild Surmises on Savage Thoughts." In C. Schrire (ed.), *Past and Present in Hunter-Gatherer Studies*. Orlando, FL: Academic Press, pp. 1–25.

Scott, James. 1985. *Weapons of the Weak: Everyday Forms of Peasant Resistance*. New Haven, CT, and London: Yale University Press.

——. 1990. *Domination and the Art of Resistance: Hidden Transcripts*. New Haven, CT, and London: Yale University Press.

Sebopeng, Pheko. 1983. Interviews at Tamasane, May 17 and 18.

Sharp, John S., and Spiegel, Andrew D. 1985. "Vulnerability to Impoverishment in South African Rural Areas: The Erosion of Kinship and Neighborhood as Social Resources." *Africa* 55:133–153.

Silberbauer, George. 1965. Report to the Government of Bechuanaland on the Bushmen Survey. Gaborone: Bechuanaland Government.

——. 1981. *Hunter and Habitat in the Central Kalahari Desert*. Cambridge, England: Cambridge University Press

Sillery, Anthony. 1952. *The Bechuanaland Protectorate*. Cape Town, South Africa, and New York: Oxford University Press.

——. 1974. *Botswana: A Short Political History*. London: Methuen.

Sims, David. 1981. *Agroclimatological Information, Crop requirements and Agricultural Zones for Botswana*. Gaborone, Botswana: Government Printer.

Smith, Andrew. 1975 [1834]. W. F. Lye (ed.), *Andrew Smith's Journal of His Expedition into the Interior of South Africa, 1834–6*. Cape Town, South Africa: Balkema.

Smith, Dorothy. 1990. *The Conceptual Practices of Power*. Toronto: University of Toronto Press.

Soja, Edward. 1988. *Postmodern Geographies: The Reassertion of Space in Critical Social Theory*. London: Verso.

Solway, Jacqueline. 1980. "Cattle and Drought in the Western Kweneng District." Gaborone, Botswana: Ministry of Agriculture, Rural Sociology Unit.

Solway, Jacqueline, and Lee, Richard. 1990. "Foragers, Genuine or Spurious? Situating the Kalahari San in History." *Current Anthropology* 31:109–146.

Spelman, Elizabeth. 1990. *Inessential Woman*. London: Woman's Press.

Spivak, Gayatri Chakravorty. 1988. *In Other Worlds: Essays in Cultural Politics*. New York: Routledge.

Syson, Lucy. 1972. "The Population of the Shoshong Area." Gaborone, Botswana: United Nations Development Plan.

Thomas, Nicholas. 1992. "The Inversion of Tradition." *American Ethnologist* 19(2):213–235.

Tlou, Thomas. 1977. "Servility and Political Control: Botlanka among the Batawana, ca 1750–1906." In Susan Miers and J. Kopytoff (eds.), *Slavery in Africa: Historical and Anthropological Perspectives*. Madison: University of Wisconsin Press, pp. 367–390.

Tobias, Phillip V. 1964. "Bushmen Hunter-Gatherers: A Study of Human Ecology." In D. H. S. Davis (ed.), *Ecological Studies in Southern Africa*. The Hague, Netherlands: Uitgevenig, pp. 67–68.

Tsing, Anna L. 1994. "From the Margins." *Cultural Anthropology* 9(3):279–298.

Tyler, Stephen 1987. *The Unspeakable: Discourse, Dialogue, and Rhetoric in the Postmodern World*. Madison: University of Wisconsin Press.

Valiente, Nouilles C. 1991. "Homme-femme: Diffenciation et complèmentaritè chez les Kua (Bochiman) de la Réserve Centrale du Kalahari au Botswana." *Bulletin annual de Museè d'Ethnographic de Genève* 31–32:1–64.

Vierich, Helga. 1979. Interim Report on Basarwa and Related Poor Bakgalagadi in Kweneng District. Gaborone, Botswana: Ministry of Local Government and Lands.

———. 1982. "Adoptive Flexibility in a Multi-Ethnic Setting: The Basarwa of the Southern Kalahari." In E. Leacocks and R. Lee (eds.), *Politics and History in Band Societies*. Cambridge, England: Cambridge University Press, pp. 213–222.

Vincent, Joan. 1986. "System and Process, 1974–1985." *Annual Review of Anthropology* 15:99–119.

Von Kaufmann, R. R. 1978. "The Tribal Grazing Land Policy's Relevance in a Drought-prone Environment" In *Proceedings of the Symposium on Drought in Botswana*. Gaborone: The Botswana Society, pp. 255–260.

Voss, Anthony E. 1990. " 'Die Bushie is Dood': Long Live the Bushie." *African Studies* 49:59–71.

Weed, Elizabeth. 1989. "Introduction: Terms of Reference." In *Coming to Terms: Feminism, Theory, Politics*. New York: Routledge,

Werbner, Richard. 1971. "Local Adaptation and the Transformation of an Imperial Concession in North-Eastern Botswana." *Africa* 11:32–41.

———. 1982. "Introduction." In R. Werbner (ed.), *Land Reform in the Making*. London: Rex Collings, pp. i–xiii.

———. 1991. "From Heartland to Hinterland. Elites and the Geo-Politics of Land in Botswana." Paper presented at the Symposium on Land in African Agrarian Systems, Center for African Studies, University of Illinois.

Wiessner, Polly. 1986. "!Kung San Networks in a Generational Perspective." In Megan Biesle, Robert Gordon, and Richard Lee (eds.), *The Past and Future of !Kung Ethnography*. Hamburg, Germany: Helmut Buske Verlag, pp. 103–136.

Williams, Raymond. 1977. *Marxism and Literature*. Oxford, England and New York: Oxford University Press.

Willoughby, W. C. 1898. Archives of Sally Oak College Library of Birmingham, files 713, 734, 770, 794.

Wilmsen, Edwin N. 1989. *Land Filled with Flies: A Political Economy of the Kalahari*. Chicago: Chicago University Press.

———. 1990. "The Real Bushman is the Male One: Labour and Power in the Creation of Basarwa Ethnicity." *Botswana Notes and Records* 22:21–37.

———. 1991. "A Battle for the Centuries: Ethnography at Odds with Its Purpose." Paper presented at the Annual Conference of the Association for Anthropology in Southern Africa, Johannesburg, South Africa.

———. 1992. "The Social Organization of Khoisan Participation in the Nineteenth Century Atlantic Slave Trade." Paper presented at the 91st Annual Meeting of the American Anthropological Association, San Francisco.

———. 1993. "The Search for 'Truth' and Authority: A Reply to Lee and Guenther." *Current Anthropology* 34:715–721.

————. 1995. "Who Were the Bushmen: Historic Process in the Creation of an Ethnic Construct." In. R. Rapp and J. Schneider (eds.), *Articulating Hidden Histories: Exploring the Influence of Eric R. Wolf.* Berkeley: University of California Press.

Wilmsen, Edwin N., and Denbow, James. 1986. "Advent and Course of Pastoralism in the Kalahari." *Science* 234:1509–1515.

————. 1990. "Paradigmatic History of San-speaking People and Current Attempts at Revision." *Current Anthropology* 31:489–524.

Wilmsen, Edwin N., and Vossen, Rainer. 1990. "Labour, Exchange, and Power in the Construction of Ethnicity in Botswana." *Critique of Anthropology* 10:7–37.

Wolf, Eric R. 1982. *Europe and the People without History.* Berkeley: University of California Press.

————. 1986. "The Vicissitudes of the Closed Corporate Peasant Society." *American Ethnologist* 13:325–329.

Worby, Eric. 1984. "The Politics of Dispossession: Livestock Development Policy and the Transformation of Property Relations in Botswana." M.A. thesis, McGill University.

Worsley, Peter. 1984. *The Three Worlds.* Chicago: University of Chicago Press.

Wylie, Diana. 1990. *A Little God: The Twilight of Patriarchy in a Southern African Chiefdom.* Middletown, MA: Wesleyan University Press.

Yellen, John. 1991. "The Present and Future of Hunter-Gatherer Studies." In C. Lamberg-Karlousky (ed.), *Archaeological Thought in America.* New York: Cambridge University Press.

Index

About the Author

PNINA MOTZAFI-HALLER is Senior Research Fellow at the Blaustein Institute for Desert Research and Lecturer in Anthropology in the Department of Behavioral Studies at Ben Gurion University of the Negev in Beer Sheva, Israel.